Principles of International Humanitarian Law

Principles of International Humanitarian Law

Jonathan Crowe

University of Queensland, Australia

Kylie Weston-Scheuber

Victorian Bar, Melbourne, Australia

Edward Elgar
Cheltenham, UK • Northampton, MA, USA

© Jonathan Crowe and Kylie Weston-Scheuber 2013

All rights reserved. No part of this publication may be reproduced, stored in a retrieval system or transmitted in any form or by any means, electronic, mechanical or photocopying, recording, or otherwise without the prior permission of the publisher.

Published by
Edward Elgar Publishing Limited
The Lypiatts
15 Lansdown Road
Cheltenham
Glos GL50 2JA
UK

Edward Elgar Publishing, Inc.
William Pratt House
9 Dewey Court
Northampton
Massachusetts 01060
USA

A catalogue record for this book
is available from the British Library

Library of Congress Control Number: 2013930508

This book is available electronically in the ElgarOnline.com
Law Subject Collection, E-ISBN 978 1 78100 273 5

ISBN 978 1 78100 272 8 (cased)
      978 1 78254 594 1 (paperback)

Typeset by Servis Filmsetting Ltd, Stockport, Cheshire

Printed on FSC approved paper

Printed and bound in Great Britain by Marston Book Services Ltd, Oxfordshire

Contents

Preface		vii
1.	The concept of armed conflict	1
2.	Sources of international humanitarian law	24
3.	Means and methods of warfare	44
4.	Protection of civilians	70
5.	Protection of combatants *hors de combat*	96
6.	Humanitarianism and human rights	115
7.	Liability of states and non-state groups	143
8.	Liability of individuals	164
Index		193

Preface

This book has two main aims. The first is to provide a clear and concise explanation of some of the central principles of international humanitarian law (also known as the law of armed conflict). The second is to bring additional clarity to the understanding of those principles by situating them in a broader philosophical, ethical and legal context. We consider a range of wider issues relevant to international humanitarian law, such as its relationship to theories of humanitarianism, the extent to which it reflects the ethical duties of participants in armed conflict and its connection to other bodies of law, such as international human rights law. We also take up positions on some contested questions concerning the interpretation of specific norms. The book should therefore prove useful for students encountering international humanitarian law for the first time, but we hope it will also hold interest for practitioners and scholars with existing knowledge of the field.

The book has had a long gestation. The idea for the work was first conceived some ten years ago as a collaboration with two other authors, Kate Parlett and Andrew Stumer. Those authors later withdrew to pursue other projects and the work has gone through many phases of development since then. However, we would like to express our sincere thanks for their contributions. Their enthusiasm in the earlier stages of the process played a large role in bringing the book to where it is today.

There are several other people whose contributions to the book we would like to acknowledge. Both authors have benefited greatly over the years from the teaching, mentoring and collegiality of Anthony Cassimatis. We would also like to mention the role of Peter Alcorn, who sadly passed away in 2009, in fuelling our enthusiasm for the study of international humanitarian law. Jonathan Crowe would like to thank the students in his courses on international humanitarian law at the University of Queensland over the last several years for their enthusiasm and probing questions. He also thanks Eve Massingham for her helpful comments on earlier drafts of some of the chapters. Both authors are grateful to Youngwon Lee for her excellent research assistance and proof editing. Finally, we would like to thank our respective partners, Cicely Bonnin and Kerry O'Brien, for their support and encouragement throughout all stages of the project.

There is no more pressing and important area of international jurisprudence than international humanitarian law. It protects people's lives and well-being on a daily basis. War is destructive by its very nature, but the law of armed conflict plays a crucial role in moderating its harmful impact on the lives of people around the globe. In many ways, it is the last-ditch hold-out position of humanity against arbitrary violence. We hope this book can make a modest contribution to the dissemination, understanding and universal acceptance of humanitarian norms. We can think of no better objective.

Jonathan Crowe
Kylie Weston-Scheuber
November 2012

1. The concept of armed conflict

International humanitarian law can be generally defined as *the body of international law governing the conduct of armed conflicts*. The notion of armed conflict is therefore central to understanding this area of law. This is true both in terms of the philosophical underpinnings of international humanitarian law and in terms of the legal rules that set out the limits of its operation. The guiding principles of international humanitarian law arise from the need to place limits on the conduct of armed conflicts. These restraints are needed due to what we will call the *morally exceptional* nature of warfare. The philosophical concept of warfare will therefore be our first focus in this chapter.

We will then turn to the legal limits on the operation of international humanitarian law. The fundamental principle here is that international humanitarian law has no operation unless an armed conflict exists. This raises the important question of what constitutes an 'armed conflict'. We will therefore examine the legal definition of armed conflict, before turning to related questions concerning the duration and scope of hostilities. Finally, we will consider the legal distinction between international and non-international armed conflicts. This distinction has historically played an important role in international law. However, as we will see, its importance is diminishing over time.

THE LOGIC OF WARFARE

It is worthwhile to begin by reflecting on the morally exceptional character of armed conflict. It is widely seen as permissible and perhaps even praiseworthy for people engaged in warfare to deliberately set out to injure and kill others. This is, to put it mildly, quite different from the moral framework that governs human interaction in everyday life. In the normal moral codes of almost every human community, setting out deliberately to injure and kill other people is one of the very worst things you can do. This common view of warfare therefore posits a radical exception to the normal moral paradigm.

Let us assume the morally exceptional status of armed conflict for present purposes and ask where that idea leads. We might call this the question of the *logic of warfare*. It is sometimes said that 'all is fair in war', meaning that all moral rules are suspended. This is the notion of *absolute warfare*. The concept of absolute warfare is often associated with the Prussian military theorist Carl von Clausewitz (1780–1861). Clausewitz famously argued that armed conflicts tend naturally to escalate towards a state of absolute warfare.[1] The idea that the sole aim of warfare is to defeat your opponent and normal moral rules do not apply leads logically to the conclusion that any and all means are justified.

In warfare, then, it seems that all bets are off. The goal of all parties in the conflict must be to secure victory and bring about the return of normal moral relations. Any measures that promote this end are permissible. Clausewitz is often interpreted as having fully endorsed this conclusion, but in fact he was ambivalent about it. He thought that the logic of warfare, if followed to its natural conclusion, means that the end justifies the means. However, he also noted that in actual wars, which are for limited purposes, absolute warfare is unsustainable, as it allows no conclusion short of total annihilation.[2] A state of absolute warfare will not truly end until one side is completely destroyed.

HUMANITARIANISM

The morally exceptional nature of warfare means that the most important goal is to bring about peace. Absolute warfare might end the conflict, but it is not the best way to secure a peaceful conclusion. Rather, it would end the war at the cost of totally destroying one of the parties. It seems, then, that we need an alternative to absolute warfare. Rather than seeking an end to war at all costs, we need to conduct armed conflicts in such a way as to leave open the possibility of a lasting peace. This is perhaps the fundamental idea behind the doctrine of *humanitarianism*. Humanitarianism brings moral limits back into war by seeking to moderate the effects of warfare in the name of human ideals.

Humanitarianism responds to the unusual situation that arises in armed conflicts by adopting an approach of moderation. Although war necessarily involves suffering, there are basic values that unite humans even in wartime. This means that even war has limits. Humans are not inclined to

---

[1] Carl von Clausewitz, *On War* (JJ Graham tr, Wordsworth 1997) 6–7 [bk I, ch I, §3].
[2] Ibid 22–3 [bk I, ch I, §25].

live in a permanent state of warfare and the wounds left by war will eventually have to be tended. It is therefore necessary to maintain a commitment to human ideals on which community may be founded following the cessation of hostilities. In this way, international humanitarian law aims to ensure respect for the most basic human values, such as dignity, community and freedom from suffering. It represents the last-ditch hold-out position of the human community against absolute warfare.

Classical Origins

The historical development of the idea that humanitarianism moderates warfare laid the foundations for the contemporary body of rules that constitutes international humanitarian law. Despite the moral strangeness of armed conflicts, human communities have long accepted the importance of mitigating the effects of warfare. For example, there is evidence that warfare between Ancient Greek city states around 700 to 450 BCE was governed by customary rules, concerned among other things with the treatment of prisoners of war and the extent to which defeated forces should be pursued.[3] The influence of these rules is apparent in Plato's *Republic*, written around 375 BCE, where it is noted that citizens of occupied territories should not be enslaved or attacked, corpses should not be robbed and conquering forces should refrain from burning houses or destroying occupied lands.[4]

Plato's central reason for approving these principles concerned the common values that united the Greek nations. He noted the importance of maintaining goodwill between states even in times of armed conflict, in order to facilitate the progress of their common culture. Although Plato was not prepared to extend this approach to wars between Greeks and other races, whom he considered 'barbarians', his emphasis on the need to maintain a sense of common value during armed hostilities, in order to pave the way for future reconciliation between the parties, foreshadowed modern humanitarianism. We will discuss the limits on the Ancient Greek idea of humanitarianism further below.

Another important antecedent to modern humanitarian theories is found in the writings of Plato's pupil, Aristotle (384–322 BCE). Aristotle's theories on law and politics have been highly influential in shaping

---

[3] Josiah Ober, 'Classical Greek Times' in Michael Howard, George J Andreopoulos and Mark R Shulman (eds), *The Laws of War: Constraints on Warfare in the Western World* (Yale University Press 1994).
[4] Plato, *Republic* (Desmond Lee tr, Penguin 1987) 197–9 [bk V, §§469–71].

modern Western legal systems. His conception of the political community has been particularly important. Aristotle viewed humans as naturally social animals, who possess a common understanding of a good and fulfilling life. According to this shared conception of the good life, called *eudaimonia*, the highest form of human existence is characterised by full participation in the political community.[5] This emphasis on shared values and the importance of community in human existence finds modern expression in the rules of international humanitarian law.

Humanitarian attitudes towards warfare can be discerned in other classical traditions. Although the Roman armies developed a reputation for fierceness in pursuit of military objectives,[6] Cicero argued in *De Officiis* in 44 BCE that certain standards must be observed in the conduct of warfare. In particular, he contended that forces should refrain from inflicting unnecessary devastation upon occupied territories, and captured opponents not guilty of excessive brutality during combat should be protected.[7] Cicero's position was motivated by the idea that there are important principles of justice common to all human communities. He emphasised that hostilities should always be conducted with the aim of securing a lasting and equitable peace. Unlike Plato, Cicero did not distinguish in this respect between his fellow Romans and members of other cultures.

Early Modern Developments

Customary rules regulating warfare persisted through to the Middle Ages, when the first attempts were made to formalise the rules. These initially took the form of official proclamations. The Ordinance for the Government of the Army, published in 1386 at the order of Richard II of England, prohibited acts of violence against women and priests, as well as the burning of houses and the desecration of churches. Proclamations to a similar effect were issued by Henry V of England in 1415 and 1419,[8] Ferdinand of Hungary in 1526, Emperor Maximilian II in 1570 and King

---

[5] For an overview of Aristotle's legal and political theory, see Jonathan Crowe, *Legal Theory* (Thomson Reuters 2009) 18–22.

[6] Robert C Stacy, 'The Age of Chivalry' in Michael Howard, George J Andreopoulos and Mark R Shulman (eds), *The Laws of War: Constraints on Warfare in the Western World* (Yale University Press 1994).

[7] Cicero, *De Officiis* (Walter Miller tr, Harvard University Press 1913) 37 [bk I, §XI], 83 [bk I, §XXIV].

[8] Theodor Meron, 'Shakespeare's Henry the Fifth and the Law of War' (1992) 86 *American Journal of International Law* 1, 23–4.

Gustavus II Adolphus of Sweden in 1621.[9] These instruments show that common international standards governing warfare were in place long before any formal agreements on the topic were concluded.

One of the most important modern works on international humanitarian law, Hugo Grotius' *On the Law of War and Peace* (1625), also dates from this period. The first two books of that work are mainly concerned with how a war may justly be commenced – in other words, the *jus ad bellum*. The third and final book, however, discusses what behaviour is permissible once war has started – that is, the *jus in bello* or international humanitarian law. Grotius' examination of the law of war is notable for his purposive view of human nature, which echoes Aristotle's emphasis on humanity's shared sense of value. In particular, Grotius emphasises that armed conflicts should always be conducted with a view to creating a lasting peace, again laying the foundations for modern humanitarianism.[10]

Grotius' writings contain many of the fundamental principles of contemporary international humanitarian law that we will encounter throughout this book. For example, he argues that combatants should take steps to avoid causing injury to civilians caught up in fighting, that prisoners of war should be treated humanely and that armed forces should avoid causing unnecessary damage to the regions through which they pass during the conflict. However, it was to be more than 200 years before these principles began to find formal expression in international legal agreements.

The preceding paragraphs by no means provide a complete account of the development of humanitarian ideas. However, they illustrate that the formal documents at the heart of modern international humanitarian law reflect a long customary tradition. This point is central to understanding the standards governing contemporary armed conflicts. Considered apart from this customary background, modern treaties concerning humanitarian law might well seem vague, incomplete and unenforceable. It is only when these documents are understood as attempts to formalise a robust tradition of unwritten principles that one appreciates why their provisions are so widely respected and obeyed.

---

[9] See generally Edoardo Greppi, 'The Evolution of International Criminal Responsibility under International Law' (1999) 835 *International Review of the Red Cross* 531; Kenneth Ögren, 'Humanitarian Law in the Articles of War Decreed in 1621 by King Gustavus II Adolphus of Sweden' (1996) 313 *International Review of the Red Cross* 438; MH Keen, *The Laws of War in the Late Middle Ages* (Routledge and Kegan Paul 1965).

[10] Hugo Grotius, *On the Law of War and Peace* (Francis W Kelsey tr, Clarendon Press 1925) vol II, 860–62 [bk III, ch XXV].

INSIDERS AND OUTSIDERS

We have already seen that the classical doctrine of humanitarianism espoused by Ancient Greek authors like Plato and Aristotle was limited in scope. The Ancient Greeks did not extend humanitarian principles to 'barbarians', but only to other Greeks. Barbarians, like women and slaves, were not considered members of the *polis* (city state or political community), which for the Greeks was equivalent to the moral community. It was assumed that non-citizens did not share common aspirations and values with citizens, so there was no need to extend them humanitarian consideration.

This feature of the Ancient Greek worldview marks a fundamental difference from modern humanitarianism. The version of the doctrine that lies behind international humanitarian law posits a *global moral community*. On this view, all humans are entitled to respect by virtue of their shared nature and values. Another way of putting this is that modern humanitarianism is committed to *cosmopolitanism*: the view that the whole world is a single moral community. The term comes from a statement attributed to the radical Ancient Greek thinker Diogenes the Cynic (c 412–323 BCE), founder of the Stoic school of philosophy: 'I am a citizen of the world [*kosmopolitês*].'

Diogenes was a great philosopher whose ideas are still influential today. However, he was a very strange man. He is reputed to have lived in a large tub and dined mainly on onions. Other stories involve him masturbating, spitting and defecating in public to mock prudish customs. He is also reputed to have wandered around in daytime with a lamp, saying, 'I am only looking for a true human being'. This story reflects the extent to which he rejected the worldview of his fellow Athenian citizens. The division between insiders and outsiders, marked by the conferral of citizenship, was firmly ingrained in Ancient Greek culture. Diogenes, however, questioned the distinction.

It may seem obvious to us today that cosmopolitanism is correct. (*Of course* we should extend the same moral standards to everyone!) However, it arguably still goes against some widespread practices and beliefs. For example, we commonly think it is legitimate to extend greater consideration to family members and fellow nationals than to those more distant from us. Is this type of partiality legitimate? There is a lively philosophical debate on these issues.[11] There is no scope to pursue the topic fully here,

---

[11] See, for example, Harry Brighouse and Adam Swift, 'Legitimate Parental Partiality' (2009) 37 *Philosophy and Public Affairs* 43; Harry Brighouse, 'Justifying

but it illustrates the potentially radical implications of cosmopolitanism as a doctrine. We should not be too quick to simply declare that 'we are all cosmopolitans now!' International humanitarian law, however, has clear affinities with the cosmopolitan outlook.

JUS AD BELLUM AND *JUS IN BELLO*

We defined international humanitarian law at the start of this chapter as *the body of international law governing the conduct of armed conflicts*. The existence of an armed conflict is therefore a necessary prerequisite for international humanitarian law to operate. It is important to note in this context that international humanitarian law is concerned with regulating the *conduct* of armed conflicts, rather than their *commencement*. It is not concerned with how a conflict started or who was to blame for it, but rather stipulates what forms of conduct are permissible once the war is ongoing.

The body of international law relating to the conduct of armed conflicts is sometimes referred to using the Latin term *jus in bello* ('law in war'). This is generally viewed as synonymous with what we now call international humanitarian law. The law relating to the commencement of armed conflicts, by contrast, is known as the *jus ad bellum* ('law to war'). It is also sometimes called the *jus contra bellum* ('law against war'), since its primary concern is to stem the proliferation of armed disputes.

The distinction between the *jus in bello* and the *jus ad bellum* is fundamental to international humanitarian law. The objective of this field of law is to set up a body of rules that applies consistently to all parties to an armed conflict. It thereby avoids the need to draw difficult and controversial distinctions between just and unjust conflicts. It also avoids passing judgment on which of the parties to a conflict may be at fault. It simply applies the same fundamental guarantees and responsibilities to everyone.

THE PRINCIPLE OF NEUTRALITY

We might call this feature of international humanitarian law the *principle of neutrality*. There is a good reason why international humanitarian law

---

Patriotism' (2006) 32 *Social Theory and Practice* 547; Igor Primoratz, 'Patriotism: A Deflationary View' (2002) 33 *Philosophical Forum* 443; Peter Singer, *Practical Ethics* (2nd edn, CUP 1993) 232–4; Mark C Murphy, *Natural Law in Jurisprudence and Politics* (CUP 2006) 168–76; Jonathan Crowe, 'Natural Law in Jurisprudence and Politics' (2007) 27 *Oxford Journal of Legal Studies* 775, 791–3.

adopts this principle. It is common for parties on both sides of a conflict to depict themselves as fighting for justice and to accuse their opponents of being at fault. If international humanitarian law imposed different rules on unjust aggressors and innocent parties, both sides of a conflict would try to exploit this for their own advantage. This would undermine the underlying goal of establishing dependable limits on warfare. The principle of neutrality therefore plays an important role in promoting universal respect for humanitarian principles.

It is worth noting, however, that the ethical underpinnings of the rules governing armed conflict are more complicated than the principle of neutrality makes it seem. International humanitarian law takes the view that it does not matter how a conflict started. The same rules apply to everyone. However, imagine that Kate is asleep in her bed when she hears a noise downstairs. She comes down to find that Andrew has broken into her house and is brandishing a gun. Kate also happens to have a gun nearby, which she keeps for self-defence. The two confront each other in Kate's living room.

Let us suppose that Kate and Andrew both see that the other is armed. They are in genuine fear for their lives. Most people would agree that Kate is entitled to defend herself from Andrew. She should probably disarm him or flee if she can, but she may use force to defend herself if necessary. Andrew, however, seems to be in a different position. He is the one who caused the altercation by wrongfully breaking into Kate's house. If Kate defends herself against Andrew and injures him, she is not culpable. However, if Andrew ends up injuring Kate, he is to blame, even if he feared for his life.

This example shows that it does make a difference who started a conflict. An innocent victim who acts in self-defence is in a different ethical position to an unjust aggressor.[12] Nonetheless, international humanitarian law sets this aside and aims at the universal acceptance of a common set of rules.[13] If the parties to a war were treated differently depending on their

---

[12] For further discussion, see Michael Walzer, *Just and Unjust Wars* (Basic Books 1977) ch 3; Jeff McMahan, 'Innocence, Self-Defence and Killing in War' (1994) 2 *Journal of Political Philosophy* 193; Jeff McMahan, 'The Ethics of Killing in War' (2004) 114 *Ethics* 693; Gerhard Øverland, 'Killing Civilians' (2005) 13 *European Journal of Philosophy* 345; Gerhard Øverland, 'Killing Soldiers' (2006) 20 *Ethics and International Affairs* 455.

[13] Compare Jeff McMahan, 'The Ethics of Killing in War' (2004) 114 *Ethics* 693, 730–33; David Luban, 'War Crimes: The Law of Hell' in Larry May (ed), *War: Essays in Political Philosophy* (CUP 2008) 270–73; Patrick Emerton and Toby Handfield, 'Order and Affray: Defensive Privileges in Warfare' (2009) 37 *Philosophy and Public Affairs* 382.

ethical status, everyone would claim to be in the right. One party might claim to be above the rules and the other would retaliate. The situation would escalate. We would be on the slippery slope to absolute warfare.

COHERENCE AND ACCEPTANCE

It is instructive in this context to distinguish two aspirations that often guide the development of legal principles. The first aspiration is to create a body of norms that exhibits coherence with underlying ethical principles. The second aspiration is to achieve general acceptance of the norms that comprise the legal system; in other words, to ensure the norms are followed. Frequently, these two objectives go hand in hand. A legal system is often more likely to be respected if it contains a coherent body of rules.[14]

Legal systems may differ, however, in the relative levels of emphasis they place on these two aspirations. A case can be made that international humanitarian law places greater emphasis on acceptance and less on consistency with underlying ethical norms than many other fields of law. Humanitarian norms often prioritise simplicity and clarity over coherence with underlying ethical principles, since the primary aim of this body of law is to secure recognition and respect from all participants in armed conflict. The principle of neutrality, as discussed in the previous section, provides an example.

We saw above that the ethical principles governing self-defence seem to suggest that different standards apply to aggressors and innocent parties. This is what Jeff McMahan calls the 'deep morality' of warfare.[15] However, as McMahan points out, the deep morality of warfare differs significantly from the law of war.[16] The international law of armed conflict, then, does not derive its legitimacy from its strict coherence with the deep morality of warfare, but rather from the need for clear and generally accepted conventions to 'mitigate the savagery of war'.[17] These conventions are typically founded in broad underlying values, but their most important feature may be that they are generally respected. It is only by maintaining clear, stable and predictable conventions concerning acceptable conduct on the battlefield that the international community can place reliable limits on warfare.

---

[14] For further discussion of the value of coherence in law, see Jonathan Crowe, 'Dworkin on the Value of Integrity' (2007) 12 *Deakin Law Review* 167.
[15] Jeff McMahan, 'The Ethics of Killing in War' (2004) 114 *Ethics* 693, 730.
[16] Ibid 730–33.
[17] Ibid 730.

DEFINING ARMED CONFLICT

We have seen that international humanitarian law only operates during an armed conflict. The legal definition of armed conflict therefore plays a critical role in this body of law. A number of important questions arise here. How do we distinguish an armed conflict from a mere civil disturbance, such as a riot? How do we determine exactly when an armed conflict commences and when it ends? These lines may often be difficult to draw, but international courts and tribunals have offered some guidance.

Common Article 2 of the Geneva Conventions of 1949 states that the Conventions will apply to 'all cases of declared war or of any other armed conflict which may arise between two or more of the High Contracting Parties, even if the state of war is not recognised by one of them'. A declaration of war is therefore not necessary for the existence of an armed conflict. International humanitarian law comes into play whenever hostilities reach a certain threshold. The concept of armed conflict is also relevant to international criminal law, as violations of the laws and customs of war can only be prosecuted when they occur in the context of a conflict. We will return to that issue below.

Common Article 2 goes on to clarify that the provisions of the Geneva Conventions also apply in cases of total or partial occupation of a state party's territory, even when the occupation is met with no resistance. This extends the reach of the Conventions to situations where an occupation occurs without a declaration of war or armed hostilities. People who are affected by such an occupation will therefore still potentially receive the guarantees afforded to protected persons under Geneva Convention IV. The obligations of occupying powers will be discussed in greater detail in Chapter 4.

An important definition of an armed conflict comes from the International Criminal Tribunal for the Former Yugoslavia (ICTY) judgment in *Prosecutor v Tadić*, the first case to be heard before that body.[18] The Appeals Chamber in *Tadić* confirmed that 'for there to be a violation of [international humanitarian law], there must be an armed conflict'.[19] The Appeals Chamber then went on to say that 'an armed conflict exists whenever there is a resort to armed force between States or protracted armed violence between governmental authorities and organised armed

---

[18] *Prosecutor v Tadić*, International Criminal Tribunal for the Former Yugoslavia (ICTY) Appeals Chamber Decision on Jurisdiction, 2 October 1995.
[19] Ibid [67].

groups or between such groups within a State'.[20] This was reaffirmed in the later case of *Prosecutor v Kunarac*.[21]

The definition proposed by the Appeals Chamber in *Tadić* recognises two distinct tests for the existence of an armed conflict. The first test refers to 'a resort to armed force between States'. This is the classic definition of an *international* armed conflict. It traditionally involves a formal declaration of warfare by one or both states, although this is not strictly necessary. The second test refers to 'protracted armed violence between governmental authorities and organised armed groups or between such groups within a State'. This formulation recognises that international humanitarian law may also apply to conflicts involving non-state groups. The test covers both conflicts involving a combination of states and non-state groups and conflicts in which no states are directly involved.

Historically, the application of international humanitarian law to insurgent groups depended on the members of the group being recognised as belligerents by either the state they were opposing or a third state. If the state to which the insurgents were opposed recognised them as belligerents, the laws of war would apply in their entirety. However, this was rare and usually occurred only when it suited the recognising state.[22] The applicability of the rules of international humanitarian law to a non-state group no longer depends upon recognition of the group by a state. Rather, it depends primarily on whether or not an armed conflict exists under international law. We will examine the extent to which international humanitarian law binds non-state groups in more detail in Chapter 7.

Protracted Armed Violence

According to the ICTY Appeals Chamber in *Tadić*, an armed conflict involving non-state groups arises only if the violence is *protracted* and the non-state groups are *organised*. What amounts to 'protracted armed violence' within the meaning of the *Tadić* definition? The ICTY Trial Chamber has clarified that 'protracted armed violence' contrasts with 'banditry, unorganised and short-lived insurrections'.[23] Rioting, for example, is not normally treated as an armed conflict, but merely a civil disturbance. This was reiterated by the Inter-American Commission on

---

[20] Ibid [70].
[21] *Prosecutor v Kunarac*, ICTY Appeals Chamber Judgment, 12 June 2002 [55]–[56].
[22] Lindsay Moir, *The Law of Internal Armed Conflict* (CUP 2002) 4–18.
[23] *Prosecutor v Tadić*, ICTY Trial Chamber Judgment, 7 May 1997 [562].

Human Rights (IACHR) in the case of *Juan Carlos Abella v Argentina*.[24] The IACHR stated that an armed conflict must be contrasted with 'disturbances with no concerted intent' and 'isolated and sporadic acts of violence'.[25]

Among the examples given by the IACHR in *Abella* of situations falling short of armed conflict were violent civilian demonstrations, students throwing stones at police, bandits holding hostages for ransom and political assassinations.[26] It may be difficult to draw the line in particular cases. However, the IACHR observed in *Abella* that 'in making such a determination, what is required in the final analysis is a good faith and objective analysis of the facts in each particular case'.[27] A legalistic adherence to any particular definition is inappropriate. Rather, a holistic assessment of the facts is required.

The *Abella* case concerned a skirmish at a military base during a time of political unrest in Argentina. The IACHR concluded that an armed conflict had occurred, even though the skirmish only lasted for 30 hours in total. Its reasoning emphasised 'the concerted nature of the hostile acts undertaken by the attackers, the direct involvement of governmental armed forces and the nature and level of the violence'.[28] The IACHR noted that the case involved a 'carefully planned, coordinated and executed' armed attack against 'a quintessential military objective – a military base'. It also cited the International Committee of the Red Cross (ICRC) recommendation that the rules of international humanitarian law 'should be applied as widely as possible'.[29] This reasoning suggests that, in borderline cases, there may be a presumption in favour of the existence of an armed conflict.

Organised Armed Groups

According to the ICTY Appeals Chamber in *Tadić*, an armed conflict involving non-state forces must involve 'organised armed groups'. Again, this standard is intended to distinguish armed conflicts from sporadic outbreaks of violence, such as riots and demonstrations. Typically, an organised armed group will have a clear chain of command. However, it is not necessary that each group involved in an armed conflict be clearly

---

[24] *Juan Carlos Abella v Argentina*, Inter-American Commission on Human Rights Case No 11.137, Report No 55/97, 18 November 1997.
[25] Ibid [149].
[26] Ibid [154].
[27] Ibid [153].
[28] Ibid [155].
[29] Ibid [152].

differentiated and defined. There may be a number of loosely related armed groups involved, as in the conflict in the former Yugoslavia.[30] The ICTY Trial Chamber in the case of *Prosecutor v Haradinaj* viewed the following factors as indicative of organisation: the existence of command structure and disciplinary rules; control of a determinate territory; access to weapons, equipment and military training; and the ability to define military strategy and use military tactics.[31]

No one factor can be considered determinative and whether hostilities involve organised armed groups must accordingly be considered on a case-by-case basis. The ICTY Appeals Chamber noted in the *Tadić* case, for example, that the main parties to the conflict in Bosnia and Herzegovina were the government of the Republic of Bosnia and Herzegovina, on the one hand, and the Bosnian Serb forces, on the other. In recognising the situation as an armed conflict under international law, the Tribunal observed that the Bosnian Serb forces exhibited various indicia of organisation, including operating under the command of the Bosnian Serb administration and occupying a determinate region. The United Nations Security Council had also taken steps to maintain peace and security in the region, including imposing an arms embargo.[32] This showed that the Bosnian Serb forces had a significant military presence and were in effective control of disputed territory.

The requirement of a certain level of organisation of a group as a prerequisite for the applicability of international humanitarian law is also significant in the context of modern terrorism. Common rhetoric in relation to the 'war on terror' might give rise to a perception that armed resistance to terrorists automatically constitutes an armed conflict. However, there is a real question as to whether the kinds of loosely organised groups that often carry out terrorist activity have the requisite internal structure, based on the characteristics outlined above, to bring international humanitarian law into play.[33]

There is precedent in both international tribunals and the decisions of state courts to recognise terrorist groups as organised armed groups for the purpose of establishing the existence of an armed conflict.[34] For example,

---

[30] *Prosecutor v Tadić*, ICTY Appeals Chamber Decision on Jurisdiction, 2 October 1995 [70].
[31] *Prosecutor v Haradinaj*, ICTY Trial Chamber Judgment, 3 April 2008 [60].
[32] *Prosecutor v Tadić*, ICTY Trial Chamber Judgment, 7 May 1997 [564], [567].
[33] International Committee of the Red Cross, *International Humanitarian Law and the Challenges of Contemporary Armed Conflicts* (ICRC 2007) 7–8.
[34] *Prosecutor v Boskoski*, ICTY Trial Chamber Judgment, 10 July 2008 [173]–[190].

the United States Supreme Court considered in *Hamdan v Rumsfeld* that the conflict that existed in Afghanistan between the United States and the terrorist group Al Qaeda in 2001 constituted a non-international armed conflict under international law, bringing it within the scope of Common Article 3 of the Geneva Conventions.[35] Although sporadic and isolated acts of terrorism will be unlikely to meet the threshold, protracted terrorist violence may well do so.

Issues also arise increasingly in contemporary conflicts involving hostilities between organised crime groups within the territory of a state or between an organised crime group and government forces. Is an organised crime group capable of satisfying the criteria for an organised armed group within the meaning of the ICTY Appeals Chamber in *Tadić*? Although this falls to be determined on a case-by-case basis, there seems no principled reason for excluding such disputes from the definition of armed conflict as long as they meet the overarching requirements mentioned above.[36]

SCOPE OF ARMED CONFLICT

The existence of an armed conflict brings international humanitarian law into operation. However, an issue may arise as to whether particular acts fall within the conflict's geographical and temporal scope. In its jurisdictional decision in the *Tadić* case, the ICTY Appeals Chamber observed that 'the temporal and geographical scope [of the conflict] extends beyond the exact time and place of hostilities'. At least some aspects of international humanitarian law apply within the 'entire territory' of the parties for the duration of the conflict.[37] It follows that 'a violation of the laws or customs of war may [. . .] occur at a time when and in a place where no fighting is actually taking place'.[38] In the case of non-international conflicts, international humanitarian law applies in so much of the territory as is under the control of one or more of the parties to the conflict.[39]

The temporal reach of international humanitarian law, on the other

---

[35] *Hamdan v Rumsfeld* 548 US 557, 629–31 (2006).
[36] International Committee of the Red Cross, *International Humanitarian Law and the Challenge of Contemporary Armed Conflicts* (ICRC 2011) 9–12.
[37] *Prosecutor v Tadić*, ICTY Appeals Chamber Decision on Jurisdiction, 2 October 1995 [67]–[68].
[38] *Prosecutor v Kunarac*, ICTY Appeals Chamber Judgment, 12 June 2002 [64].
[39] *Prosecutor v Tadić*, ICTY Appeals Chamber Decision on Jurisdiction, 2 October 1995 [64], [70].

hand, extends from the initiation of hostilities until 'a general conclusion of peace is reached'.[40] Declaration of an armistice or ceasefire does not have the effect of terminating an armed conflict unless it constitutes a peace agreement and is followed by a general cessation of hostilities. A temporary cessation of hostilities does not mean international humanitarian law ceases to apply. The Geneva Conventions specifically provide for the temporal application of international humanitarian law in respect of particular groups. Prisoners of war, for example, gain the protection of Geneva Convention III from the time they fall into the power of the enemy until their final release and repatriation.[41]

The provisions of Geneva Convention IV apply from the outset of the conflict until the general close of military operations. Those aspects of Geneva Convention IV governing occupied territories are further stipulated to apply for one year after the general close of military operations, with the exception of some articles that apply until the occupying power ceases to exercise the functions of government.[42] The position has now been clarified by Additional Protocol I of 1977, which states that all provisions applicable to occupation continue to operate until the occupation terminates.

Connection to the Conflict

A further issue arises in the context of international criminal law. The ICTY has held that a charge of violating the laws and customs of war can only be established if the acts have an appropriate connection to the armed conflict. It is not enough that the acts occur at the same time and place as the conflict. Rather, they must take place *in the context of* the conflict.[43] In the words of the ICTY Appeals Chamber: 'The existence of an armed conflict must, at a minimum, have played a substantial part in the perpetrator's ability to commit [the crime, the] decision to commit it, the manner in which it was committed or the purpose for which it was committed.'[44]

This requirement is necessary to distinguish acts committed during an armed conflict that properly fall within international humanitarian law from those that properly fall under domestic law. For example, an ordinary theft or assault during wartime would not fall within international

---

[40] Ibid [70].
[41] Geneva Convention III, art 5.
[42] Geneva Convention IV, art 6.
[43] *Prosecutor v Tadić*, ICTY Appeals Chamber Decision on Jurisdiction, 2 October 1995 [69].
[44] *Prosecutor v Kunarac*, ICTY Appeals Chamber Judgment, 12 June 2002 [58].

humanitarian law, but would be dealt with under domestic law, as it would be in peacetime. On the other hand, ethnically motivated assaults during the Yugoslavian and Rwandan conflicts have been treated as violations of international humanitarian law, since the motivation was related to the conflict.[45]

The ICTY Appeals Chamber has made it clear that an act may be sufficiently related to the conflict to enliven international humanitarian law, even though it does not occur 'in the midst of battle'.[46] The Appeals Chamber judgment in *Kunarac* sets out a list of factors that may be considered in assessing whether an act is related to the conflict. These include: the fact that the perpetrator is a combatant; the fact that the victim is a non-combatant; the fact that the victim is from a group associated with the enemy; the fact that the act may be said to serve the ultimate goal of a military campaign; and the fact that the crime is committed as part of or in the context of the perpetrator's official duties.[47]

The *Kunarac* case concerned a systematic campaign of rape and other forms of abuse perpetrated by Bosnian Serb military personnel against Bosnian Muslim women during the armed conflict in the former Yugoslavia. The ICTY Trial Chamber had no difficulty in establishing a connection between the assaults and the conflict. The crimes were both facilitated and motivated by the conflict; as the Trial Chamber observed, 'Muslim civilians were killed, raped or otherwise abused as a direct result of the armed conflict and because the armed conflict apparently offered blanket impunity to the perpetrators'.[48] This finding was later endorsed by the ICTY Appeals Chamber.[49]

TYPES OF ARMED CONFLICTS

International humanitarian law has traditionally distinguished between international and non-international armed conflicts. Prior to the Geneva

---

[45] See, for example, *Prosecutor v Delalic*, ICTY Trial Chamber Judgment, 16 November 1998; *Prosecutor v Kvocka*, ICTY Trial Chamber Judgment, 2 November 2001; *Prosecutor v Jean Paul Akayesu*, International Criminal Tribunal for Rwanda Trial Chamber Judgment, 2 September 1998.

[46] *Prosecutor v Tadić*, ICTY Appeals Chamber Decision on Jurisdiction, 2 October 1995 [69]; *Prosecutor v Kunarac*, ICTY Appeals Chamber Judgment, 12 June 2002 [60].

[47] *Prosecutor v Kunarac*, ICTY Appeals Chamber Judgment, 12 June 2002 [59].

[48] *Prosecutor v Kunarac*, ICTY Trial Chamber Judgment, 22 February 2001 [568].

[49] *Prosecutor v Kunarac*, ICTY Appeals Chamber Judgment, 12 June 2002 [64].

Conventions of 1949, it was generally thought that civil conflicts were outside the scope of international law. They were a matter for states to deal with internally. However, there was growing international awareness of the need for regulation in this area, fuelled by the bloody and protracted nature of conflicts such as the Spanish Civil War (1936–1939). The importance of placing limits on internal armed conflicts has only increased since then. Since the Second World War, the vast majority of armed conflicts have been non-international in character.[50]

The requirements of international humanitarian law still differ between international and non-international conflicts. However, the distinction has for some time been diminishing in importance, as we will see in more depth below. It is now widely accepted that some common guarantees apply in conflicts of both types.[51] Common Article 3 of the Geneva Conventions was the first, and for some time the only, provision to bring non-international conflicts within the reach of international humanitarian law. It was supplemented by the adoption of Additional Protocol II to the Geneva Conventions in 1977.

The rationale behind the protections contained in Common Article 3 is that there are certain principles of humanity so fundamental that they apply to combatants and civilians in all kinds of conflict. Prior to 1949, the Geneva Conventions assisted only persons caught up in international conflicts. Belligerent groups in civil conflicts were widely perceived as domestic criminals and attempts by the Red Cross Movement to aid those belligerents as inadmissible aid.[52] For this reason, suggestions that the Conventions in their entirety should be applied to non-international conflicts were rejected; their implementation would have greatly restricted states in their capacity to deal with insurgents, including having to treat them as prisoners of war, rather than using ordinary criminal procedures.[53] Common Article 3 is accordingly limited to the most fundamental of principles underlying the Geneva Conventions; it could not be said that

---

[50] Jean-Marie Henckaerts and Louise Doswald-Beck, *Customary International Humanitarian Law* (CUP 2005) xxviii; Lindsay Moir, *The Law of Internal Armed Conflict* (CUP 2002) 1; Dan Smith, *The State of War and Peace Atlas* (Penguin 1997) 90–95; International Committee of the Red Cross, *International Humanitarian Law and the Challenge of Contemporary Armed Conflicts* (ICRC 2011) 6.

[51] *Prosecutor v Tadić*, ICTY Appeals Chamber Decision on Jurisdiction, 2 October 1995 [96]–[127].

[52] Jean S Pictet et al (eds), *Commentary on the Geneva Conventions* (ICRC 1960) vol 3, 28–9.

[53] Ibid 32.

torture or mutilation, for example, are reasonable measures for a state to suppress a rebellion against it by an insurgent group.[54]

A distinction needs to be drawn in this context regarding the scope of Common Article 3 and Additional Protocol II. Common Article 3 has the broader scope of the two. It applies to armed conflicts 'not of an international character' occurring in the territory of a state party. Additional Protocol II, on the other hand, applies to armed conflicts not covered by Additional Protocol I that take place in the territory of a state party between its armed forces and dissident armed forces or other armed groups. The non-state groups in question must be under responsible command, and control enough of the state's territory to carry out 'sustained and concerted military operations' and to implement the Protocol.[55] The more limited scope of Additional Protocol II occurred as a result of fears by a number of states who negotiated the text of the Additional Protocols that an expansive field of application would limit their ability to deal effectively with internal disturbances.

It therefore appears that Additional Protocol II will technically only apply to armed conflicts where one of the parties is a state, whereas the principles expressed in Common Article 3 potentially apply to conflicts where no states are involved. It has been suggested that both state and non-state participants in internal armed conflicts are bound by Common Article 3 by virtue of its customary law status.[56] Additional Protocol II is also expressly stated not to apply to 'internal disturbances and tensions, such as riots, isolated and sporadic acts of violence' and other similar incidents.[57] It therefore reiterates the overarching definition of armed conflict discussed earlier in this chapter.

Definitional Issues

We have seen that the definition of armed conflict offered by the ICTY Appeals Chamber in *Tadić* has two limbs, corresponding to international and non-international conflicts. An international armed conflict, according to this definition, is a conflict between the armed forces of two or

---

[54] Ibid 36–7.
[55] Additional Protocol II, art 1(1).
[56] For discussion, see Sandesh Sivakumaran, 'Binding Armed Opposition Groups' (2006) 55 *International and Comparative Law Quarterly* 369, 371–5. Compare *Nicaragua v United States (Merits)*, International Court of Justice (ICJ) Judgment, 27 June 1986 [218]–[219]. We will return to this issue in Chapter 7.
[57] Additional Protocol II, art 1(2).

more states.[58] A non-international armed conflict, on the other hand, is a conflict between a state and an organised armed group within the state's territory or between two or more non-state groups within a state's territory.

The distinction between international and non-international conflicts is not always straightforward. For example, it may depend whether a particular entity is legally recognised as a state. Would a war between China and Taiwan be international or non-international? What about border skirmishes between Somaliland and Puntland? The answer potentially depends on how one interprets the criteria for statehood under international law. We will examine that topic in more detail in Chapter 7.

The ICTY Appeals Chamber described the conflict in the former Yugoslavia as having 'both internal and international aspects'.[59] This shows that the distinction may be ambiguous, even in the absence of disputes concerning statehood. The status of the Yugoslavian conflict was complicated by the multiple state and non-state parties involved. In some cases, a non-international armed conflict may *become* international at a certain point in its history. This is often referred to as an 'internationalised' conflict. A conflict may become internationalised because of the creation of a new state or states during the conflict. Alternatively, internationalisation may occur when a third-party state militarily intervenes in a non-international conflict or when one or more participants in a non-international conflict come to act 'on behalf of' a third-party state.[60]

The Test of Control

When is a party to a non-international conflict deemed to be acting 'on behalf of' a third-party state, thereby internationalising the conflict? Two tests for resolving this question have been mooted. The first test arises from the International Court of Justice (ICJ) decision in the case of *Nicaragua v United States*.[61] In that case, the ICJ held a party is acting on behalf of a state if the state has 'effective control' over the group.[62] This is a high standard, requiring the state to issue the group with instructions

---

[58] *Prosecutor v Tadić*, ICTY Appeals Chamber Judgment, 15 July 1999 [84].
[59] *Prosecutor v Tadić*, ICTY Appeals Chamber Decision on Jurisdiction, 2 October 1995 [77].
[60] Ibid; *Prosecutor v Tadić*, ICTY Appeals Chamber Judgment, 15 July 1999 [88]–[97].
[61] *Nicaragua v United States (Merits)*, ICJ Judgment, 27 June 1986.
[62] Ibid [115].

to commit specific acts. It is not enough that the state provides technical support or financial assistance.

The primary issue before the ICJ in *Nicaragua* was not whether the conflict in question was international or non-international, but rather whether the United States could be held responsible for acts performed by a non-state guerrilla group fighting against the Nicaraguan government. However, the ICTY Appeals Chamber in *Tadić* treated the test as relevant to the classification of armed conflicts. The ICJ in *Nicaragua* presented the effective control test as generally applicable to determining state responsibility for the actions of non-state groups. The ICTY Appeals Chamber, on the other hand, ruled that the test only applies to the control of *individuals* and *disorganised* groups.[63]

According to the Appeals Chamber, control of *organised* groups is assessed using the weaker 'overall control' test.[64] The overall control test asks whether the state 'wields general control over the group, not only by equipping and financing [it], but also by coordinating or helping in the general planning of its military activity'.[65] It does not require that the state issues directions to perform specific acts, but merely that the state has an overall relationship of influence and control over the group. The rationale for the two different tests seems to be that the actions of organised groups are generally more predictable than those of disorganised groups or individuals. It is therefore reasonable to hold a state responsible for the actions of an organised group based on an overall relationship of control, while for disorganised groups and individuals specific directions are needed.

The Appeals Chamber further held that 'where the controlling State in question is an adjacent State with territorial ambitions on the State where the conflict is taking place [. . .] it may be easier to establish the threshold'.[66] This suggests a holistic approach to determining whether a non-state group is acting on behalf of a state. If a third-party state has an obvious interest in the success of a rebel group operating on the territory of another state, an inference may more easily be drawn based on technical and material assistance that the group is operating on the third party's behalf.

---

[63] *Prosecutor v Tadić*, ICTY Appeals Chamber Judgment, 15 July 1999 [99]–[100].
[64] Ibid [120].
[65] Ibid [131].
[66] Ibid [140].

Wars of National Liberation

Additional Protocol I to the Geneva Conventions generally applies to the same types of armed conflicts covered by Common Article 2: namely, international conflicts between state parties.[67] However, Article 1(4) of Additional Protocol I extends its scope to a type of conflict not covered by Common Article 2: 'armed conflicts in which peoples are fighting against colonial domination and alien occupation and against racist regimes in exercise of their right of self-determination'. Conflicts falling into this category are commonly called *wars of national liberation*. They are deemed international conflicts for the purposes of Additional Protocol I, although they would otherwise count as internal conflicts.

Article 96(2) of Additional Protocol I provides that state parties are not obliged to observe its provisions in relation to states or other parties to a conflict that do not accept it as binding. Article 96(3) then sets out a procedure whereby non-state groups engaged in wars of national liberation may formally undertake to apply the Protocol. These provisions effectively mean that the Protocol is not binding in wars of national liberation unless the non-state groups involved have recognised its application.

The definition of a war of national liberation in Article 1(4) is open to interpretation. It makes reference to the concept of self-determination, which itself is not very clearly delineated under international law. Furthermore, it is very much open to dispute whether a particular armed group is fighting against 'colonial domination', 'alien occupation' or a 'racist regime'. These kinds of terms tend to feature in political rhetoric rather than being framed for technical accuracy. They are therefore unsuited to determining legal questions such as the status of an armed conflict. Furthermore, it is unlikely that a state would be willing to voluntarily label itself as colonial, alien or racist when facing internal armed dissent. The inclusion of wars of national liberation in Additional Protocol I has therefore long been controversial. The scope of the provision remains poorly defined.

The Future of the Distinction

It has been suggested by a number of judges and commentators that the distinction between international and non-international armed conflicts is gradually diminishing in importance.[68] Some, but certainly not all, rules

---

[67] Additional Protocol I, art 1(3).
[68] For a helpful overview, see Emily Crawford, 'Unequal Before the Law:

governing international armed conflicts have become applicable to internal conflicts as a matter of customary international law.[69] Furthermore, the nature of contemporary armed conflicts means the distinction is not always obvious, as the Yugoslavian conflict illustrates.

Non-international conflicts not infrequently possess an extraterritorial aspect – for example, incursions over state borders – and may feature the involvement of international forces either fighting alongside the parties or acting in a peacekeeping capacity. Conflicts may also arise between a state and a non-state party operating from the territory of another state but not under that state's authority or control, such as the 2006 conflict between Israel and Hezbollah forces operating from within Lebanon.[70]

The increasingly diverse nature of armed conflict continues to challenge the delineation of the boundaries between types of conflict. The ICTY Appeals Chamber commented in the *Tadić* decision on jurisdiction that since the 1930s the distinction between international and non-international conflict has become increasingly blurred. The Appeals Chamber attributed this to various factors, including the increasing frequency and protracted nature of civil conflicts, sometimes involving the whole population of the state where they occur. The increasing interdependence of states in the modern world also means that armed violence within one state will impact on the interests of other nations, making them more likely to have an interest in the resolution of such internal conflicts.[71]

Finally and perhaps most importantly, the Appeals Chamber pointed to the emergence of human rights doctrines and to their gradual assumption of importance relative to traditional notions of state sovereignty:

> Why protect civilians from belligerent violence, or ban rape, torture or the wanton destruction of hospitals, churches, museums or private property, as well as proscribe weapons causing unnecessary suffering when two sovereign States are engaged in war, and yet refrain from enacting the same bans or providing the same protection when armed violence has erupted 'only' within the territory of a sovereign State?[72]

The Case for the Elimination of the Distinction Between International and Non-International Armed Conflicts' (2007) 20 *Leiden Journal of International Law* 441.

[69] Jean-Marie Henckaerts and Louise Doswald-Beck, *Customary International Humanitarian Law* (CUP 2005) xxix.

[70] International Committee of the Red Cross, *International Humanitarian Law and the Challenge of Contemporary Armed Conflicts* (ICRC 2011) 9–11.

[71] *Prosecutor v Tadić*, ICTY Appeals Chamber Decision on Jurisdiction, 2 October 1995 [97].

[72] Ibid [97].

Developments in technology have contributed significantly to the expansion of international humanitarian law to cover a broader range of conflicts. Now more than ever, the suffering of people embroiled in conflicts around the world is instantly transmitted to wide international audiences through the internet and social media platforms. These new technologies have given the notion of cosmopolitanism referred to earlier in this chapter new meaning, as it allows us to witness the experiences of other global citizens in a way that could not have been imagined in Diogenes' time.

The atrocities perpetrated on a large scale during the civil conflict in Rwanda in the 1990s, and the international community's failure to act, brought home to people around the world the need for civilians to be granted protection in internal conflicts, regardless of principles of state sovereignty. More recently, media coverage of hostilities between state governments and national liberation forces has highlighted the suffering of citizens and reinforced the need for certain minimum standards of protection to apply to victims of all conflicts, regardless of their nature.

While these developments do not mean that *all* rules applicable to international conflicts now apply to non-international conflicts, it is certainly the case that a number of rules and principles now apply regardless of the nature of the conflict. These rules include protection of civilians from hostilities, protection of civilian objects, and the prohibition of certain means of warfare and methods of conducting hostilities.[73] In 2005, a study commissioned by the ICRC found that of 161 customary principles of international humanitarian law, 148 applied in non-international as well as international armed conflicts.[74] The recognition of these principles of customary international law may mean that the distinction between types of conflict is of much less significance that it has been in the past.

---

[73] Ibid [126]–[127].
[74] Jean-Marie Henckaerts and Louise Doswald-Beck, *Customary International Humanitarian Law* (CUP 2005). The figures are reported in International Committee of the Red Cross, *International Humanitarian Law and the Challenge of Contemporary Armed Conflicts* (ICRC 2011) 12.

2. Sources of international humanitarian law

We have seen that international humanitarian law is *the body of international law governing the conduct of armed conflicts*. This chapter examines the historical development and main sources of international humanitarian law. We begin by briefly discussing the sources of international law generally, focusing on those topics that are most relevant to international humanitarian law. We will then distinguish between the two main branches of international humanitarian law, known as the Hague law and the Geneva law, before tracking the development of this body of law from the 1860s to the present day.

We will see that international humanitarian law centres on a number of important international conventions, such as the Hague Regulations of 1899, the Geneva Conventions of 1949 and the two Additional Protocols of 1977. These general documents are supplemented by a number of other sources of law, including specialised conventions on particular issues and types of weapons, the rules of customary international law, the decisions of international tribunals, the writings of prominent academic authors and the pronouncements of bodies such as the United Nations (UN) General Assembly.

SOURCES OF INTERNATIONAL LAW

The traditional starting point for examining the sources of international law is Article 38(1) of the Statute of the International Court of Justice (ICJ). It requires the ICJ to apply in its decisions the following sources of international law:

- international conventions;
- international custom;
- 'the general principles of law recognised by civilised nations';
- as a supplementary source, judicial decisions and 'the teachings of the most highly qualified publicists'.

Article 38(1) is widely acknowledged as an authoritative statement of the sources of international law. The ICJ Statute goes on to affirm that states appearing before the ICJ may elect to have their dispute heard *ex aequo et bono* (according to the right and the good).[1] This would allow the ICJ to dispense with the usual rules of international law. However, no parties have ever opted to invoke that provision.

International Conventions

A *convention* or *treaty* is an agreement between two or more states. This source of law therefore reflects the traditional model of international law as governing relationships between states. An important feature of international conventions is that they are only binding upon the states who are parties to them.[2] This represents a potential limitation on the applicability of the rules of international law. However, the consensual character of treaty law is less of a problem for international humanitarian law than it is for some other areas of international law. This is because the Geneva Conventions of 1949, which contain many of the fundamental rules of international humanitarian law, have now been ratified by all 194 recognised states. They are therefore universally applicable.

Other important international humanitarian law conventions enjoy various levels of endorsement by states. The sources of international humanitarian law applicable in an armed conflict will therefore depend on which conventions have been ratified by the states involved. The two Additional Protocols of 1977, for example, boast 171 and 166 parties respectively at the time of writing. This represents a sizable proportion of the international community. Unfortunately, a number of influential and strategically important states – such as India, Indonesia, Israel, Iran, Malaysia, Pakistan, Sri Lanka, Thailand and the United States – have yet to ratify either of the Additional Protocols. There are therefore significant gaps in their applicability to specific armed conflicts.

International Custom

The existence of a rule of customary international law traditionally requires two elements:

- general and consistent state practice in support of the rule; and
- a sense of legal obligation regarding the rule (*opinio juris*).

---

[1] Statute of the International Court of Justice, art 38 (2).
[2] Vienna Convention on the Law of Treaties, art 34.

The first of these requirements calls for general and consistent state practice observing the rule, but not absolute or 'rigorous conformity'.[3] The practice of states specifically affected by the rule will be particularly significant.[4] The element of *opinio juris* further requires that states do not observe the practice merely as a matter of habit, but because they regard it as a binding norm. These elements are often difficult to assess in practice. Fortunately, the International Committee of the Red Cross (ICRC) has produced a comprehensive study of customary international humanitarian law that seeks to document relevant state practice and codify the corresponding customary rules.[5] The ICRC study is not necessarily decisive as a statement of international law, but it provides a highly persuasive starting point for examining the customary rules governing armed conflict.

Customary international humanitarian law plays an important role in mitigating the problems posed by the consent-based character of treaty law. Customary international law does not depend on the consent of states. It is presumed to bind all members of the international community. A treaty provision that attains customary law status can therefore effectively become binding on states who are not parties.[6] There is also significant support for the view that customary international humanitarian law is binding upon armed groups who are not affiliated with any state.[7] The main exception to the universally binding character of customary international law is the principle known as the *persistent objector rule*. It has long been recognised that a state that persistently objects to a norm of customary international law from the point of its creation will not be bound by it.[8]

States can modify by treaty the customary legal rules that apply between them, but this modification only applies to interactions between those parties. Furthermore, some customary rules cannot be modified by agreement. These are known as norms of *jus cogens*. They are peremptory norms recognised by the international community from which no

---

[3] *Nicaragua v United States (Merits)*, International Court of Justice (ICJ) Judgment, 27 June 1986 [186].

[4] *North Sea Continental Shelf Cases*, ICJ Judgment, 20 February 1969 [73].

[5] Jean-Marie Henckaerts and Louise Doswald-Beck, *Customary International Humanitarian Law* (CUP 2005).

[6] Vienna Convention on the Law of Treaties, art 38.

[7] See, for example, *Nicaragua v United States (Merits)*, ICJ Judgment, 27 June 1986 [218]–[219]. We will return to this issue in Chapter 7.

[8] *Anglo-Norwegian Fisheries Case*, ICJ Judgment, 18 December 1951.

derogation is permitted.[9] There is dispute over exactly which aspects of international law rise to the level of *jus cogens* norms. However, it is widely agreed that the prohibitions on genocide, torture, slavery, war crimes and crimes against humanity fall into this category.[10] These examples are all potentially relevant to armed conflicts.

Additional Sources

The notion of *general principles of law* allows international courts and tribunals to have reference to the underlying principles of domestic legal systems. This is most commonly used for procedural and evidential matters, although it has sometimes been employed by international bodies as a basis for adopting substantive rules.[11] Article 38(1) also mentions judicial decisions and 'the teachings of the most highly qualified publicists'. This is a reference to the writings of academic experts.

There is no doctrine of *stare decisis* in international law. However, past decisions of international courts and tribunals are considered persuasive, as are the writings of eminent commentators. These are recognised as supplementary sources of international law. There is a wide range of international courts and tribunals that have handed down decisions relevant to international humanitarian law. However, some of the international bodies of most relevance to this field of law are as follows:

- The International Court of Justice, which is the official judicial organ of the UN. The ICJ was preceded by the Permanent Court of International Justice, the official judicial body of the League of Nations.
- The international military tribunals established to try war crimes following the Second World War, including the International Military Tribunal at Nuremberg and the International Military Tribunal for the Far East.
- The International Criminal Tribunal for the Former Yugoslavia and the International Criminal Tribunal for Rwanda, which were established by the UN following the armed conflicts in those regions.

---

[9] Vienna Convention on the Law of Treaties, art 53.
[10] M Cherif Bassiouni, 'International Crimes: *Jus Cogens* and *Obligatio Erga Omnes*' (1996) 59 *Law and Contemporary Problems* 63, 68.
[11] See, for example, *Case Concerning the Temple of Preah Vihear*, ICJ Judgment, 15 June 1962. For further discussion of this issue, see Chapter 7.

- Other ad hoc international criminal tribunals established for particular countries with UN cooperation, including the Special Court for Sierra Leone and the Extraordinary Chambers in the Courts of Cambodia.
- Regional human rights tribunals, such as the European Court of Human Rights and the Inter-American Court of Human Rights, which are sometimes called upon to rule on matters arising from armed conflicts.
- The International Criminal Court, established in 2002 to prosecute serious crimes under international law, including war crimes.

UN General Assembly Resolutions are another significant source of pronouncements on international law. Some General Assembly Resolutions purport to state or codify international law, while others are aspirational in content. It is important to distinguish the two types. Resolutions of the former type may hold persuasive force as interpretations of international law. Examples of General Assembly Resolutions relevant to the conduct of armed conflicts include Resolution 1653 (XVI) of 1961, dealing with the legal status of nuclear weapons, and Resolution 2444 (XXIII) of 1968, urging respect for the fundamental principles of international humanitarian law.

HAGUE LAW AND GENEVA LAW

We saw in the last chapter that international humanitarian law is concerned with the *jus in bello* as distinct from the *jus ad bellum*. International humanitarian law itself is then often divided into two sections. These are commonly called the *Hague law* and the *Geneva law*, after the main international treaties containing the applicable rules. According to this distinction, the Hague law is concerned with regulating the means and methods of warfare employed by the parties to an armed conflict, while the Geneva law is concerned with protecting vulnerable parties who find themselves affected by warfare.

The Hague law gains its name from the 1899 and 1907 Hague Conventions and the accompanying Hague Regulations. These documents are directly concerned with regulating the conduct of armed exchanges, for example by restricting the types of weapons that can be used and prohibiting particular military strategies. The Geneva law, by contrast, is now contained primarily in the four Geneva Conventions of 1949 and their two Additional Protocols of 1977. These Conventions specify minimum standards of treatment for specific classes of people rendered vulnerable by armed conflicts, such as the sick and wounded, prisoners of war and civilians caught up in hostilities.

The traditional distinction between these two fields of law is reflected to some extent in the structure of this book. Chapter 3, on the means and methods of warfare, deals substantially with the Hague law, while Chapters 4 and 5, relating to the protection of civilians and combatants, focus largely, although not exclusively, on the Geneva rules. However, it is impossible to maintain a rigid distinction between the two areas. There are many points where the categories overlap. Furthermore, both sets of rules reflect a common concern for mitigating the potentially devastating consequences of armed conflicts. They are therefore best regarded as comprising a unified collection of legal rules and principles, under the general heading of international humanitarian law.

EARLY DEVELOPMENTS

The origins of international humanitarian law as a distinctive branch of international law can be traced to three important developments during the 1860s, two of which centred on international conferences aimed at mitigating the suffering caused by warfare. The earlier of these two meetings, which occurred in Geneva in 1864, is particularly notable, since it not only led to the adoption of the first international convention dealing specifically with humanitarian issues, but also established the important role of what is now the Red Cross and Red Crescent Movement within the humanitarian field.

The Red Cross Movement

The International Committee of the Red Cross was founded in Geneva in 1863 by a group of local citizens. At the forefront of the organisation was Jean Henri Dunant, whose 1862 book, *A Memory of Solferino*, provided the impetus that led to the body's creation.[12] In 1859, Dunant found himself in the village of Castiglione in Northern Italy immediately following the Battle of Solferino, in which over 40,000 combatants were wounded. He joined other volunteers in tending the injured soldiers and was so moved by the experience that he wrote an account of it. Dunant's recollections of the combatants' suffering convinced many Europeans that something had to be done to improve conditions for those affected by

---

[12] Henri Dunant, *A Memory of Solferino* (ICRC 1986).

armed conflicts. The years following the founding of the ICRC in Geneva saw the establishment of a number of national Red Cross organisations across the continent.

Dunant's aims for the Red Cross Movement were twofold. Most importantly, he wanted the various national Red Cross organisations to play a practical and immediate role in providing medical services to wounded combatants and others caught up in armed conflicts. However, he also wanted to encourage nations to agree to a treaty recognising the Red Cross bodies and setting out standards for protecting the wounded. Following intensive lobbying by ICRC members and like-minded individuals, the Swiss government agreed to convene the 1864 Geneva meeting mentioned above.

The Early Geneva Documents

The 1864 Geneva Conference culminated in the adoption of the Convention for the Amelioration of the Condition of the Wounded in Armies in the Field, which conferred protected status during armed conflicts upon ambulances, hospitals and medical personnel, imposed a duty on forces to care for wounded combatants and acknowledged and protected the distinctive Red Cross symbol of 'a red cross on a white ground'. The duty to care for the wounded was imposed on all parties regardless of affiliation.

The 1864 Geneva Convention was followed by several treaties attempting to broaden its scope. An 1899 treaty adapted the 1864 agreement to protect wounded or shipwrecked sailors. A major revision of the 1864 regime occurred in 1906 and this was extended the following year to naval activities. These early instruments laid the foundations for what became known as the Geneva branch of international humanitarian law, concerned with protecting specific groups rendered vulnerable by armed conflicts, such as the sick and injured. However, as we will see, the early agreements were to undergo considerable revision before the principles in this field of law took on their current form.

The Lieber Code

While the ICRC was agitating in Geneva for international action to protect the wounded, important developments in international humanitarian law were also occurring on the other side of the globe. The American states were, at the time, embroiled in the Civil War, which lasted from 1861 until 1865. In 1863, the leader of the Northern forces, United States President Abraham Lincoln, issued a famous order to his troops, entitled Instructions for the Government of Armies of the United States in the Field.

Lincoln's order became known as the Lieber Code, after its primary author, a German-born lawyer named Francis Lieber. It represented an ambitious attempt to set out detailed guidelines for the conduct of all aspects of land-based warfare. Although the Code was a purely internal document and was somewhat undermined by the discretion given to commanders in the name of military necessity, it nevertheless influenced later international attempts to regulate the means and methods of warfare.

The St Petersburg Declaration

Another important event in the development of international humanitarian law took place in 1868, when the Russian government invited a commission of international military experts to St Petersburg to discuss growing concern about the use in warfare of a recently developed range of light explosives. The explosives in question were designed to put only one combatant out of action, but typically inflicted far more serious wounds than an ordinary rifle bullet and therefore greatly increased the suffering experienced by the victim. The St Petersburg meeting responded to this development by adopting a declaration forbidding the use in hostilities of explosives under 400 grams in weight.

Although the St Petersburg Declaration was directed at a very specific issue, the reasoning endorsed by the delegates provided the basis for further developments in regulating the means and methods of warfare. The commission emphasised the importance of alleviating the suffering of combatants and noted that the infliction of injury during armed conflicts was permissible only to the extent that it was necessary to overcome enemy resistance. Since the explosives under discussion increased the suffering of the wounded without providing any direct military advantage compared to the use of ordinary bullets, the St Petersburg delegates agreed to proscribe their use.

Both the Lieber Code and the St Petersburg Declaration have served as important models for the development of what has become known as the Hague law, concerned with mitigating the suffering caused to combatants in warfare by limiting the varieties of weapons and tactics that forces can employ against one another. As the popular name suggests, this body of law has found its most prominent expression in a series of agreements arising from conferences held in the Dutch city of The Hague. The historical background to these important treaties is examined in the following section.

THE HAGUE PEACE CONFERENCES

Following the St Petersburg Declaration, the Russian government continued to encourage international discussion on rules and customs concerning warfare. It was at Russia's instigation that delegates from a number of states arrived at The Hague in 1899 to debate measures aimed at preventing the outbreak of further wars in Europe. The stated focus of the Hague Peace Conference was firmly on the *jus contra bellum*. The main issue scheduled for discussion concerned the creation of compulsory arbitration mechanisms for disputes between nations, in order to forestall recourse to armed hostilities. However, the delegates also discussed the need for standards governing the conduct of warfare.

The First Hague Peace Conference

The most positive outcome reached at the Hague Conference of 1899 related not to compulsory international arbitration, but to the means and methods of warfare. In the former area, while it was resolved that arbitration between hostile states should be encouraged, no agreement was reached regarding a compulsory regime. In the latter field, however, delegates agreed upon a Convention with Respect to the Laws and Customs of War on Land, which was accompanied by a wide-ranging collection of Regulations.

The 1899 Hague Regulations represented an ambitious attempt to codify the existing customs governing the conduct of land warfare. The drafters based the Regulations on a number of sources, including the Lieber Code and a draft declaration that had been proposed at a conference in Brussels in 1874. Inspiration was also drawn from the reasoning underlying the St Petersburg Declaration. The resulting document clarified many important issues concerning the conduct of warfare, including treatment of prisoners of war, the obligations of occupying powers and restrictions on specific types of weapons and military tactics. The most notable omission from the Regulations was the treatment of the sick and injured, which had been covered by the 1864 Geneva Convention.

The influence of the St Petersburg Declaration was evident in the Preamble to the 1899 Hague Convention on land warfare. The Preamble recognised that the damage inflicted in war should not exceed that necessary to achieve military objectives. The influence of St Petersburg was also apparent in an important paragraph of the Preamble that became known as the Martens Clause, after its author, the distinguished Russian delegate, Fyodor Fyodorovich Martens (also known as Friedrich Martens and Frédéric de Martens).[13] The Martens Clause provided that, in situations not envisaged by the drafters of the Hague documents, military commanders were not entitled to act arbitrarily, but should abide by 'the laws of humanity and the dictates of the public conscience'. Although the precise legal implications of this provision continue to be debated,[14] it clearly emphasises the underlying humanitarian principles endorsed by the St Petersburg delegates.

The 1899 Hague Peace Conference also continued the work of the St Petersburg committee in another respect. Just as the St Petersburg Declaration had targeted a specific type of light explosive, the Hague delegates agreed to adopt an additional declaration prohibiting the use of a newly developed variety of rifle ammunition, known as dum-dum bullets. The reasoning underlying the Hague agreement directly reflected the arguments of the St Petersburg committee. Since dum-dum ammunition, which was designed to flatten and expand upon entering the human body, was likely to severely aggravate the suffering of wounded combatants without resulting in any direct military advantage, the Hague delegates decided its use in armed hostilities should not be allowed.

The Second Hague Peace Conference

It was envisaged at the 1899 Hague Conference that regular follow-up meetings would be held. This agreement resulted in the Second Hague Peace Conference, which was convened in 1907. The Second Hague Conference reiterated the desire for lasting peace that motivated the previous meeting, but made few changes to the 1899 Regulations on land warfare. The Regulations were adapted to cover an emerging form of aerial bombardment, whereby forces threw explosives from balloons upon troops stationed below. This, however, had been provisionally prohibited in 1899.

The main advances achieved at the 1907 Hague Conference related to naval warfare. The delegates adopted a number of conventions in this area. The two most notable were the Convention Concerning Bombardment by Naval Forces in Times of War, which adapted to naval operations the

---

[13] For further background on Martens and his contributions to international law, see Vladimir V Pustogarov, 'Fyodor Fyodorovich Martens (1845–1909): A Humanist of Modern Times' (1996) 312 *International Review of the Red Cross* 300.

[14] Antonio Cassese, 'The Martens Clause: Half a Loaf or Simply Pie in the Sky?' (2000) 11 *European Journal of International Law* 187; Rupert Ticehurst, 'The Martens Clause and the Laws of Armed Conflict' (1997) 317 *International Review of the Red Cross* 125.

rules about bombardment contained in the 1899 Regulations, and the Convention Relative to the Laying of Automatic Submarine Contact Mines, which restricted the use of mines and torpedoes to protect commercial shipping operations. Several other conventions also regulated matters affecting commercial shipping. The 1907 Hague Conference was followed by a conference in London two years later focusing specifically on naval warfare, but it failed to reach any formal outcome.

THE LEAGUE OF NATIONS PERIOD

The 1907 Hague Conference closed with delegates anticipating a third meeting. However, it never eventuated, due to the outbreak of the First World War in 1914. The period between the First and Second World Wars brought few lasting improvements to the Hague rules. The creation of the League of Nations in 1920, following the conclusion of the Versailles Peace Conference the previous year, led to a number of initiatives aimed at preserving world peace, but had little impact on the law of warfare.

The main exception was the adoption in 1925 at a meeting in Geneva of a Protocol prohibiting the use in armed conflicts of chemical agents, such as chlorine, phosgene and mustard gas. These types of agents had been widely and controversially employed during the First World War. The prohibition also extended to bacteriological agents, which in 1925 had not been adapted for military use, but were recognised as a possible feature in future conflicts. The Protocol illustrates the continual efforts of international humanitarian law to stay abreast of technological innovations in warfare.

Developments in the Geneva law during this period were more extensive. In 1929, the ICRC initiated an international meeting in Geneva that led to some important additions to the rules contained in the 1864 and 1906 Geneva treaties. The delegates drew on the experiences of the First World War in compiling a considerably refined agreement regarding the treatment of the sick and wounded in land warfare. The conference also gave rise to a separate instrument governing the treatment of prisoners of war. Standards governing the treatment of prisoners had been included in the 1899 Hague Regulations, but the relevant provisions lacked detail and sat uneasily with the emphasis of the Hague documents on balancing restrictions on warfare with the demands of military necessity.

The 1929 Geneva Convention Relative to the Treatment of Prisoners of War improved the Hague rules in many respects. As well as including far more detail in response to the events of the First World War, the Geneva instrument incorporated strong provisions dealing with such issues as reprisals against prisoners and acknowledged the role of the Red Cross Movement in monitoring and documenting captured combatants. The 1929 agreement on prisoners of war dominated the field until 1949, when the entire body of the Geneva rules was revised. The following section examines the important developments of the 1949 Geneva Conference in light of their historical background.

THE 1949 GENEVA CONFERENCE

The content of the four Geneva Conventions of 1949 will be covered later in this book, particularly in Chapters 4 and 5. The present discussion focuses on the historical context and main themes of the conference at which the instruments were adopted. Like the 1864 Geneva Conference, the 1949 meeting was instigated by the ICRC in cooperation with the Swiss government. The meeting's purpose was to update the previous Geneva treaties in light of developments in the Second World War (1939–1945) and the Spanish Civil War, which took place between 1936 and 1939.

The Spanish Civil War, in particular, highlighted an important lacuna in the previous international humanitarian law instruments. Prior to 1949, international humanitarian law had been exclusively concerned with regulating armed conflicts involving two or more nations. Civil wars between a state and a non-state group operating in its territory were thought to be domestic matters outside the reach of international law. The Spanish War, in which both combatants and civilians had been brutally treated, served as a reminder that internal conflicts, too, should be constrained by legal rules.

In response to this issue, the 1949 Geneva Conference decided to insert into each of the four updated treaties a common provision dealing with non-international armed conflicts, which has become known as Common Article 3. The provision contains a number of fundamental rules that are stated to apply 'as a minimum' to armed conflicts that are not international in character. Common Article 3 represented a critical step in the development of international humanitarian law, as it was the first time an international instrument had established guidelines for the conduct of internal armed conflicts. It remained the sole provision expressly covering such conflicts until 1977.

The first three Geneva Conventions of 1949 superseded previous Geneva treaties. Geneva Convention I protects wounded and sick combatants in conflicts on land, superseding the agreements of 1864 and 1906. Geneva Convention II deals with wounded, sick and shipwrecked combatants at sea, replacing the Geneva treaties of 1899 and 1907, while Geneva

Convention III deals with prisoners of war, surpassing the agreement of 1929. By contrast, Geneva Convention IV on the Protection of Civilian Persons in Time of War broke new ground by extending detailed protections to civilians caught up in military hostilities. Although the treatment of civilians in wartime had been covered to some extent in the Hague documents, Geneva Convention IV, like the 1929 Convention on prisoners of war, represented a considerable advance on the Hague rules.

The delegates' decision to adopt a separate treaty on the protection of civilians reflected events in both the Spanish Civil War and the Second World War, where advancing forces came across large numbers of civilians, with scant guidelines in place as to how they should be treated. Convention IV was also inspired by the lengthy periods of occupation experienced by a number of European nations during the Second World War. The experiences of the Second World War were reflected in several other changes enacted by the 1949 Conventions. For example, Geneva Convention III recognised that members of organised resistance movements, which had operated throughout Europe during the Second World War, should be accorded special protection under certain conditions.

UNITED NATIONS INITIATIVES

The 1949 Geneva Conference was followed by another period of relative stasis in international humanitarian law. The United Nations was created in 1945 to succeed the failed League of Nations, but its initial years yielded little action to improve the rules governing armed conflicts. The main exception was the adoption in 1954 at an international conference hosted in The Hague by the United Nations Educational, Scientific and Cultural Organisation (UNESCO) of a Convention for the Protection of Cultural Property in the Event of Armed Conflict. The Convention represented a notable development, as it gave detailed attention to yet another area covered to some extent in the 1899 Hague Regulations, but in need of more complete consideration. However, few other significant advances were made in international humanitarian law until the early 1960s, when high-profile conflicts such as the Vietnam War again brought the topic to worldwide attention.

Nuclear Weapons

The closing stages of the Second World War saw an ominous development in the means and methods of warfare with the first hostile use of nuclear weapons. Although the issue received extensive attention in the early years of the UN – indeed, the first ever resolution of the UN General Assembly concerned the regulation of nuclear energy – the organisation's efforts were initially directed at encouraging nuclear disarmament, rather than clarifying the legal position regarding the use of nuclear weapons during wartime. This focus altered somewhat with General Assembly Resolution 1653 (XVI) of 1961, which declared that the use of nuclear weapons in warfare would be illegal and called upon member nations to conclude a treaty to that effect.

Unfortunately, no such treaty has ever eventuated. However, the Resolution signalled the possibility of a more active role for the UN in urging the development of humanitarian principles. A number of other resolutions on nuclear weapons followed. General Assembly Resolution 2444 (XXIII) of 1968 affirmed that the general principles of international humanitarian law govern nuclear weapons. Every year since 1996, the General Assembly has reiterated its earlier call for states to negotiate a binding nuclear weapons convention, but to no effect. We will examine the status of nuclear weapons under international humanitarian law in greater detail in Chapter 3.

Resolution 2444 (XXIII)

In 1968, which the UN declared Human Rights Year, the organisation convened a conference in Tehran, Iran, to discuss issues relating to human rights. Towards the end of the meeting, the delegates adopted a resolution that suggested a new chapter in the UN's attitude towards international humanitarian law. Resolution XXIII asked the General Assembly to direct the Secretary-General to enquire into potential improvements to existing humanitarian law conventions and the possible need for additional treaties dealing with emerging humanitarian issues. The General Assembly adopted Resolution 2444 (XXIII) in December 1968. The Resolution invited the Secretary-General, in consultation with the ICRC, to undertake the studies suggested by the Tehran delegates.

General Assembly Resolution 2444 (XXIII) was notable not only for the ongoing role envisaged for the UN Secretariat in developing international humanitarian law, but also for its endorsement of the fundamental principles that had been agreed upon at the International Conference of the Red Cross held in Vienna in 1965. Those principles, which again reflected the conception of international humanitarian law that motivated the St Petersburg Declaration, centred on the following propositions:

- The right of parties to an armed conflict to take steps to injure enemy combatants is not unlimited.

- Civilian populations must never be targeted in armed hostilities.
- Efforts must always be made to distinguish between combatants and civilians in order to protect the latter.
- The general principles of international humanitarian law govern the use of nuclear and other weapons of mass destruction.

Following Resolution 2444 (XXIII), the Secretary-General produced a series of annual reports assessing the current state of international humanitarian law and suggesting potential changes. The reports were generally well received by the General Assembly, which passed several resolutions endorsing the Secretary-General's recommendations. On the whole, however, the recommendations generated little sustained attention. The notable exceptions concerned relatively specific issues, such as the protection of journalists and the status of wars of national liberation. It is significant that the UN consistently recognised these wars as international armed conflicts and stressed that combatants on all sides were entitled to the full protection of the Geneva Conventions.

The activities of the UN during the 1960s demonstrated the potential for that organisation to take a leading role in promoting and developing international humanitarian law, although the practical impact of some of these initiatives was ultimately limited. The approach adopted by the UN clearly reflected the humanitarian ideals expressed in the reasoning of the St Petersburg delegates and the work of the ICRC. It is also noteworthy that the UN frequently treated issues relating to international humanitarian law as elements of the organisation's work in advancing human rights. For instance, Resolution 2444 (XXIII), which arose from the 1968 Tehran Conference on human rights, was entitled Respect for Human Rights in Armed Conflicts.

Bacteriological Weapons

One notable feature of UN debates on international humanitarian law during the 1960s was deliberation on the status of bacteriological weapons. The employment of bacteriological agents in armed hostilities had been envisaged in the 1925 Geneva Protocol, but the terms of that document were necessarily vague, since such agents had not been adapted to warfare at the time it was drafted. Furthermore, many states had never ratified the 1925 Protocol, undermining its potential effectiveness. Discussion about this issue in the UN General Assembly and elsewhere culminated in an important 1972 Convention on bacteriological, biological and toxin weapons. The rules and principles governing this topic will be examined further in Chapter 3.

THE 1977 ADDITIONAL PROTOCOLS

The international awareness of the need for revisions to international humanitarian law that resulted from UN and ICRC activities during the 1960s culminated in a diplomatic conference in Geneva in 1974. The event was again hosted by the Swiss government. The ICRC played an important role, presenting draft documents aimed at updating central aspects of international humanitarian law. The delegates refined the ICRC documents in four annual sessions between 1974 and 1977, producing two treaties designated as Additional Protocols I and II to the Geneva Conventions of 1949. The Protocols were adopted at the 1977 session and many states ratified them later that year.

Additional Protocol I sought to update and extend the rules relating to the conduct of international armed conflicts (controversially defined to encompass wars of national liberation, as we saw in Chapter 1).[15] It covers issues relating to both the means and methods of warfare and the protection of vulnerable parties. Additional Protocol II, meanwhile, is directed at non-international armed conflicts, making it the first instrument devoted exclusively to that area. Additional Protocol II therefore continued the extension of international humanitarian law that began with the adoption of Common Article 3. The application of international humanitarian law to non-international conflicts had gained considerable support by 1977, but it was by no means uncontroversial. Several delegates at the conference recorded objections to the entire second Protocol. Even today, the number of states to have ratified Protocol II lags slightly behind the figure for Protocol I.

Like Common Article 3, both Additional Protocols reinforce the principle that certain activities, such as murder, torture, taking of hostages and summary execution, are prohibited in both international and non-international conflicts. A number of other protections are common to conflicts of both types. The wounded, sick and shipwrecked must be respected and protected in all circumstances and measures must be taken to locate and collect them.[16] Humanitarian relief activities must be permitted regardless of the type of conflict.[17] Attacks on the civilian population and objects needed for their survival are absolutely prohibited.[18] Special protection is also accorded to medical units and transport, which may not

---

[15] Additional Protocol I, art 1(4).
[16] Additional Protocol I, art 10, 33; Additional Protocol II, art 7, 8.
[17] Additional Protocol I, arts 69–71; Additional Protocol II, art 18.
[18] Additional Protocol I, arts 48, 50–60, ; Additional Protocol II, arts 13–16.

be attacked or destroyed.[19] Some of these protections are more detailed in Additional Protocol I than in Additional Protocol II, but the same principles appear in both contexts.

There are also a number of provisions in Additional Protocol I that have no counterpart in Additional Protocol II. For example, Additional Protocol I provides that captured combatants are entitled to be treated as prisoners of war and are therefore protected by Geneva Convention III.[20] There is no direct equivalent to prisoner of war status under Additional Protocol II, although the treaty does afford significant protections to captured fighters. We will consider this issue in more detail in Chapter 5.

The organic nature of civil conflicts, often involving large proportions of the population of a nation or region, poses a challenge in terms of the important principle that members of the civilian population not be targeted. This is especially the case where members of opposing forces live and operate freely within their communities, meaning that the distinction between civilian and combatant populations may sometimes be difficult to draw. Nonetheless, the principle of distinction, according to which civilian objects must be distinguished from military targets and spared from direct attack, is reflected in both Additional Protocols.[21] The protection applies to all civilians so long as they do not take a 'direct part in hostilities'.[22] We will consider the principle in greater depth in Chapter 3.

We noted in Chapter 1 that the boundaries between international and non-international conflicts are increasingly blurred. Insofar as the protections in the Additional Protocols have been recognised as principles of customary international law, the differences between the two treaties have lost some of their significance.[23] The extent to which particular humanitarian principles have come to form part of customary international law as it applies to international and non-international conflicts will be considered in the context of the various types of protection detailed in Chapters 3, 4 and 5.

---

[19] Additional Protocol I, arts 8, 9, 12, 21–31; Additional Protocol II, art 11.
[20] Additional Protocol I, art 45.
[21] Additional Protocol I, art 48; Additional Protocol II, art 13(2). See also Jean-Marie Henckaerts and Louise Doswald-Beck, *Customary International Humanitarian Law* (CUP 2005) 3–8.
[22] Additional Protocol I, art 51(3); Additional Protocol II, art 13(3).
[23] Jean-Marie Henckaerts and Louise Doswald-Beck, *Customary International Humanitarian Law* (CUP 2005) xxix.

THE 2005 ADDITIONAL PROTOCOL

The Geneva Convention of 1864 established the Red Cross emblem to symbolise the neutral status granted by international humanitarian law to medical services and relief societies participating in the provision of care for civilians and the wounded. By the end of the nineteenth century, the Red Cross, the Red Crescent and the Red Lion and Sun were all in use by states to signify the protected status of medical and other humanitarian objects. The Geneva Conventions of 1949 recognised all three emblems and reserved them for humanitarian purposes,[24] although the Red Lion and Sun has since fallen into disuse.

Although the emblems were not intended to have any religious connotations, they have been viewed in that light by some states.[25] This perception has inhibited understanding of the neutrality of the Red Cross and Red Crescent Movement and the willingness of some states to utilise the emblems. Accordingly, a third Additional Protocol to the Geneva Conventions was adopted in 2005, establishing a third emblem: the Red Crystal. This emblem may be utilised in the same way as the Red Cross and Red Crescent emblems. At the time of writing, there were 59 state parties to the Additional Protocol III.

CURRENT CHALLENGES

International humanitarian law faces a number of ongoing challenges. These include the challenges posed by new and emerging types of weapons, the changing face of armed conflict and the political dynamics of the international community. We saw above that some of the earliest developments in international humanitarian law concerned responses to new types of weapons. The Additional Protocols covered a number of issues traditionally regarded as falling within Hague law, such as the principles governing bombardment. However, they were silent on the use of specific types of weapons.

The status of weapons such as napalm and landmines had been discussed at the 1974–1977 diplomatic conference and other international meetings, but delegates were unable to reach the agreement necessary to

---

[24] Geneva Convention I, art 44.
[25] For discussion, see René Provost, 'The International Committee of the Red Widget? The Diversity Debate and International Humanitarian Law' (2007) 40 *Israel Law Review* 614.

incorporate such matters into the Additional Protocols. The issue was followed up at a conference on conventional weapons convened by the UN, which occurred over two sessions in 1979 and 1980. Towards the end of the 1980 session, the conference adopted a Convention on Certain Conventional Weapons, with three annexed Protocols. The Convention entered into force in 1983. It now has five optional Protocols placing restrictions on the use of different types of conventional weapons, including landmines and cluster munitions. The structure and content of the Convention will be examined in greater detail in Chapter 3.

The status of specific types of weapons under international humanitarian law is an enduring topic of international discussion. Nuclear weapons, for example, continue to generate much debate. The ICJ was presented with an opportunity to clarify this issue in 1996, when the World Health Organization requested an advisory opinion on the legality of nuclear armaments. However, the Court did little to advance the debate, noting that the use of nuclear weapons would often contravene humanitarian rules due to their indiscriminate nature, but refusing to offer a definitive view on their legal status.[26] Other recent developments in relation to specific types of weapons include the Chemical Weapons Convention of 1993, which entered into force in 1996, and the Ottawa Landmines Convention of 1997, which came into force in 1999.

Armed conflicts continue to arise, defying the aspirations of the *jus ad bellum*. Civil conflicts, in particular, continue to proliferate. Conflicts involving non-state groups have always posed a challenge for international humanitarian law. Many contemporary civil conflicts involve a number of different state and non-state parties, some of which may be loosely affiliated or have overlapping command structures. These conflicts may occur wholly within the territory of a state or spill over national boundaries.

The respect shown for international humanitarian norms in these conflicts is highly variable. Organisations such as the ICRC and the UN continue to work to disseminate humanitarian principles. However, the informal recruitment policies and loose command structures that characterise many contemporary conflicts make it difficult to disseminate and enforce humanitarian standards among combatants. Reprisals against captured combatants and civilian populations, including campaigns of torture and rape, are widespread. The problem is exacerbated in some conflicts by the use of independent contractors outside the military hierarchy.

---

[26] *Legality of the Threat or Use of Nuclear Weapons*, ICJ Advisory Opinion, 8 July 1996.

Attempts to gauge compliance with international humanitarian law are themselves beset by problems, due to difficulties in gaining access to areas where hostilities are occurring. There is, however, cause for optimism. In many respects, support for humanitarian principles within the international community appears stronger than ever before. As mentioned previously, the Geneva Conventions of 1949 have now been accepted by every recognised state, while the two Additional Protocols of 1977 have been ratified by the vast bulk of the international community. Leading human rights instruments, such as the two International Covenants on Civil and Political Rights and Economic, Social and Cultural Rights are also widely recognised, while treaties such as the Ottawa Landmines Convention of 1997 have gained significant support in a relatively short time.

We saw in the previous chapter that international humanitarian law emphasises the basic values that unite human societies. Its continued effectiveness therefore depends not so much upon the formal status of the applicable legal documents, as on the continuation of the international spirit of cooperation that those documents reflect. Should states consistently decide to bypass international institutions in favour of unilateral responses to perceived threats or humanitarian crises, the cooperation necessary to maintain respect for humanitarian standards could become increasingly tenuous. On the other hand, the universal recognition afforded to the principles of the Geneva Conventions shows that the aspirations reflected in this body of law are still very much alive.

3. Means and methods of warfare

The preceding chapters have dealt with the concept of armed conflict and the history and sources of international humanitarian law. The present chapter begins our exploration of the substantive rules of international humanitarian law by examining the limitations placed on the means and methods of warfare. We will look first at the role of combatants as the primary agents of warfare, examining the legal significance of combatant status. We will then examine the main duties of combatants when conducting armed attacks, beginning with the fundamental principles governing this area and then turning to particular kinds of prohibited weapons and forbidden tactics. The chapter concludes by briefly examining environmental and cultural protection under the law of armed conflict.

AGENTS OF WARFARE

International humanitarian law encourages a clear and reliable division between combatants and non-combatants. This reflects the fundamental role played by the *principle of distinction* in this body of law. The principle of distinction requires combatants to distinguish at all times between military targets and civilian objects and stipulates that only military targets may be the object of attack. This principle is undermined if attacking forces cannot readily distinguish combatants from other parties.

The importance of the distinction between combatants and non-combatants is reflected in Article 43(2) of Additional Protocol I to the Geneva Conventions, which provides that '[m]embers of the armed forces of a Party to a conflict [. . .] are combatants, that is to say, they have the right to participate directly in hostilities'. This stipulation makes it clear that international humanitarian law regards combatants as the primary agents of warfare. In the following sections, we will look first at the definition of a combatant set out in the Conventions, before discussing the exact significance of combatant status under international law.

Who is a Combatant?

The classic definition of combatant status under international humanitarian law is found in Article 4 of Geneva Convention III. That provision sets out the categories of people who are entitled to prisoner of war status. The first category comprises members of the regular armed forces of a party to the conflict. The second category covers members of other armed groups, such as militias and volunteer corps, who:

- are under responsible command;
- bear a fixed, distinctive sign recognisable at a distance;
- carry arms openly; and
- respect the requirements of international humanitarian law.

A broadly similar definition, albeit with some differences, is found in Articles 43 and 44 of Additional Protocol I. That definition covers all armed forces or groups under the command of a party to the conflict who are subject to an internal disciplinary system and distinguish themselves from the civilian population or, where this is not possible, carry arms openly whenever engaging in or preparing to engage in an attack.[1] The main difference between the definitions is that whereas Geneva Convention III seems to require combatants to systematically distinguish themselves from civilians, Additional Protocol I recognises that in some cases they may only do so when launching an attack.

The types of situations envisaged in Additional Protocol I where it is not possible for combatants to distinguish themselves from civilians include resistance movements in occupied territories, wars of national liberation and civilians spontaneously taking up arms as the last line of defence (*levée en masse*).[2] Combatants falling into these categories are likely to find it highly impractical or perilous to consistently carry arms openly and bear a uniform or fixed, distinctive sign. We noted in Chapter 1 that the application of Additional Protocol I to wars of national liberation has long been controversial. A similar point applies to the expansion of combatant status outlined above.

---

[1] Additional Protocol I, arts 43(1), 44(3).
[2] Yves Sandoz, Christophe Swinarski and Bruno Zimmermann (eds), *Commentary on the Additional Protocols* (Martinus Nijhoff 1987) 509.

Significance of Combatant Status

We saw above that Article 43(2) of Additional Protocol I designates combatants as the primary agents of warfare under international humanitarian law. Beyond that, however, the provision is open to two divergent interpretations. The pivotal question here is what Article 43(2) means when it says that combatants 'have the right to participate directly in hostilities'. One way of interpreting this provision would be to infer that *only* combatants have the right to participate in hostilities. This would make it a violation of international humanitarian law for a non-combatant to engage directly in armed conflict.

An example of this interpretation can be found in §950v(15) of the *Military Commissions Act of 2006*, the United States statute passed to govern military commissions hearing charges against detainees at Guantanamo Bay. That provision made it a crime under United States law, punishable by death, to intentionally kill 'one or more persons, including lawful combatants, in violation of the law of war'. In March 2007, the provision was used as the basis for a charge against Australian detainee David Hicks, based on the allegation that he attempted to shoot anti-Taliban forces during the war in Afghanistan.[3]

It was not alleged that Hicks fired on civilians, which is a serious violation of international humanitarian law. Rather, the allegation was that he attempted to kill members of opposing armed forces. On the face of it, this seems odd. After all, attacking opposing forces is part and parcel of armed conflict. There were numerous soldiers on both sides of the conflict doing what Hicks was alleged to have done. The basis for the charge, however, seems to have been that, according to the United States government's interpretation of international law, Hicks was not entitled to take part in hostilities. He was what the *Military Commissions Act of 2006* described as an 'unlawful enemy combatant'.[4]

The charge against Hicks under §950v(15) was dropped before trial. The United States Congress subsequently enacted a revised *Military Commissions Act of 2009*, which removed the term 'unlawful enemy combatant', replacing it with 'unprivileged enemy belligerent'.[5] This change in terminology seems to signal a shift in the United States government's stance on whether non-combatants are prohibited under international

---

[3] For further discussion, see Jonathan Crowe, 'Combatant Status and the "War on Terror": Lessons from the Hicks Case' (2008) 33 *Alternative Law Journal* 67.
[4] *Military Commissions Act of 2006*, §948a.
[5] Ibid.

humanitarian law from taking up arms. However, the crime of 'murder in violation of the law of war', previously contained in §950v(15), remains largely unchanged.[6]

Our view is that it is a mistake to interpret Article 43(2) of Additional Protocol I as prohibiting non-combatants from participating in hostilities. It bears noting that there is no provision in the Geneva Conventions or Additional Protocols expressly stating such a prohibition. Article 43(2) is as close as we get. Other provisions that expressly deal with civilians engaging in hostilities, such as Article 51(3) of Additional Protocol I, merely say they lose their immunity from attack while doing so.

What, then, is the point of Article 43(2)? We suggest that the provision serves two purposes. The first is to reinforce the importance of the distinction between combatants and non-combatants, by designating combatants as the primary (although not necessarily sole) agents of warfare. The second is to emphasise that combatants may not be tried or punished merely for taking part in hostilities. On this interpretation, the provision states that combatants 'have the right to participate directly in hostilities', not to imply that non-combatants lack that right, but to emphasise that captured combatants cannot be executed or otherwise penalised merely for being on the wrong side of the conflict. Article 43(2) therefore reinforces the prohibition on reprisals against prisoners of war.[7]

Another way of putting the point is as follows. Article 43(2) refers to a 'right to participate directly in hostilities', but the term 'right' is notoriously ambiguous. The American jurist, Wesley Newcomb Hohfeld, famously argued that the term is commonly used in at least four distinct senses.[8] One possible interpretation of Article 43(2) would be that it confers what Hohfeld calls a 'privilege' or 'liberty': combatants are free to participate in hostilities and non-combatants are not. However, we suggest the provision is better understood as conferring what Hohfeld terms an 'immunity'. Combatants enjoy immunity against punishment merely for taking part in hostilities. Non-combatants have no such immunity, but this does not mean they are prohibited from taking up arms.

Non-combatants who take up arms are bound by the same legal rules as any other fighter. They cannot directly attack civilians or their

---

[6] *Military Commissions Act of 2009*, §950t(15).
[7] Geneva Convention III, art 13.
[8] Wesley Newcomb Hohfeld, 'Some Fundamental Legal Conceptions as Applied in Judicial Reasoning' (1913) 23 *Yale Law Journal* 16; Wesley Newcomb Hohfeld, 'Fundamental Legal Conceptions as Applied in Judicial Reasoning' (1917) 26 *Yale Law Journal* 710. For an overview, see Jonathan Crowe, *Legal Theory* (Thomson Reuters 2009) ch 8.

property; they cannot mount their attacks in a disproportionate way; they cannot mistreat civilians or captured combatants; they cannot use prohibited weapons or tactics. Like recognised combatants, they can lawfully be targeted by opposing forces.[9] They may also be liable to prosecution under the law of the detaining power for their hostile actions, since they do not benefit from the combatant immunity recognised in Article 43(2). However, provided that non-combatants abide by the ordinary laws of war, they are not prohibited under international law from engaging in hostilities. There is no firm basis in the conventions for such a prohibition.

Unprivileged Belligerents

The definitions of combatant status in both Geneva Convention III and Additional Protocol I are framed primarily as prerequisites for prisoner of war status. As discussed above, the conventions do not state that only combatants are permitted to engage in hostilities. We have argued against the view that non-combatants are prohibited from taking up arms. However, if a non-combatant becomes directly involved in the conflict and is subsequently captured, she or he will not be entitled to prisoner of war status. This is why fighters who do not qualify as combatants are sometimes called 'unprivileged belligerents'.

The benefits of prisoner of war status are discussed in Chapter 5. We will see that the protections are extensive and detailed. The fact that unprivileged belligerents do not qualify for prisoner of war status if captured therefore provides a real disincentive for non-combatants to take up arms. Nonetheless, it would be wrong to think that unprivileged belligerents are entirely unprotected by international humanitarian law. In fact, under international humanitarian law, *nobody* goes entirely unprotected. Those who are not entitled to prisoner of war status benefit from other safeguards.

There are at least two additional layers of protection available to captured belligerents who do not benefit from prisoner of war status under Geneva Convention III. The first is the 'protected persons' regime in Part III of Geneva Convention IV, which extends detailed protections to people who fall into the hands of a party to a conflict of which they are not nationals.[10] However, the 'protected persons' regime will not extend to unprivileged belligerents who find themselves in the hands of their own

---

[9] Additional Protocol I, art 51(3).
[10] See the detailed discussion in Chapter 4.

state or its allies.[11] It is also possible to override some of the protections on security grounds.[12]

The second additional layer of protection is contained in Article 75 of Additional Protocol I, which lists the 'fundamental guarantees' that protect all persons who fall into the hands of a party to an armed conflict. Additional Protocol I, like Geneva Convention IV, only applies in international armed conflicts. The equivalent level of protection in non-international conflicts is expressed in Articles 4–5 of Additional Protocol II, which are less detailed than Article 75, but cover many of the same basic issues. These articles, in turn, elaborate on the guarantees set out in Common Article 3 of the Geneva Conventions. Together, these provisions represent the minimum level of protection to which *everyone* is entitled in times of armed conflict, even unprivileged fighters.

It has been suggested by some commentators that these basic tenets of international humanitarian law do not apply to people who provide support for terrorism.[13] However, there is no basis for this in the applicable treaties. The closest we get is the security-based exceptions contained in Geneva Convention IV, but even those provisions are subject to express guarantees of humane treatment and procedural justice.[14] Nor is there any scope to argue that the Conventions did not anticipate the use of terrorism in warfare. Terrorism in wartime is hardly a recent phenomenon. Indeed, it is explicitly mentioned and condemned in Geneva Convention IV, as well as both Additional Protocols.[15] A strong case can be made that terrorists, like other people caught up in warfare, should be afforded at least the basic level of protection set out in the provisions discussed above.[16]

Combatant Status in Non-International Conflicts

It is sometimes said that there is no such thing as combatant status in non-international conflicts.[17] The reasoning behind this claim runs as follows.

---

[11] Geneva Convention IV, art 4.
[12] Geneva Convention IV, arts 5, 42.
[13] See, for example, John C Yoo, 'Terrorists Have No Geneva Rights', *Wall Street Journal*, 26 May 2004, A16.
[14] Geneva Convention IV, arts 5, 43.
[15] Geneva Convention IV, art 33; Additional Protocol I, art 51(2); Additional Protocol II, art 4(2)(d).
[16] For discussion, see Jan Klabbers, 'Rebel with a Cause? Terrorists and Humanitarian Law' (2003) 14 *European Journal of International Law* 299.
[17] Gary Solis describes this interpretation as the 'traditional view'. See Gary Solis, *The Law of Armed Conflict* (CUP 2010) 191.

First, the definition of combatant status is found in Article 4 of Geneva Convention III and Article 43 of Additional Protocol I. Neither of those provisions applies to non-international armed conflicts. Second, the main benefits associated with being a combatant are entitlement to prisoner of war status if captured and immunity from trial and punishment for taking part in hostilities. Neither of those protections is enjoyed by fighters in non-international conflicts. They are not covered by the protections afforded to prisoners of war under Geneva Convention III[18] and may be prosecuted domestically for their hostile actions.

There are, however, some obvious dangers to denying the existence of combatant status in internal conflicts. The most troubling consequence of this claim is perhaps that it risks undermining respect for the principle of distinction. There can be no doubt that the principle of distinction applies in non-international conflicts. Article 13(2) of Additional Protocol II prohibits attacks against individual civilians or the civilian population. This prohibition is recognised as a principle of customary international law applying in conflicts of all kinds.[19] The prohibition implies that a distinction can meaningfully be drawn between combatants and civilians for the purposes of planning military attacks.

The view that combatant status does not exist in non-international conflicts also risks giving the impression that captured fighters in such conflicts are entirely at the mercy of the enemy. This is far from the case, even though the provisions of Geneva Convention III and Additional Protocol I do not apply. Captured fighters in internal conflicts are afforded a range of protections under international law, including those contained in Common Article 3 to the Geneva Conventions and Articles 4, 5 and 6 of Additional Protocol II. We will discuss these provisions at greater length in Chapter 5.

DUTIES OF COMBATANTS

A number of the basic obligations of combatants under international humanitarian law are already implicit in the definition of combatant status discussed above. Combatants must distinguish themselves from the civilian population wherever possible. This should generally involve wearing a fixed, distinctive sign. They must carry arms openly whenever

---

[18] Geneva Convention III, art 2.
[19] Jean-Marie Henckaerts and Louise Doswald-Beck, *Customary International Humanitarian Law* (CUP 2005) 3–8.

mobilising or launching an attack.[20] Combatants must respect the rules of international humanitarian law, although a failure to do so does not make them subject to reprisals or deprive them of prisoner of war status.[21] They must also be subject to a system of responsible command which enables those who violate the law to be held accountable.[22]

There are a range of other basic duties conferred on combatants by international humanitarian law. We will consider a number of these in the following sections. The discussion will be structured around the fundamental principles of international humanitarian law that govern this area. We will see that the conduct of combatants is governed by a web of distinct but mutually supporting legal doctrines. These doctrines provide the framework within which military commanders must make operational decisions. They also impose limits on the permissible conduct of ordinary combatants.

Superfluous Injury

The first of these fundamental principles is the prohibition on the infliction of superfluous injury or unnecessary suffering. The basic idea here is that attacking forces are proscribed from inflicting injury on opposing combatants beyond what is necessary to remove them from active combat. According to Article 22 of the Hague Regulations, '[t]he right of belligerents to adopt means of injuring the enemy is not unlimited'. This principle appears in very similar terms in Article 35(1) of Additional Protocol I. Article 35(2) then states that '[i]t is prohibited to employ weapons, projectiles and material and methods of warfare of a nature to cause superfluous injury or unnecessary suffering'.[23]

The International Committee of the Red Cross (ICRC) study on customary international humanitarian law describes the prohibition on inflicting superfluous injury or unnecessary suffering as a fundamental rule applicable in both international and non-international armed conflicts.[24] We saw in Chapter 2 that the prohibition on inflicting superfluous injury was first codified in the St Petersburg Declaration of 1868. The main aim of that declaration was to prohibit explosive bullets, but its Preamble contains a wide-ranging statement concerning the limits that customary rules

---

[20] Additional Protocol I, art 43(3).
[21] Additional Protocol I, art 43(2).
[22] Additional Protocol I, art 43(1).
[23] See also Hague Regulations, art 23.
[24] Jean-Marie Henckaerts and Louise Doswald-Beck, *Customary International Humanitarian Law* (CUP 2005) rule 70.

place on the conduct of warfare. In particular, the Preamble affirms the following basic principles:

> That the progress of civilization should have the effect of alleviating as much as possible the calamities of war;
>
> That the only legitimate object which States should endeavour to accomplish during war is to weaken the military forces of the enemy;
>
> That for this purpose it is sufficient to disable the greatest possible number of [combatants];
>
> That this object would be exceeded by the employment of arms which uselessly aggravate the sufferings of disabled [combatants], or render their death inevitable;
>
> That the employment of such arms would, therefore, be contrary to the laws of humanity.

There are numerous historical examples of weapons that have been banned or criticised for causing unnecessary suffering. In medieval times, some authorities, including the Catholic Church, condemned the crossbow for causing unnecessary injury.[25] The St Petersburg Declaration, as we have seen, was aimed at explosive bullets, designed to leave a small entry wound but explode inside the body. In a similar vein, the 1899 Hague Peace Conference agreed to ban dum-dum bullets, which were designed to flatten and expand inside the target. In more recent times, criticism has been directed at landmines, cluster munitions, chemical weapons and nuclear weapons on similar grounds. We will consider the legal status of these forms of weaponry in greater detail below.

Military Necessity

The prohibition on causing unnecessary suffering is closely linked to the doctrine of military necessity. According to this principle, a party making an attack is permitted to use only that degree of force required to achieve the anticipated military objective that will result in minimum loss of life and property. Military necessity is sometimes depicted as a permissive doctrine; that is, as permitting a party to do whatever is necessary

---

[25] Robert C Stacy, 'The Age of Chivalry' in Michael Howard, George J Andreopoulos and Mark R Shulman (eds), *The Laws of War: Constraints on Warfare in the Western World* (Yale University Press 1994) 30.

to achieve the desired military outcome. However, it is better viewed as a restrictive doctrine. A party may do what is *necessary* to achieve the objective *and no more*.

Numerous expressions of the doctrine of military necessity can be found in international instruments. According to the Preamble of Hague Convention IV of 1907, the treaty aims to 'diminish the evils of war, as far as military requirements permit'. Article 23 of the Hague Regulations forbids parties from seizing or destroying enemy property, unless 'imperatively demanded by the necessities of war'. Similarly, Article 54 states that underwater power and communications cables between occupied and neutral territories are not to be seized or destroyed 'except in the case of absolute necessity'.

Article 6 of the 1945 Charter of the International Military Tribunal at Nuremberg refers to the crime of '[w]anton destruction of cities, towns, or villages [. . .] not justified by military necessity'. Similar terms are used at various points in the Geneva Conventions and Additional Protocols. The first section of Part III of Geneva Convention IV, for example, allows parties to 'take such measures of control and security in regard to protected persons as may be necessary as a result of the war'.[26] Article 54 of Additional Protocol I likewise provides that civilian crops and livestock may not be destroyed or removed, except by parties in their own territory 'where required by imperative military necessity'.[27]

The Principle of Distinction

We saw at the start of this chapter that the principle of distinction requires military commanders to distinguish at all times between military targets and civilian objects. Only legitimate military targets may be attacked. Article 48 of Additional Protocol I makes it clear that this principle takes the form of an absolute prohibition, stating that parties 'shall at all times distinguish between civilian objects and military objectives and [. . .] shall direct their operations only against military objectives'.[28]

The principle of distinction stipulates that military attacks may never be directed at civilian persons or objects, regardless of whether this might lead to a military advantage. It therefore places a further limitation on the scope of permitted attacks under the doctrine of military necessity. According to military necessity, as we have seen, a party may do what is

---

[26] Geneva Convention IV, art 27. See also art 53.
[27] Additional Protocol I, art 54(5).
[28] See also Additional Protocol II, arts 13–14.

necessary to achieve a military objective and no more. The principle of distinction supplements this with a further restriction: attacks may never be directed at civilian objects, even if such a strategy would produce a military benefit.

The stark dichotomy the principle of distinction establishes between civilians and combatants is open to question on an ethical level. It might be thought that combatants are always legitimate targets of armed attacks, either because they have consented to take part in the conflict and therefore to be targeted or, more plausibly, because they are actual or potential aggressors who may be attacked in self-defence. Likewise, it might seem that civilians are innocent bystanders to the conflict and therefore may never be attacked. However, neither of these assumptions will hold in all cases.

Combatants may be poorly educated and uninformed about the background to the armed conflict. They may join the armed forces because they are conscripted or because their social and economic prospects are limited. They may join up in peacetime without foreseeing being involved in any war, let alone the actual conflict that arises. They are often young and may not fully understand the implications of military service. They may play a very limited role in the actual conduct of hostilities.

Civilians, on the other hand, may sometimes play a crucial role in bringing about or conducting the war. Political leaders, in particular, will often be largely responsible for initiating, funding and planning the conflict. Ordinary citizens may vote or publicly campaign in favour of war. They may actively support the armed forces in a range of different ways. The diversity among both combatants and civilians therefore undermines any sharp ethical distinction between the groups.[29] It may also make a difference, as we saw in Chapter 1, why and by which side the conflict was started.

These issues, however, take nothing away from the case for respecting the principle of distinction. The principle seeks to place clear and consistent limits on the conduct of warfare.[30] International humanitarian law

---

[29] For further discussion, see Michael Walzer, *Just and Unjust Wars* (Basic Books 1977) ch 3; Jeff McMahan, 'Innocence, Self-Defence and Killing in War' (1994) 2 *Journal of Political Philosophy* 193; Jeff McMahan, 'The Ethics of Killing in War' (2004) 114 *Ethics* 693; Gerhard Øverland, 'Killing Civilians' (2005) 13 *European Journal of Philosophy* 345; Gerhard Øverland, 'Killing Soldiers' (2006) 20 *Ethics and International Affairs* 455.

[30] Compare Jeff McMahan, 'The Ethics of Killing in War' (2004) 114 *Ethics* 693, 730–33; David Luban, 'War Crimes: The Law of Hell' in Larry May (ed), *War: Essays in Political Philosophy* (CUP 2008) 270–73.

could have adopted a less stark rule, according to which civilians could be attacked under certain circumstances or if the military advantage is great enough. Derogations from the principle of distinction would then be permitted where justified by military necessity. However, a relaxed interpretation of the principle would carry serious risks for the security of civilian populations, leaving them open to attacks and reprisals for perceived military gain. It would lack the salience of the current legal framework in setting practical limits on hostilities and would deprive the international community of a clear basis for condemning attacks on civilian objects.

The principle of distinction also plays an important role in protecting humanitarian workers, such as medical personnel and Red Cross officials, from becoming the object of military attacks. Humanitarian workers are crucial to the efforts of the Red Cross to alleviate the harms of armed conflict. The principle of distinction makes it absolutely clear that there is never any excuse for targeting such persons. Anything less than this would seriously undermine the already tenuous security such workers enjoy when going about their duties. Anyone who risks her or his life to mitigate the suffering of those affected by armed conflict deserves the best protection international law can offer.

Proportionality

The principle of distinction provides that only military objectives may be directly targeted in armed conflict. However, an attack on a legitimate military objective may sometimes cause incidental damage to civilian persons or objects. These harmful side effects are regulated in international humanitarian law by the doctrine of proportionality. This doctrine prohibits attacks that may be expected to cause injury to civilian life or property that is excessive in relation to the anticipated military advantage.

A clear statement of the doctrine of proportionality can be found in Article 51(5)(b) of Additional Protocol I, which prohibits attacks 'which may be expected to cause incidental loss of civilian life, injury to civilians, damage to civilian objects, or a combination thereof, which would be excessive in relation to the concrete and direct military advantage anticipated'. The doctrine holds customary law status in both international and non-international armed conflicts.[31] It places a duty on forces to assess

---

[31] Jean-Marie Henckaerts and Louise Doswald-Beck, *Customary International Humanitarian Law* (CUP 2005) rule 14.

the impact of an attack on civilian objects and refrain from attacking if the principle would be violated.[32]

We will consider the protections given to civilians against the effects of armed attack in more detail in Chapter 4. It is helpful for current purposes, however, to clarify the relationship between the doctrine of proportionality and the other principles discussed above. The doctrine of proportionality is evidently closely linked to the notion of military necessity. Proportionality entails that an attack that causes incidental damage to civilian objects can be justified only where the damage is proportionate to a concrete and direct military advantage; in other words, where military necessity demands it.

The doctrine of proportionality also resembles military necessity in another respect: both doctrines are subject to the principle of distinction. Proportionality can never be used to justify a direct attack on civilian persons or objects, even if a case could be made that a proportionate military advantage would thereby be gained. It only applies to attacks directed at military objectives that may impact incidentally on civilians. The legal framework therefore mandates the following procedure for military commanders: first, abide by the principle of distinction by ensuring attacks are directed only at legitimate military targets; second, assess proportionality, making sure that a planned attack on a military objective will not cause unreasonable damage to civilian objects.

Why, then, does international humanitarian law distinguish between direct attacks on civilians, which are absolutely prohibited, and attacks that incidentally impact on civilians, which are subject to proportionality? Why not apply a proportionality test in all cases? One obvious reason is that assessments of proportionality are often not clear cut. We have seen that international humanitarian law aims to set out clear rules that can be generally accepted. A blanket ban on directly attacking civilians facilitates this aim much better than placing reliance on the notion of proportionality, which requires a balancing exercise and therefore creates scope for argument in particular cases. Any relaxation of the prohibition on targeting civilians would hold clear potential for abuse. It would leave civilian populations perpetually at risk of attacks in the name of military necessity.

The distinction between direct attacks and incidental harms against civilian objects also seems to have some basis in what philosophers call the *doctrine of double effect*. This principle holds that it is sometimes permissible to cause a harm as a foreseen, but unintended, side effect of an act, although it would not be permissible to intentionally cause the same

---

[32] Additional Protocol I, art 57(2).

harm, either as an end in itself or as a means to an end.[33] The basic idea is that, other things being equal, it is generally worse to intentionally harm someone than it is to harm someone as an unintended side effect of an otherwise reasonable act. There is therefore a higher threshold for justifying the former kind of harm than the latter.

A classic example is as follows:

> *Highway:* Cicely is overseeing the construction of a new highway. She knows that highways invariably cause a certain number of road accidents, which often involve death and serious injury. Nonetheless, she goes ahead with the construction of the road.[34]

Cicely foresees that serious accidents may occur as a result of her action in building the highway. Nonetheless, if such an accident does occur, we would not normally hold her morally culpable for it, as we would if she intentionally set out to harm someone. (We are assuming that she took reasonable safety precautions in designing and constructing the road.) The example therefore suggests that there is at least sometimes a moral difference between harming someone intentionally and harming them as a side effect. However, the nature and scope of this distinction have long been disputed.

Indiscriminate Attacks

The principle of distinction and the doctrine of proportionality are further supplemented by a general prohibition on indiscriminate attacks. Article 51(4) of Additional Protocol I states that '[i]ndiscriminate attacks are prohibited.' The provision then goes on to clarify that attacks are considered indiscriminate if they:

- are not directed at a specified military objective;
- employ a method that *cannot be directed* at a specific military objective; or

---

[33] For further discussion of the principle, see Jonathan Crowe, 'Does Control Make a Difference? The Moral Foundations of Shareholder Liability for Corporate Wrongs' (2012) 75 *Modern Law Review* 159, 166–70. See also Joseph M Boyle, Jr, 'Toward Understanding the Principle of Double Effect' (1980) 90 *Ethics* 527; Philippa Foot, 'The Problem of Abortion and the Doctrine of Double Effect' in *Virtues and Vices and Other Essays* (OUP 1978).

[34] For discussion, see Jonathan Crowe, 'Does Control Make a Difference? The Moral Foundations of Shareholder Liability for Corporate Wrongs' (2012) 75 *Modern Law Review* 159, 166–7. See also John Finnis, *Fundamentals of Ethics* (Georgetown University Press 1983) 91–2.

- apply a method or means of combat *the effects of which cannot be limited* to a specific military objective.

The three limbs of this definition each cover a specific type of case. The first limb deals with attacks that are indiscriminate in the sense that they are not directed at a specific, identifiable military target. This limb therefore reinforces the principle of distinction, providing that every attack must have a legitimate military objective as its end. The second limb deals with attacks that use a type of weapon or a method of targeting that is incapable of being spatially limited to a specific military objective. This means that attacks that are ostensibly directed at a particular military objective will still be indiscriminate if the means or method of attack employed is incapable of being confined to that target.

The third limb covers attacks whose effects cannot be confined to a specific military objective. This overlaps with the second limb discussed above, but it also covers attacks that may be capable of being confined to a military target at the time they are launched, but will have subsequent effects extending beyond that objective. In other words, the second limb can be understood as covering attacks that are *spatially* indiscriminate, while the third limb covers those that are *temporally* indiscriminate.

Consider, for example, a scenario where landmines are deployed directly in the path of advancing forces. Let us assume that the landmines are not self-destructing or self-deactivating and no clean-up operation is planned. The use of landmines in such circumstances is directed at a specific military target. However, unexploded mines are likely to remain in the ground long after the advancing forces have moved on. This therefore seems to be a method of warfare the temporal effects of which cannot be limited to a specific objective. It will fall under the third limb of the definition discussed above.

The prohibition on indiscriminate attacks may be derived in at least two ways from the other principles of international humanitarian law discussed above. The first route derives from the principle of distinction. That principle states that military forces must distinguish at all times between civilian and military objects. It follows that the means and methods of attack they employ must be capable of observing that distinction. The connection between these two principles is expressly noted in Article 51(4). The second route to the prohibition on indiscriminate attacks draws on the doctrines of military necessity and proportionality. Those principles state that a party may legitimately do only what is necessary and proportionate to achieve a military objective. An attack that employs methods that cannot be confined to the target will often violate those doctrines.

It should be emphasised, however, that the prohibition on indiscriminate attacks is not subject to proportionality calculations. This reflects its close relationship to the principle of distinction. We saw previously that civilian persons and objects may never be directly attacked, regardless of any military advantage that may be gained from doing so. Likewise, Article 51(4) of Additional Protocol I makes it clear that the prohibition on indiscriminate attacks is absolute. An indiscriminate attack of any of the three kinds identified in that provision may never be launched, even if the anticipated damage to civilian objects flowing from such an attack is proportionate to the military benefits.

There is some degree of conceptual tension between the prohibition on indiscriminate attacks and the doctrine of proportionality. There is a sense in which any attack that raises the issue of proportionality will necessarily violate the prohibition on indiscriminate means and methods. Proportionality only arises where an attack that is aimed at a legitimate military target will have incidental effects on civilian objects. However, such an attack is, by definition, one that is not capable of being limited *solely* to the military target. It therefore seems to fall foul of the prohibition on indiscriminate attacks.

If this analysis were correct, the doctrine of proportionality would have no room to operate, since any attack that might raise it would be prohibited as indiscriminate. The principles need to be interpreted in such a way to avoid this contradiction. The best resolution, in our view, is to interpret the prohibition on indiscriminate attacks as requiring that the means and methods employed must be *reasonably capable* of being limited to a specific military target. This does not require that an attack has absolutely no effects whatsoever on the civilian population. Rather, it must be capable of being reasonably confined to the military objective and any flow on effects must be proportionate.[35] This interpretation seems consistent with how the prohibition is generally understood and applied.

Bombardment and Targeting

Article 51(5)(a) of Additional Protocol I specifically designates area bombardment as an indiscriminate method of attack. It is therefore prohibited. The provision applies to 'an attack by bombardment or other means, which treats several distinct military objectives as a single objective in an area that also contains civilian objects'. There is therefore a duty on military commanders to target bombing campaigns at a specific military

---

[35] Compare Additional Protocol I, art 51(5)(b).

objective, rather than targeting multiple objectives in a way that includes civilian objects. The rules and practices governing this area are often called the rules of targeting.

The issue of bombardment has long been a point of contention in international humanitarian law. The 1923 Draft Hague Rules on Aerial Warfare represented an early attempt to clarify the area, but they never came into force. Article 24 of the Draft Rules stated that '[a]erial bombardment is legitimate only when directed at a military objective'. The issue was revived following the Second World War. The aerial bombardment of cities such as London, Hamburg, Coventry and Dresden sparked concern that such tactics may not comply with military necessity and the principle of distinction.

Modern warfare has seen the emergence of technologically assisted 'smart bombs' to aid with targeting. This has greatly reduced casualties. However, military commanders must still make complex and difficult judgments concerning the likely impact of a planned bombardment on both military and civilian objects and assess the appropriateness of the attack in light of that information. These decisions are often made with imperfect information, in a limited time frame and with high stakes for all concerned. Mistakes still occur. The complex dynamics of military operations make international humanitarian law difficult to apply with precision. Its exact requirements continue to be debated.

PROHIBITED WEAPONS

We saw earlier in this chapter that international humanitarian law has often sought to respond to concern over the harmful and disproportionate effects of specific forms of weaponry, ranging from crossbows to explosive bullets and more modern innovations, such as chemical and biological weapons. The following paragraphs look in more detail at some of the specific forms of weapons prohibited or restricted under international humanitarian law. Some of these weapons, such as chemical agents and landmines, are the subjects of specific treaties. Others need to be dealt with primarily by applying the general principles of international humanitarian law. Nuclear weapons provide an example.

Chemical and Biological Weapons

There have long been moves to ban the use of chemical and biological weapons in warfare, based largely on the prohibition against unnecessary suffering. An early attempt was made in Article 23 of the Hague

Regulations, which provides that '[i]t is especially forbidden to employ poison or poisonous weapons'. The 1925 Geneva Protocol subsequently prohibited the use of chemical agents, such as chlorine, phosgene and mustard gas, in addition to bacteriological agents, which were then in the early stages of development. This was a response to the widespread use of chemical weapons during the First World War. The 1925 Protocol was widely ratified, although there were regular breaches.

The main treaties governing this area today are the 1972 Biological and Toxin Weapons Convention and the 1993 Chemical Weapons Convention. Both enjoy substantial, but not universal, international support. Parties to the 1972 Convention undertake not to develop or stockpile bacteriological agents or toxins. However, the Convention is hampered by the lack of any enforcement or monitoring arrangements. Parties to the 1993 Convention agree not to develop or stockpile chemical weapons. Unlike the 1972 Convention, the 1993 Convention includes an implementation and monitoring regime. The 1972 Convention has 165 state parties at the time of writing, while the 1993 Convention has 188 parties. The ICRC study on customary international humanitarian law has found the use of poisonous, biological and chemical weapons in warfare to be prohibited as a matter of international custom in both international and non-international armed conflicts.[36]

Landmines and Cluster Munitions

The use of landmines in warfare has long been controversial, due to the serious health and safety problems mines have caused in many nations (particularly in Africa and Asia). The main treaties in this area are the 1980 Convention on Certain Conventional Weapons and the 1997 Ottawa Landmines Convention. Protocol II to the 1980 Convention, which has been ratified by 91 states at the time of writing, prohibits the indiscriminate use of mines. It also requires that remotely delivered mines have self-destructing or self-deactivating mechanisms or, alternatively, that remotely controlled mechanisms be used to render the mines inoperative when the military objective is no longer present.

The 1997 Ottawa Convention imposes a total ban on antipersonnel landmines. It is therefore much stronger than Protocol II to the 1980 Convention and enjoys more extensive international support, with 160 state parties at the time of writing. A number of influential states have not

---

[36] Jean-Marie Henckaerts and Louise Doswald-Beck, *Customary International Humanitarian Law* (CUP 2005) rules 72–4.

ratified the 1997 Convention, but many of them have agreed to observe the lower standards imposed by the 1980 Protocol. These currently include China, India, Israel, Pakistan, Russia and the United States. According to the ICRC study on customary rules of international humanitarian law, international custom prohibits the indiscriminate use of landmines and requires parties using mines to remove or disable them.[37] This corresponds to the position under the 1980 Protocol.

Cluster munitions are dealt with under Protocol V to the 1980 Convention, which covers explosive remnants of war, and the 2008 Convention on Cluster Munitions. Protocol V to the 1980 Convention, with 78 state parties, was adopted in 2003 and entered into force in 2006. It requires parties to keep records on the use of explosive remnants of war, including unexploded cluster bomblets, and remove or destroy them as soon as possible in areas under their control. The 2008 Convention goes further, banning the use, stockpiling and production of cluster munitions. It currently has 71 state parties.

Nuclear Weapons

Nuclear weapons serve as a helpful case study to illustrate the practical implications of the general principles of international humanitarian law discussed in the previous section. The legitimacy of the use of nuclear weapons in warfare has long been controversial. Nuclear armaments were notoriously employed upon the Japanese cities of Hiroshima and Nagasaki during the Second World War. It has often been claimed that the bombings hastened the end of the conflict and therefore avoided far greater combatant and civilian casualties. However, their legality was and is highly questionable.[38]

There is no operative international treaty specifically banning the use of nuclear weapons in warfare. The Nuclear Non-Proliferation Treaty of 1970 (with 189 state parties at the time of writing) aims to limit the spread of nuclear weapons, but stops well short of a complete ban. The Comprehensive Nuclear Test Ban Treaty goes much further, banning all nuclear explosions in both civilian and military contexts. It was adopted

---

[37] Ibid rules 81–3.
[38] The District Court of Tokyo, ruling in 1963 on a lawsuit by survivors of the Hiroshima and Nagasaki bombings, found that the attacks violated fundamental principles of the law of war. However, the claimants were ultimately unsuccessful, since they lacked standing to obtain damages under international law and a claim under domestic law was barred by sovereign immunity. See *Ryuichi Shimoda v State* (1964) 8 *Japanese Annual of International Law* 231.

by the United Nations (UN) General Assembly on 10 September 1996, but is yet to enter into force and seems unlikely to do so in the near future. A model nuclear weapons convention has been circulating in various forms since 1997, but has yet to attain any formal status.

The UN General Assembly has regularly cast doubt upon the legality of using nuclear weapons in warfare. We saw in Chapter 2 that General Assembly Resolutions stating existing legal principles may hold persuasive force as interpretations of international law. General Assembly Resolution 1653 (XVI) of 1961 declared the use of nuclear weapons in warfare to be illegal and urged states to adopt a treaty to this effect. General Assembly Resolution 2444 (XXIII) of 1968 affirmed that 'the general principles of international humanitarian law [including the principle of distinction] govern the use of nuclear and other weapons of mass destruction'. The General Assembly has repeated its call for a binding nuclear weapons convention every year since 1996.

The International Court of Justice (ICJ) issued an Advisory Opinion on the *Legality of the Threat or Use of Nuclear Weapons* in 1996.[39] However, the Advisory Opinion produced no definite outcome on the legality of nuclear weapons. The ICJ judges split 7-7 on the central issue, with the ruling being adopted by the President's casting vote. The finding was that the use or threat of nuclear weapons would 'generally' infringe international humanitarian law, but might be permissible in 'extreme' cases of self-defence. The equivocal nature of the decision drew strong criticism in some quarters.[40]

A strong case can be made that the use of nuclear weapons in warfare is prohibited under international humanitarian law in almost all conceivable circumstances. The conclusion derives from the fundamental principles discussed in the previous section. The principle of distinction means that a nuclear weapon may only be used if it is capable of being targeted only at a specific military objective. The prohibition on indiscriminate attacks likewise entails that nuclear weapons may only be employed where their short-term *and* long-term effects can be reasonably confined to the military target.

---

[39] *Legality of the Threat or Use of Nuclear Weapons*, ICJ Advisory Opinion, 8 July 1996.

[40] See, for example, Timothy McCormack, 'A *Non Liquet* on Nuclear Weapons: The ICJ Avoids the Application of General Principles of International Humanitarian Law' (1997) 316 *International Review of the Red Cross* 76; Louise Doswald-Beck, 'International Humanitarian Law and the Advisory Opinion of the International Court of Justice on the Legality of the Threat or Use of Nuclear Weapons' (1997) 316 *International Review of the Red Cross* 35.

The doctrine of proportionality prohibits attacks that may be expected to cause injury to civilian life or property that is excessive in relation to the anticipated military advantage. Where a number of options exist, there is an obligation to choose the one involving the least risk of civilian damage.[41] The prohibition on superfluous injury, along with the doctrine of military necessity, likewise rules out the use of weaponry that will cause unnecessary suffering to combatants.[42] It is also relevant to note the provisions of international humanitarian law relating to environmental protection, which we will consider in more detail shortly. According to Article 35(3) of Additional Protocol I, '[i]t is prohibited to employ methods or means of warfare which are intended, or may be expected, to cause widespread, long-term and severe damage to the natural environment'.[43]

The cumulative effect of these principles is that the use of a nuclear weapon in warfare will only be permissible if the weapon is capable of being targeted only at a specific military objective; its short-term and long-term effects can be reasonably limited to the military target; and there is no other way to target the objective that would involve less risk to civilians, combatants and the environment. It is extremely difficult to imagine these conditions being satisfied, especially given the well-documented long-term health and environmental effects resulting from nuclear radiation.

Other Prohibited Weapons

A range of other weapons are specifically prohibited or restricted by international treaties. A number of these are covered by the various Protocols to the 1980 Convention on Certain Conventional Weapons. An example is weapons that leave fragments inside the body too small to be detected by x-ray. Fragmentary weapons of this type are prohibited by Protocol I to the 1980 Convention on Certain Conventional Weapons, which has 110 state parties at the time of writing. The ICRC study on customary international humanitarian law has concluded that this prohibition has customary law status.[44]

The use of incendiary weapons (flamethrowers and the like) is heavily restricted. Protocol III to the 1980 Convention on Certain Conventional Weapons (with 106 state parties at the time of writing) expressly prohibits the use of such weapons against civilians or civilian objects. This, of

---

[41] Additional Protocol I, art 57(3).
[42] Additional Protocol I, art 35(2).
[43] See also Additional Protocol I, arts 54–56.
[44] Jean-Marie Henckaerts and Louise Doswald-Beck, *Customary International Humanitarian Law* (CUP 2005) rule 79.

course, is simply an application of the principle of distinction. However, the Protocol also bans the use of incendiary weapons on military targets located near a concentration of civilians. This arguably goes further than the general principles of international humanitarian law, since it rules out any attempt to justify such an attack based on the doctrine of proportionality. The ICRC study has found a similar position prevails under customary international humanitarian law.[45]

Laser weapons designed to permanently blind combatants are prohibited. These are dealt with under Protocol IV to the 1980 Convention on Certain Conventional Weapons, which currently has 100 state parties. According to the ICRC study, weapons designed to permanently blind combatants are also banned as a matter of international custom in both international and non-international armed conflicts.[46]

RUSES AND PERFIDY

This chapter has so far focused primarily on the means of warfare. We turn now to the methods of warfare (that is, the tactics and strategies that armed forces may employ). It is important to distinguish in this context between ruses of war, which are permitted by international humanitarian law, and perfidy, which is prohibited. The prohibition on perfidy can be found in Article 23 of the Hague Regulations, which states '[i]t is especially forbidden [. . .] to make improper use of a flag of truce, of the national flag or [. . .] insignia or uniform of the enemy, as well as the distinctive badges of the Geneva Convention'. Article 24, by contrast, states that '[r]uses of war and the employment of measures necessary for obtaining information about the enemy [. . .] are considered permissible'.

A more recent definition of perfidy can be found in Article 37(1) of Additional Protocol I, which provides that '[a]cts inviting the confidence of an adversary to lead [her or] him to believe that [she or] he is entitled to, or obliged to accord, protection under the rules of [international humanitarian law], with intent to betray that confidence, shall constitute perfidy'. Some examples are then given, including:

- feigning an intent to negotiate by using a flag of truce or surrender;
- feigning incapacitation by wounds or sickness;
- feigning civilian or non-combatant status;

---

[45] Ibid rules 84–5.
[46] Ibid rule 86.

- feigning protected status by using Red Cross, UN or neutral insignia.

The definition of perfidy can be contrasted with Article 37(2) of Additional Protocol I, which holds that '[r]uses of war are not prohibited. Such ruses are acts which are intended to mislead an adversary [. . .] but which infringe no rule of [international humanitarian law] [. . .] because they do not invite the confidence of an adversary with respect to protection under that law'. Examples of ruses set out in the provision include the use of camouflage, decoys, mock operations and misinformation.

The prohibition on perfidy makes it a violation of international humanitarian law to pretend to hold protected status in order to invite the confidence of the enemy. A flagrant example of perfidy would be using an ambulance marked with the Red Cross emblem to covertly transport troops and launch an armed attack. It is likewise prohibited for combatants on the battlefield to play dead, feign injury or express an intention to surrender in order to lull the enemy into a false sense of security. The reason for these prohibitions should be obvious: the protections international humanitarian law affords to vulnerable groups will be of little avail if they are abused for military purposes.

A less blatant recent example of misuse of the Red Cross emblem in armed conflict arose in the context of the civil war in Colombia. On 2 July 2008, Colombian security forces rescued 15 hostages, including former presidential candidate Ingrid Betancourt, who had been held for up to ten years by the Revolutionary Armed Forces of Columbia (FARC). The rescue was widely hailed as a daring coup: it involved the use of bogus communications to persuade FARC rebels to release the hostages to a group posing as aid workers. Photographs and video footage taken of personnel about to embark on the rescue mission appeared to show one man wearing a bib bearing Red Cross insignia.

The use of the Red Cross symbol in this context constitutes a clear violation of international humanitarian law, notwithstanding that the purpose of the ruse was to rescue hostages. Apart from the fact that the Geneva Conventions limit use of the Red Cross emblem to medical and humanitarian workers,[47] wearing the emblem in order to pose as an aid worker constitutes perfidy under Article 37 of Additional Protocol I.[48] Indeed, it would seem to be perfidious for the military members of the rescue group to pose as aid workers at all, regardless of whether Red Cross emblems

---

[47] See, for example, Geneva Convention I, art 44.
[48] See also Additional Protocol I, art 38.

were used. These fundamental principles apply in all forms of warfare. Article 12 of Additional Protocol II prohibits the improper use of the protected emblems in non-international conflicts.

There might seem to be room for dispute here as to what is meant in Article 37 by the phrase 'inviting the confidence of an adversary [. . .] with intent to betray that confidence'. The classic case of perfidiously inviting the confidence of the enemy is where that confidence is abused in order to launch an armed attack. However, is this a necessary component of perfidy? What if the confidence is invited as a way of gaining information or rescuing hostages? It seems fairly clear that inviting the confidence of the enemy by feigning protected status is perfidious regardless of why the trick is employed. This is consistent with the rationale for the prohibition. Any attempt to gain an advantage by impersonating a vulnerable person endangers the protection of such persons in the future.

FORBIDDEN ORDERS

It is forbidden under international humanitarian law for military commanders to issue certain commands to their forces. Orders of 'take no quarter' (that is, that there be no survivors) are prohibited, as is the raising of a red flag to indicate such an order to opposing soldiers. There is no excuse for targeting combatants who are seeking to surrender. Article 40 of Additional Protocol I accordingly provides that '[i]t is forbidden to order that there shall be no survivors'. This prohibition can also be found in Article 23 of the Hague Regulations. It is recognised as a rule of customary international law.[49]

In a similar way, it is prohibited to order attacks on combatants who have surrendered. According to Article 41(1) of Additional Protocol I, '[a] person who is recognised or [. . .] should be recognised to be *hors de combat* shall not be made the object of attack'. Article 41(2) then clarifies that a person is *hors de combat* (literally, 'outside the fight') if she or he has been captured, shows an intention to surrender, or is unconscious or incapacitated. Article 23 of the Hague Regulations contains a similar requirement.[50] This rule explains why it is prohibited to order that no quarter be given: such an order would constitute a pre-emptive instruction to attack persons who are *hors de combat*.

---

[49] Jean-Marie Henckaerts and Louise Doswald-Beck, *Customary International Humanitarian Law* (CUP 2005) rule 46.
[50] See also ibid rule 47.

ENVIRONMENTAL PROTECTION

International humanitarian law contains a number of rules protecting the natural environment from the consequences of armed attack. Some of these principles protect the natural environment in its own right, while others protect the environment in light of its importance to the health and welfare of civilians. A principle of the former kind appears in Article 35(3) of Additional Protocol I, according to which '[i]t is prohibited to employ methods or means of warfare which are intended, or may be expected, to cause widespread, long-term and severe damage to the natural environment'.

Article 35(3) may be contrasted with Articles 54–56 of Additional Protocol I, which aim to protect aspects of the environment necessary for the health and survival of civilians. These provisions occur in the part of Additional Protocol I concerning protection of civilian objects. Article 55(1), for example, provides that:

> Care shall be taken in warfare to protect the natural environment against widespread, long-term and severe damage. This protection includes a prohibition of the use of methods or means of warfare that are intended or may be expected to cause such damage to the natural environment and thereby to prejudice the health or survival of the population.

Similar principles are codified in the ICRC study on customary international humanitarian law.[51] The ICRC study also emphasises that the usual limitations on the conduct of warfare operate to protect the natural environment. No feature of the natural environment may be directly attacked unless it is a military objective. Any incidental damage to the natural environment must pass the test of proportionality.

A classic example of a military attack directed at the natural environment is the United States policy of chemical deforestation during the Vietnam War, using Agent Orange and other toxic herbicides. The harmful effects of these measures on the health and welfare of civilian populations has been widely documented.[52] The chemical deforestation policy seems a clear example of a method of warfare with widespread, long-term and severe implications for the natural environment, as well as having incidental impacts on both civilians and the environment that are inconsistent with proportionality.

---

[51] Ibid rules 43–5.
[52] For a helpful overview, see Diane Niblack Fox, 'Chemical Politics and the Hazards of Modern Warfare: Agent Orange' in Monica J Casper (ed), *Synthetic Planet: Chemical Politics and the Hazards of Modern Life* (Routledge 2003).

CULTURAL PROTECTION

Protecting culturally significant buildings and objects from warfare has long been a concern of international humanitarian law. According to Article 27 of the Hague Regulations, 'all necessary steps must be taken to spare, as far as possible, buildings dedicated to religion, art, science, or charitable purposes [and] historic monuments'. Article 53 of Additional Protocol I contains similar protections, providing that '[i]t is prohibited to commit any acts of hostility directed against the historic monuments, works of art or places of worship which constitute the cultural or spiritual heritage of peoples; to use such objects in support of the military effort; [or] to make such objects the object of reprisals'.

According to Rule 38 of the ICRC study on customary international humanitarian law, parties to a conflict must take special care to avoid damage to cultural objects that are not military targets. Cultural property must not be attacked, unless required by military necessity. Rule 39 likewise provides that cultural property must not be used for purposes likely to expose it to destruction, unless imperatively required by military necessity, while Rule 40 makes clear that wilful damage, theft or vandalism of cultural property is prohibited. Each of these customary rules is held to apply in both international and non-international armed conflicts. An obligation on occupying powers to prevent and remedy the illicit export of cultural property is also stated to apply in international conflicts.[53]

The 1954 Hague Convention on Cultural Property, with 124 state parties at the time of writing, was a reaction to the destruction of European cultural heritage during the Second World War. The Convention imposes both positive and negative duties to protect cultural property. Article 4(1) obliges parties to refrain from 'any use of the property and its immediate surroundings or of the appliances in use for its protection for purposes which are likely to expose it to destruction or damage in the event of armed conflict'. Protocol II to the Hague Convention, adopted in 1999, strengthens and clarifies the Convention in response to the destruction of cultural property in armed conflicts in Somalia, Iraq, Kuwait and Yugoslavia. The Protocol entered into force in 2004 and currently has 61 state parties.

---

[53] Jean-Marie Henckaerts and Louise Doswald-Beck, *Customary International Humanitarian Law* (CUP 2005) rule 41.

4. Protection of civilians

The previous chapter examined the principles of international humanitarian law regulating the means and methods of warfare. In this chapter and the next, we examine protections afforded by international humanitarian law to certain classes of person. This chapter examines how civilians are protected under humanitarian law, while in Chapter 5 we will consider the protections afforded to combatants placed *hors de combat*. As we shall see, the definitions of 'combatant' and 'civilian' are interrelated. There is also some overlap between the protections provided to persons of both categories.

We begin this chapter with an examination of the key protections afforded to civilians and civilian property under international humanitarian law, focusing on the principles of distinction and humane treatment. We then consider the doctrine of military necessity, the related concept of proportionality and the obligation on both attacking and defending parties to take precautionary measures for the protection of civilians. We then look at the prohibition on reprisals, before examining the protections afforded to certain categories of civilian under humanitarian law, namely civilians in occupied territories, interned civilians, the sick and wounded, women, children and journalists.

FUNDAMENTAL PRINCIPLES

A central doctrine of international humanitarian law relating to civilians is the principle of distinction. We encountered this principle in our discussion of the duties of combatants in Chapter 3. The principle stipulates that parties to a conflict must consistently distinguish combatants and military targets on the one hand from civilian persons and objects on the other. Only the former may be the object of attack. Attacks must never be directed against civilians or civilian objects.[1] Acts or threats of violence designed to spread terror among the civilian population are also prohibited.[2]

---

[1] Additional Protocol I, art 48; Additional Protocol II, art 13(2).
[2] Additional Protocol I, art 51(2); Additional Protocol II, art 13(2).

The principle of distinction was first set out in the Preamble to the St Petersburg Declaration, which stated that the only legitimate object in war is to weaken the military forces of the enemy. It was subsequently recognised in the Hague Regulations[3] and restated in both Additional Protocols of 1977.[4] It is also a principle of customary international law applicable in both international and non-international conflicts.[5] The International Court of Justice has described it as one of the 'intransgressible principles of international customary law'.[6] The principle mandates a distinction in terms of both people (combatants and civilians) and property (military and civilian objects).

Another fundamental doctrine of international humanitarian law relevant to civilians is the principle of humane treatment. We saw in Chapter 1 that international humanitarian law is founded on the notion that there are certain principles of humanity so fundamental that they apply in all situations. Common Article 3 of the Geneva Conventions gives expression to this principle. It provides that civilians 'shall in all circumstances be treated humanely', without any adverse distinction founded on race, colour, religion, sex, birth, wealth or any other similar criteria.[7] The provision then sets out the fundamental guarantees applicable to persons affected by all types of armed conflict. These guarantees have since been reiterated and extended by provisions in both Additional Protocols.[8]

A variety of acts are prohibited under Common Article 3, including violence to life and person, taking of hostages, outrages upon personal dignity (in particular humiliating and degrading treatment) and sentences imposed without due process of law. International humanitarian law further provides that persons prosecuted for offences related to the armed conflict must be tried according to recognised principles of judicial procedure.[9] Women who are detained should be held in separate quarters and supervised by women. Families are to be accommodated together wherever possible.[10]

---

[3] Hague Regulations, art 25.
[4] Additional Protocol I, art 48; Additional Protocol II, art 13(2).
[5] Jean-Marie Henckaerts and Louise Doswald-Beck, *Customary International Humanitarian Law* (CUP 2005) rules 1, 7.
[6] *Legality of the Threat or Use of Nuclear Weapons*, International Court of Justice (ICJ) Advisory Opinion, 8 July 1996 [79].
[7] See also Additional Protocol I, art 9(1); Additional Protocol II, art 2(1).
[8] See also Additional Protocol I, art 75; Additional Protocol II, arts 4–6.
[9] Geneva Conventions, art 3; Additional Protocol I, art 75(4); Additional Protocol II, art 6.
[10] Additional Protocol I, art 75(5); Additional Protocol II, art 5(2)(a).

THE CONCEPT OF A CIVILIAN

International humanitarian law defines civilian status by a process of exclusion. Article 50 of Additional Protocol I, for example, provides that a civilian is any person who does not fall within the categories of combatants recognised in Article 4 of Geneva Convention III or Article 43 of Additional Protocol I.[11] The definitions of combatant status in those provisions were discussed in detail in Chapter 3. The latter provision covers armed forces or groups under the command of a party to the conflict who are subject to an internal disciplinary system and distinguish themselves from the civilian population or, where this is not possible, carry arms openly when preparing for or launching an attack.[12]

Article 50 of Additional Protocol I further provides that in case of doubt as to a person's status, the person shall be considered a civilian.[13] The civilian population then comprises all persons who are civilians.[14] The fact that there may be persons present within a civilian population who do not come within the definition of civilians does not deprive the population as a whole of its civilian character.[15] If soldiers on leave visiting their families are present in a village, the community as a whole does not lose its immunity from armed attack. It is possible for a person to lose her or his civilian status by taking a direct part in hostilities.[16] However, indirect contributions to the war effort, such as providing food or clothing to combatants, do not deprive a person of civilian protections.

Although Additional Protocol II refers to civilians without defining the term, arguably the notion of a civilian in that context should be defined by reference to the definition of a non-international armed conflict and interpreted as anyone who is not a member of the state forces or organised armed groups involved in armed exchanges. A definition of a civilian as 'anyone who is not a member of the armed forces or of an organized armed group' was adopted by consensus in a committee of the diplomatic conference preceding the adoption of the Additional Protocols of 1977.

---

[11] See also Jean-Marie Henckaerts and Louise Doswald-Beck, *Customary International Humanitarian Law* (CUP 2005) rule 5.
[12] Additional Protocol I, arts 43(1), 44(3).
[13] Additional Protocol I, art 50(1).
[14] Additional Protocol I, art 50(2).
[15] Additional Protocol I, art 50(3).
[16] Additional Protocol I, art 51(3); Additional Protocol II, art 13(3).

However, it was omitted from Additional Protocol II at the last minute as a result of efforts to simplify the text.[17]

The changing nature of warfare over recent decades has blurred the line between combatants and civilians in some cases. As weaponry has become more technically advanced, civilians have increasingly become involved in providing the expertise to operate it. There has also been a rise in the use of private contractors to supply military functions. Additionally, the increasing prevalence of internal armed conflicts has created environments in which civilians may become more directly involved with armed groups than is typical in conflicts between states, for example by providing logistical support and intelligence.[18] Despite these difficulties, however, the distinction between civilians and combatants remains central to international humanitarian law. We noted in Chapter 3 that any relaxation of the distinction would carry serious risks for the safety of civilian populations.

Military Objectives

We have seen that the concept of a civilian is defined by reference to combatant status. A civilian is effectively any person who does not qualify as a combatant. Similarly, the concept of a civilian object must be understood by reference to the contrasting notion of a military objective. Civilian objects are formally defined in Additional Protocol I as all objects which are not military objectives.[19] For an object to constitute a military objective, it must satisfy two criteria. First, it must make an effective contribution to military action by its nature, location, purpose or use. Second, its total or partial destruction, capture or neutralisation must offer a definite military advantage in the circumstances at the time.[20]

It is clear from this definition that an object cannot automatically or intrinsically constitute a military objective. It will depend upon the uses to which it is put and the circumstances at the time of attack. An annex to a set of draft rules produced by the International Committee of the Red Cross (ICRC) in 1956 listed airfields, naval bases, plants providing energy for national defence, military communication lines and stores of arms

---

[17] Jean-Marie Henckaerts and Louise Doswald-Beck, *Customary International Humanitarian Law* (CUP 2005) 19.

[18] For discussion, see Andreas Wenger and Simon JA Mason, 'The Civilianization of Armed Conflict: Trends and Implications' (2008) 872 *International Review of the Red Cross* 835.

[19] Additional Protocol I, art 52(1).

[20] Additional Protocol I, art 52(2).

and supplies as examples of military objectives.[21] However, the drafters of the Additional Protocols of 1977 could not agree on a list of indicative examples. As a consequence, the Protocols themselves do not contain any further guidance. The more closely related an object is to the conduct of hostilities, the more likely it is to constitute a military objective, but in each case it will depend on the circumstances.

Certain types of objects, such as military weapons, fortifications, depots and transportation, are highly likely to contribute to military action and therefore serve as legitimate targets.[22] However, the situation becomes complicated when objects ordinarily used for civilian purposes, such as houses or schools, are employed for military ends. Some types of infrastructure, such as transportation and communication networks, may be used for both civilian and military purposes simultaneously. An area of land or building may also serve multiple purposes, some military and some not. In each case, whether the object constitutes a military objective will depend upon the two-part definition outlined above. In case of any doubt about the use of an ordinarily civilian object, the presumption should be that it is not being employed for military purposes.[23]

PROHIBITED ATTACKS

We saw above that the principle of distinction absolutely prohibits attacks on civilians. A clear example of a prohibited attack can be found in the case of *Prosecutor v Rajić* before the International Criminal Tribunal for the Former Yugoslavia (ICTY).[24] The accused was charged with ordering an attack against the village of Stupni Do in the Republic of Bosnia-Herzegovina. Stupni Do was a small village and there was no evidence that it housed any legitimate military target. The only armed resistance was provided by some local villagers who spontaneously took up arms against the attack. Soldiers under Rajić's command forced civilians from their homes, robbed them, sexually assaulted Muslim women and killed at least 37 people. The Prosecutor accepted a guilty plea to four counts of grave breaches of the Geneva Conventions. The charges included wilful killing,

---

[21] Yves Sandoz, Christophe Swinarski and Bruno Zimmermann (eds), *Commentary on the Additional Protocols* (Martinus Nijhoff 1987) 632.
[22] Ibid 636.
[23] Additional Protocol I, art 52(3).
[24] *Prosecutor v Rajić*, International Criminal Tribunal for the Former Yugoslavia (ICTY) Trial Chamber Judgment, 8 May 2006.

inhuman treatment, appropriation of property and extensive destruction not justified by military necessity.

The principle of distinction imposes obligations on both attacking and defending forces. Defending forces must not place civilian persons or objects near military targets in order to render the targets immune from attack.[25] Nonetheless, if defending forces violate this rule, it is still unlawful to directly target the civilian objects.[26] During the Persian Gulf War in 1991, for example, Iraqi forces stationed two fighter aircraft next to the historic Temple of Ur in the hope that the possibility of damaging the temple would deter attacks on the aircraft.[27] This strategy clearly violated Iraq's obligations under the law of armed conflict, but it did not remove the status of the temple as a civilian object. The legality of any attack on the aircraft in such circumstances would have to be assessed by reference to the doctrine of proportionality. We will return to this topic at greater length below.

International humanitarian law also imposes limitations on means and methods of warfare that would adversely affect civilian infrastructure. The starvation of civilians as a method of warfare is expressly prohibited.[28] Parties may not attack objects indispensable to the survival of the civilian population, such as foodstuffs, agricultural areas, crops, livestock, drinking water installations and irrigation works.[29] The protection does not apply if the objects in question are used solely to sustain the armed forces or in direct support of military action.[30] Attacks may not be directed at dangerous forces such as dams and nuclear generators which, if damaged, may wreak havoc upon the civilian population.[31] A corresponding obligation is placed on defending forces not to locate military objectives in such dangerous locations. Special protection also extends to objects of cultural or spiritual significance to civilians, including historic monuments, works of art or places of worship.[32] It is prohibited to employ such objects in support of military objectives.

International humanitarian law prohibits not only direct attacks against civilian objects, but also attacks that are indiscriminate. The concept of

---

[25] Additional Protocol I, art 51(7).
[26] Additional Protocol I, art 51(8).
[27] For discussion, see Michael W Lewis, 'The Law of Aerial Bombardment in the 1991 Gulf War' (2003) 97 *American Journal of International Law* 481, 487–8.
[28] Additional Protocol I, art 54(1); Additional Protocol II, art 14.
[29] Additional Protocol I, art 54(2); Additional Protocol II, art 14.
[30] Additional Protocol I, art 54(3).
[31] Additional Protocol I, art 56; Additional Protocol II, art 15.
[32] Additional Protocol I, art 53; Additional Protocol II, art 16.

indiscriminate attacks was discussed in Chapter 3. Indiscriminate attacks are those which are not directed at a specific military objective, are incapable of being directed at a specific military objective or the effects of which cannot be limited to a specific objective.[33] Indiscriminate attacks are prohibited because they cannot distinguish between civilian and military objects. They are therefore incapable of respecting the principle of distinction. We argued in Chapter 3 that the prohibition is best understood as requiring that means and methods of attack must be reasonably capable of being limited to a specific military objective.

Proportionality

The principle of distinction means that direct attacks on civilians are absolutely prohibited. This does not mean, however, that civilians may never legitimately be killed or injured as a result of armed conflict. An attack on a military objective may cause what is sometimes called 'collateral damage' to civilian objects. The principle of military necessity, which we encountered in Chapter 3, provides that an attacking force is permitted to use only that degree of force required to achieve a military objective that will result in minimum loss of combatant and civilian life and property. If this principle is observed, an attack that causes incidental injury to civilians or damage to civilian objects may be permissible.

The principle of proportionality, also discussed in Chapter 3, provides a further constraint on the kinds of attacks that may be carried out. Proportionality prohibits attacks that may be expected to cause damage to civilians and civilian objects that is excessive in relation to the anticipated military advantage.[34] The advantage anticipated must be exclusively military and it must also be 'concrete and direct'.[35] Proportionality therefore cannot be used to justify an attack deliberately targeting civilian objects, even if it might conceivably result in a military advantage. A military advantage can only consist of gaining ground or destroying or weakening the enemy armed forces and cannot be constituted by creating conditions conducive to surrender by targeting the civilian population.

It will sometimes be clear whether an attack is proportionate or disproportionate when weighed against the anticipated military advantage, but in other cases the competing factors will be more evenly poised. In

---

[33] Additional Protocol I, art 51(4).
[34] Additional Protocol I, art 51(5)(b). See also Jean-Marie Henckaerts and Louise Doswald-Beck, *Customary International Humanitarian Law* (CUP 2005) rule 14.
[35] Additional Protocol I, art 51(5)(b).

the cases of uncertainty, the balance should weigh in favour of protection of civilian persons and objects. This is consistent with the overarching principle in Article 57(1) of Additional Protocol I that '[i]n the conduct of military operations, constant care shall be taken to spare the civilian population'.[36] If the risk of disproportionate loss of civilian lives and property becomes apparent in the course of an attack already in progress, the attack must be cancelled or suspended.[37] Where a range of different options exists to target a particular military objective, the attacking force has a duty to choose the option that presents the least danger to civilian lives and property.[38]

Technological developments in precision weaponry have both positive and negative implications for compliance with the principles of distinction and proportionality. On the one hand, increased precision allows for more accurate targeting and therefore reduces the risk of collateral damage to civilians and civilian objects. On the other hand, increased precision may open up to attack targets that would not previously have been available, creating the potential for greater incidental harm to civilians.[39] The increasing significance of 'information warfare' also produces new challenges for implementing the principles of distinction and proportionality. The ability to shut down parts of a nation's computer network may yield significant military advantages, but could also produce serious negative consequences for the civilian population through disruptions to traffic control, telecommunications, banking networks and other critical infrastructure.[40]

Precautionary Measures

International humanitarian law requires attacking forces to refrain from attacks that will violate the principles of distinction and proportionality. These negative obligations, however, are only part of the picture. Parties to a conflict also have positive duties to protect the civilian population. Combatants engaged in military operations in proximity to civilian objects must employ precautionary measures to limit the risk to civilian life and

---

[36] See also Additional Protocol II, art 13(1).
[37] Additional Protocol I, art 57(2)(b).
[38] Additional Protocol I, art 57(3).
[39] Michael N Schmidt, 'Precision Attack and International Humanitarian Law' (2005) 859 *International Review of the Red Cross* 445, 453.
[40] For discussion, see Mark R Shulman, 'Discrimination in the Laws of Information Warfare' (1999) 37 *Columbia Journal of Transnational Law* 939.

property.[41] These measures apply to both attacking and defending forces. Attacking forces must do everything feasible to verify that targets of attack are legitimate military objectives. They must also take all feasible precautions in the choice of means and methods of attack with a view to minimising incidental damage to civilian objects.[42] Feasible precautions, in this context, are those that are practicable or practically possible in all the circumstances at the time, taking into account both humanitarian and military considerations.[43]

An attacking force must give advance warning, wherever possible, of attacks that may cause damage to the civilian population. The obligation to provide advance warning has a long history and was recognised in the Lieber Code.[44] However, a warning is only required where circumstances permit, so it is not mandated where an element of surprise is necessary for the operation to succeed or to ensure the security of the attacking party.[45] In cases where protected objects, such as ambulances and hospitals, are improperly used in hostilities, a party may only attack those objects where a warning is given to the defending party to cease the improper use and, after a reasonable time for compliance, the warning has been ignored.[46] The fact that sick and wounded members of the armed forces are cared for in hospitals does not deprive the facilities of their protected status.[47]

Defending forces must remove civilians and civilian objects from the vicinity of military objectives to the maximum extent feasible. They must also avoid locating military objectives within or near densely populated areas and take all other necessary precautions to protect the civilian population from the dangers of military operations.[48] Defending forces are particularly prohibited from using human shields.[49] This refers to the

---

[41] Additional Protocol I, art 57; Additional Protocol II, art 13; Amended Protocol II to the Convention on Certain Conventional Weapons, art 3; Protocol II to the Hague Convention for the Protection of Cultural Property, arts 6 and 7; Jean-Marie Henckaerts and Louise Doswald-Beck, *Customary International Humanitarian Law* (CUP 2005) rule 15.
[42] Additional Protocol I, art 57(2)(a).
[43] Protocol II to the Convention on Certain Conventional Weapons, art 3(4); Amended Protocol II to the Convention on Certain Conventional Weapons, art 3(10); Protocol III to the Convention on Certain Conventional Weapons, art 1(5).
[44] Lieber Code, art 19.
[45] Hague Regulations, art 26; Additional Protocol I, art 57(2)(c).
[46] Geneva Convention I, art 21; Additional Protocol II, art 11(2).
[47] Geneva Convention IV, art 19.
[48] Additional Protocol I, art 58.
[49] Geneva Convention III, art 23; Geneva Convention IV, art 28; Additional Protocol I, art 51(7).

location of civilians or persons not taking part in combat in the vicinity of military objectives with the intention of trying to prevent opposing forces targeting those objectives. The use of human shields in armed conflict has received wide international condemnation.[50]

Reprisals and Collective Punishments

Reprisals involve the purported right of a party to respond to a violation of the laws of armed conflict with force or other retributive measures. Reprisals against civilians and their property are prohibited under international humanitarian law.[51] The prohibition expressly extends to attacks against places of worship, food and water supplies, the natural environment, dams, dykes and nuclear power stations.[52] Reprisals against cultural property of importance to the heritage of a people are also forbidden.[53]

Various other groups and objects are expressly protected against being the subject of reprisals. These include wounded, sick and shipwrecked persons; medical units, transport and personnel; and religious personnel.[54] Prisoners of war also may not be the object of reprisals.[55] These detailed provisions, however, are merely specifications of the general principle that protected categories of persons and objects may never be attacked in retaliation for violations of humanitarian norms. This principle is widely regarded as part of the customary law governing both international and non-international conflicts, although state practice on the issue is not completely uniform.[56]

The concept of reprisals was widely used during the Second World War to justify attacks on civilian populations. There has been a consistent trend since that time towards condemnation of the practice.[57] This point applies equally to international and non-international conflicts. The prohibition

---

[50] Jean-Marie Henckaerts and Louise Doswald-Beck, *Customary International Humanitarian Law* (CUP 2005) 337–8.
[51] Geneva Convention IV, art 33; Additional Protocol I, art 20, 51(6). See also United Nations General Assembly Resolution 2675 (XXV) of 1970.
[52] Additional Protocol I, arts 53–56.
[53] Hague Convention for the Protection of Cultural Property, art 4(4).
[54] Geneva Convention I, art 46; Geneva Convention II, art 47; Additional Protocol I, art 20.
[55] Geneva Convention III, art 13.
[56] Jean-Marie Henckaerts and Louise Doswald-Beck, *Customary International Humanitarian Law* (CUP 2005) 521.
[57] Ibid 519–23. For further discussion, see *Prosecutor v Kupreskic*, ICTY Trial Chamber Judgment, 14 January 2000 [527]–[536].

on reprisals does not appear expressly in Additional Protocol II, but it is implicit in Common Article 3 and the requirement that the fundamental protections contained therein apply at any time and place whatsoever.[58] It is also closely connected to the principle of distinction. The ICTY Appeal Chamber expressed the view in the *Tadić* decision that the prohibition against civilian reprisals is a principle of customary law applying regardless of the type of conflict.[59]

International humanitarian law also protects civilians from punishment for acts that they have not personally committed. Collective penalties – those imposed upon groups of persons for acts of parties with whom they are associated – are prohibited.[60] This prohibition is reflected in customary law applying to all categories of armed conflicts.[61] The principle of individual criminal responsibility, which is itself a norm of customary international law,[62] further militates against punishment on a collective basis. The prohibition on collective punishment extends to internment and assigned residence of inhabitants of occupied territories pursuant to Article 78 of Geneva Convention IV.[63] These are exceptional measures only to be taken on consideration of individual cases and on the basis that the person in question poses a threat to security of the occupying power.

CIVILIANS IN OCCUPIED TERRITORIES

Civilians living in territories that come to be occupied by enemy armed forces are in a particularly vulnerable position. Historically, civilian populations have been subject to serious abuse in these circumstances. The protection of civilians in occupied territories is addressed by Part III of Geneva Convention IV through what is known as the *protected persons regime*. Part III contains a detailed scheme for protecting the rights of persons who find themselves under the control of a foreign or enemy power.

---

[58] Jean-Marie Henckaerts and Louise Doswald-Beck, *Customary International Humanitarian Law* (CUP 2005) 526–9.
[59] *Prosecutor v Tadić*, ICTY Appeals Chamber Decision on Jurisdiction, 2 October 1995 [111]–[112].
[60] Geneva Convention III, art 87; Geneva Convention IV, art 33; Additional Protocol II, art 4(2)(b).
[61] Jean-Marie Henckaerts and Louise Doswald-Beck, *Customary International Humanitarian Law* (CUP 2005) rule 103.
[62] Ibid rule 102.
[63] *Prosecutor v Mucić*, ICTY Trial Chamber Judgment, 16 November 1998 [578].

The protections of Part III of Geneva Convention IV extend to 'protected persons', defined in Article 4 as persons who 'in any manner whatsoever, find themselves, in case of a conflict or occupation, in the hands of a Party to the conflict or Occupying Power of which they are not nationals'. The requirement that persons be 'in the hands of' a party to the conflict has been interpreted broadly. It does not require that the persons in question be physically detained. It is enough that they are located in territory that is under the control of a party to the conflict or another occupying power.[64]

The requirement that protected persons be in the hands of a party 'of which they are not nationals' has also been interpreted widely. The ICTY Appeals Chamber ruled in the *Tadić* case that the key factor in applying this phrase is not legal citizenship or nationality, but rather the wider allegiances of the groups in question, having regard to religion, ethnicity and other social divides relevant to the armed conflict.[65] The issue in *Tadić* was whether residents of an occupied territory were entitled to be treated as protected persons, even though they were of the same nationality as the occupying forces. The ICTY held that the occupying forces could not rely on shared nationality to avoid their obligations.

Status as a protected person commonly arises in the context of occupation of territory by a party to the conflict without the consent of the host state. The occupying power is required to respect the laws and institutions of the occupied territory as far as possible. However, the application of the regime has been rendered less straightforward by the types of occupation that have arisen in recent years, for example the occupation of Afghanistan and Iraq by the United States and allied forces, with the consent of host governments. An ICRC report issued in 2012 elaborated upon some of the debates on the application of occupation law to contemporary forms of occupation.[66] The expert views canvassed in the report show that the relevance of consent in this area is a contested issue.[67]

The protected persons regime aims to ensure that civilians who find themselves in the hands of enemy powers are afforded certain fundamental guarantees. They are entitled to respect for their persons, honour,

---

[64] Jean S Pictet et al (eds), *Commentary on the Geneva Conventions* (ICRC 1960) vol 4, 50.
[65] *Prosecutor v Tadić*, ICTY Appeals Chamber Judgment, 15 July 1999 [166]–[168].
[66] Tristan Ferraro (ed), *Occupation and Other Forms of Administration in Foreign Territory* (ICRC 2012).
[67] Ibid 20–23.

family rights, religious practices and customs. They are to be treated humanely and protected against all acts or threats of violence, insults and public curiosity. They must be treated with equal consideration, without any adverse distinction based, in particular, on race, religion or political opinion. Women are to be protected against rape, prostitution or indecent assault.[68]

Protected persons are also offered guarantees against physical or moral coercion; physical suffering or extermination; collective penalties, intimidation and terrorism; and being taken hostage.[69] An occupying power has an obligation to ensure the provision of adequate food and medical supplies to protected persons in occupied territory. The power cannot requisition supplies for its own needs without taking account of the civilian population and ensuring fair value for any supplies requisitioned.[70]

The fundamental guarantees outlined in Article 75 of Additional Protocol I offer further protection for persons affected by an armed conflict or occupation and in the power of a party to the conflict who are not entitled to more favourable treatment under the Geneva Conventions or Additional Protocol I. Any residents of occupied territories who find themselves beyond the reach of Geneva Convention IV can rely on this provision. This might occur, for example, if residents of a particular region find themselves in the hands of a party to the conflict that is allied with their state of nationality, as such a situation is explicitly removed from the application of Geneva Convention IV.[71]

Persons falling within Article 75 are protected against violence to life, health or physical or mental well-being, including murder, torture, corporal punishment and mutilation; outrages upon personal dignity, including humiliating or degrading treatment, enforced prostitution or indecent assault; taking of hostages; and collective punishments. The provision also contains robust guarantees of due process for anyone charged with a crime. Similar protections applying in non-international conflicts can be found in Articles 4–6 of Additional Protocol II, although those provisions contain less detail.

We noted above that Geneva Convention IV does not protect persons in the hands of a power allied with their own state. The protected persons regime also does not typically assist residents of occupied territories who are nationals of the new occupying state, although if they belong to a

---

[68] Geneva Convention IV, art 27.
[69] Geneva Convention IV, arts 31–34.
[70] Geneva Convention IV, art 55.
[71] Geneva Convention IV, art 4.

minority religious, ethnic or cultural group a case could be made that they fall within the principle set out in the *Tadić* case. Geneva Convention IV provides that nationals of the occupying state who previously sought refuge in the territory of the occupied state may not be arrested, prosecuted, convicted or deported from the occupied territory except for offences preceding the outbreak of hostilities.[72] The fundamental guarantees set out in Article 75 would also apply in such circumstances.

Stateless persons and refugees might sometimes be treated as enemy aliens where their state of origin is engaged in conflict with the state in whose territory they find themselves. However, Article 44 of Geneva Convention IV provides that persons who do not *in fact* enjoy the protection of any state are not to be treated as enemy aliens exclusively on the basis of their nationality. This means that an alien in the territory of a party cannot be treated adversely by reason of her or his association with an enemy power if in fact she or he does not enjoy the diplomatic protection of the state at war with the state in which she or he is located. Article 73 of Additional Protocol I expressly extends the guarantees afforded to protected persons by Geneva Convention IV to individuals who were considered stateless persons and refugees prior to the commencement of hostilities.

Internment and Displacement of Civilians

The internment of civilians was a significant feature of the Second World War and led to widespread mistreatment. International humanitarian law recognises that internment of civilians may in some cases be necessary for security, but seeks to place the practice within strict limits. Article 79 of Geneva Convention IV provides that protected persons shall not be interned except for imperative security reasons or due to the commission of an offence. The protections for interned civilians are substantially identical to those afforded to prisoners of war, which will be considered in Chapter 5. There are also some protections afforded to interned civilians under Geneva Convention IV that have no direct parallels for prisoners of war. For example, the family life of civilian internees must be preserved as far as possible and they should be allowed to receive regular visitors, especially close relatives.[73] They may not generally be put to work, except on a voluntary basis.[74]

---

[72] Geneva Convention IV, art 70.
[73] Geneva Convention IV, arts 82, 116.
[74] Geneva Convention IV, art 95.

International humanitarian law in both international and non-international conflicts provides that the civilian population is not to be displaced for reasons related to the conflict unless the security of civilians or imperative military reasons require it. The basic principles in this area are set out in Article 49 of Geneva Convention IV and reiterated in both Additional Protocols.[75] Measures must be taken in all cases to ensure shelter, hygiene, safety and nutrition for displaced persons. Civilians in occupied territory must not be compelled to leave that territory by the occupying power; likewise, the occupying power must refrain from relocating its own civilians to the occupied region.

SICK AND WOUNDED CIVILIANS

Part II of Geneva Convention IV provides special protections for the sick and wounded and applies not only to protected persons but to the whole population of countries in conflict. The application of this part does not, therefore, rely upon considerations of nationality or relationship with a party to the conflict. Sick and wounded persons are defined as those who, due to trauma, disease or other physical or mental disorder or disability, are in need of medical assistance or care and who refrain from any act of hostility.[76] Sick and wounded persons are to be the object of particular protection and respect. Similar protections are extended to infirm persons and expectant mothers.[77]

Sick and wounded persons must receive the medical care and attention they need to the fullest extent practicable and with as little delay as possible.[78] They must not be the object of reprisals.[79] Each party has an obligation to search for the dead and wounded, assist shipwrecked persons and others in grave danger and protect them against ill treatment.[80] There is, however, no obligation to rescue the wounded and shipwrecked if this would place the rescuers themselves in serious peril.

Sick, wounded, infirm or pregnant internees may only be transferred if the journey would not be seriously detrimental to them, unless the transfer

---

[75] Additional Protocol I, art 85(4)(a); Additional Protocol II, art 17. See also Jean-Marie Henckaerts and Louise Doswald-Beck, *Customary International Humanitarian Law* (CUP 2005) rules 129–31.
[76] Additional Protocol I, art 8.
[77] Geneva Convention IV, art 16; Additional Protocol I, art 10.
[78] Additional Protocol I, art 10; Additional Protocol II, art 7.
[79] Additional Protocol I, art 20.
[80] Geneva Convention IV, art 16.

is required for their own safety.[81] The Geneva Conventions encourage the parties to a conflict to provide additional protection for wounded and vulnerable persons beyond the obligations imposed upon them. Parties may enter agreements for the mutual recognition of medical zones and hospitals in their territories and neutralised zones in the area of hostilities to shelter sick and other vulnerable persons from the effects of warfare.[82]

Medical Personnel

Medical personnel from both the civilian population and the military are subject to special protections under international humanitarian law. These are vital in ensuring that care is available for the sick and wounded and those who provide it are adequately protected. Medical personnel are those whose function is exclusively to search for, collect, transport, diagnose or treat the wounded, sick and shipwrecked or to administer medical units or medical transports.[83] Medical personnel are not to be the object of attack. Nobody engaged in medical activities can be compelled to act contrary to the rules of medical ethics or to give any information regarding people she or he has treated if that would be harmful to patients or their families, except as required by the law of her or his own party.[84]

Hospitals, medical units and medical transport also must not be the object of attack.[85] State parties must provide hospitals with certification that they are civilian hospitals and may also authorise the marking of hospitals with the Red Cross and associated symbols in order to facilitate this protection. Hospitals should be situated as far as possible from military objectives. The protection afforded to hospitals and other medical units continues unless they are used to commit acts against the opposing forces and ends only after due warning has been given to cease the improper use.[86]

Aircraft carrying the wounded or medical personnel and equipment also receive protection, but only on routes agreed between the parties and on the condition that they do not fly over enemy territory.[87] They shall be

---

[81] Geneva Convention IV, art 127.
[82] Geneva Convention IV, arts 14, 15, 17.
[83] Additional Protocol I, art 8.
[84] Additional Protocol I, art 16; Additional Protocol II, art 10.
[85] Geneva Convention IV, arts 18, 21; Additional Protocol I, arts 8, 12, 21, 23.
[86] Geneva Convention IV, art 19; Additional Protocol I, art 13.
[87] Geneva Convention I, art 36; Geneva Convention II, art 39; Geneva Convention IV, art 22. See also Additional Protocol I, arts 24–30.

permitted to fly unmolested over neutral territory with the consent of the third party concerned.[88] The aircraft must not be used to acquire a military advantage, to collect or transmit intelligence data or to carry arms or people apart from the sick and wounded and military personnel.[89]

An occupying power must provide civilian medical personnel with the assistance necessary to perform their functions.[90] Occupying powers are required to maintain health and hygiene in the occupied territory with the cooperation of national and local authorities. They are also responsible for maintaining hospitals and their services. Medical personnel are to be allowed to carry out their duties, while medical facilities, personnel and equipment are to be granted the recognition mentioned above.[91]

Medical personnel in occupied territory and areas where fighting is taking place are to wear on their left arm an armlet bearing the emblem of the Red Cross, as well as carrying photographic identification stamped by the responsible authority.[92] Hospitals must likewise maintain an up-to-date list of their medical personnel.[93] These measures facilitate the recognition of medical personnel and therefore the provision of the special protections set out for them in the Geneva Conventions.

The Role of the Protected Emblems

We saw in Chapter 2 that the Geneva Conventions and Additional Protocols give special status to four protected symbols: the Red Cross, the Red Crescent, the Red Lion and Sun (which is no longer used) and the recently adopted Red Crystal. These emblems play an indispensable role in protecting humanitarian workers during armed conflicts. The emblems should be displayed on the flags and equipment used by medical services,[94] while medical and religious personnel should bear them on armlets and identity cards.[95] Members of armed forces who are trained to

---

[88] Geneva Convention I, art 37; Geneva Convention II, art 40; Additional Protocol I, art 31.
[89] Additional Protocol I, art 28.
[90] Geneva Convention IV, art 20; Additional Protocol I, art 15; Additional Protocol II, art 9.
[91] Geneva Convention IV, art 56.
[92] Additional Protocol I, art 18(3).
[93] Geneva Convention IV, art 20.
[94] Geneva Convention I, art 39; Geneva Convention II, art 43; Additional Protocol I, art 18.
[95] Geneva Convention I, art 40; Geneva Convention II, art 42; Additional Protocol I, art 18.

carry out duties as stretcher bearers, hospital orderlies and nurses should only wear the emblem while carrying out medical duties.[96]

Parties to the conflict are required to take necessary steps to make the protected emblems indicating medical units and establishments clearly visible to opposing forces in order to avoid them being targeted.[97] It is generally prohibited to use the emblems for any purpose other than identifying medical personnel and objects.[98] The exceptions are use in peacetime for activities of national Red Cross organisations and to identify ambulances and aid stations providing free treatment to the sick and wounded. The symbols may not be used at any time for a non-humanitarian purpose.[99] We saw in Chapter 3 that it is strictly forbidden to display the protected emblems when engaging in hostilities.

Misuse of the protected emblems has long been a problem recognised by international humanitarian law. Traditionally, efforts to preserve the sanctity of the emblems have centred on combating perfidious uses, where the emblems are deliberately misused to obtain a military advantage.[100] Nowadays, however, the ubiquity of the Red Cross emblem in popular culture also poses another type of problem: its use on television and in movies, as well as in computer games and on the internet, poses the risk that its protective function will gradually be diluted. The problem here is not deliberate abuse of the emblem in the context of armed conflict, but rather its casual or inadvertent misuse in peacetime contexts unconnected to its humanitarian function under the Geneva Conventions.

The task of making combatants, officials and members of the public aware of the importance of the protected emblems has not been aided by inappropriate uses in peacetime. A famous example arose in relation to the 1987 James Bond film, *The Living Daylights*, which depicted opium being smuggled in sacks marked with the Red Cross and a man being kidnapped in a helicopter bearing the emblem. More recently, similar issues have arisen from depictions of the Red Cross symbol in computer games and on the internet. The Red Cross is widely used in war-based computer games to denote medical equipment or installations, and is sometimes shown on personnel or vehicles taking part in combat. The use of the emblem in these contexts led the Canadian national Red Cross society to write to game manufacturers in early 2006, but the practice has proved difficult to change.

---

[96] Geneva Convention I, art 41.
[97] Geneva Convention I, art 42; Geneva Convention II, art 43.
[98] Geneva Convention I, art 44; Additional Protocol I, art 18.
[99] Geneva Convention I, art 44.
[100] The prohibition on perfidy was discussed in detail in Chapter 3.

The contemporary importance of the internet for information and entertainment has introduced a new challenge in counteracting unauthorised use of the protected emblems. A report submitted to the World Intellectual Property Organization by the Red Cross Movement in 2002 noted a range of misuses of the protected emblems in domain names and on websites, including their association with pornography, online retailers and political groups.[101] The transnational and rapidly evolving nature of online information makes these types of abuses particularly difficult to counteract. It is tempting to view misuses of the protected emblems in peacetime as trivial compared to perfidious uses in wartime. However, the effectiveness of the emblems relies on participants in armed conflicts recognising and respecting their protective function. Their misuse in peacetime threatens to dilute this significance, fuelling a blasé attitude that encourages wartime abuses.

OTHER VULNERABLE GROUPS

Common Article 3 of the Geneva Conventions makes it clear that the protection afforded by international humanitarian law to civilians and other persons placed *hors de combat* is available to all parties without distinction. Any denial of humane treatment based on 'race, colour, religion or faith, sex, birth or wealth, or any other similar criteria' is expressly prohibited. This principle is reiterated in both Additional Protocols.[102] In some cases, however, the law of war sets out special protections for groups of people who are rendered particularly vulnerable within the context of armed conflict. The protections for sick and wounded civilians set out above might perhaps be viewed in this light. Other groups afforded special recognition and protection include women, children and journalists. The principles applying to each of these groups are discussed in the following sections.

Protections for Women

The number of women serving in the armed forces has grown consistently since the Second World War.[103] Nonetheless, the most common

---

[101] World Intellectual Property Organization, *Cyber Misuse of the Protected Names and Emblems of the International Red Cross and Red Crescent Movement: A Case for Special Protection* (WIPO 2002).
[102] Additional Protocol I, art 9(1); Additional Protocol II, art 2(1).
[103] Charlotte Lindsay, *Women Facing War: International Committee of the Red Cross Study on the Impact of Armed Conflict on Women* (ICRC 2001) 23.

way for women to be caught up in armed conflict is still as civilians. The high number of civilian casualties in modern conflicts and the fact that women generally comprise the majority of the civilian population during wartime[104] mean that the effect of armed conflict on women is significant. In times of war, women frequently struggle to provide for themselves and their families, particularly where food and other necessities are in short supply or where a male breadwinner has been killed or is engaged in combat. Women and children frequently bear the brunt of shortages of food and water, with limited provisions available being diverted to soldiers.[105]

The fact that women hold less political and economic power than men means that they are frequently disempowered when it comes to decisions about engaging in conflict, although these decisions will have a significant impact upon them. The role of carer is occupied primarily by women in most societies, so women are often less mobile than men in the face of danger. Women are often subjected to ill treatment by opposing forces, as well as allied forces and even members of their own side. In particular, women are at risk of rape and sexual assault, a fact that has, in the past, elicited little public recognition. International humanitarian law protects all persons against sexual assault, but women are disproportionately targeted for assaults of this nature during armed conflicts of all types.[106]

We saw above that the protection of international humanitarian law is afforded to all persons without distinction based on sex.[107] In no circumstances are women to be treated less favourably than men.[108] However, the Geneva Conventions and Additional Protocols also contain a number of provisions recognising the specific challenges and vulnerabilities faced by women in wartime. The Geneva Conventions state in several places that women are to be treated 'with all consideration due to their sex' or 'with all regard due to their sex'.[109] These provisions are somewhat vague in and of themselves, but they are supplemented by more specific protections.

---

[104] Ibid 103.
[105] Ibid 77–9.
[106] United Nations Human Rights Council, *Fifteen Years of the United Nations Special Rapporteur on Violence against Women* (UNHRC 2009) 21–5.
[107] Geneva Conventions, art 3; Additional Protocol I, art 9(1); Additional Protocol II, art 2(1).
[108] Geneva Convention III, arts 14, 88.
[109] Geneva Convention I, art 12; Geneva Convention II, art 12; Geneva Convention III, art 14.

90   *Principles of international humanitarian law*

For example, women must be respected and protected against rape, forced prostitution and other forms of indecent assault.[110]

The prohibition against rape and sexual assault under international law has been strengthened by the inclusion of these offences as crimes in the statutes of the International Criminal Tribunals for the Former Yugoslavia[111] and Rwanda.[112] Subsequently, a number of perpetrators of rape and sexual assault have been successfully prosecuted for sexual crimes against women during wartime.[113] Sexual crimes have also been enumerated in the Statute of the International Criminal Court.[114] The inclusion of rape as an offence that can constitute a crime against humanity if committed in the context of a widespread or systematic attack against a civilian population is particularly significant. As the term 'crime against humanity' is traditionally reserved for the most serious violations of international law, this development recognises rape and sexual assault as serious crimes that hold devastating consequences for both victims and their communities.

International humanitarian law provides that women who are interned are to be held in separate quarters to male internees (except where family accommodation is provided) and must be supervised and searched by female guards.[115] These provisions help to guard against the risk of ill treatment, particularly sexual violence, as well as respecting women's privacy and dignity. Special protections are also provided for nursing and expectant mothers, and mothers of dependent children.[116] These measures include guarantees concerning the provision of food and protection, special priority in hearing of cases following arrest, immunity from the

---

[110] Geneva Convention I, art 12; Geneva Convention II, art 12; Geneva Convention III, arts 14, 25, 88, 97, 108; Geneva Convention IV, arts 27, 38, 76, 85, 97, 124; Additional Protocol I, arts 70, 75, 76; Additional Protocol II, arts 5(2) and 6(4). Rape was also prohibited in the Lieber Code, art 44.
[111] Statute of the International Criminal Tribunal for the Former Yugoslavia, art 5(g).
[112] Statute of the International Criminal Tribunal for Rwanda, arts 3(g), 4(e).
[113] See, for example, *Prosecutor v Akayesu*, International Criminal Tribunal for Rwanda (ICTR) Trial Chamber Judgment, 2 September 1998; *Prosecutor v Delalic*, ICTY Trial Chamber Judgment, 16 November 1998; *Prosecutor v Furundzija*, ICTY Trial Chamber Judgment, 10 December 1998; *Prosecutor v Kvocka*, ICTY Trial Chamber Judgment, 2 November 2001; *Prosecutor v Kunarac*, ICTY Trial Chamber Judgment, 22 December 2001.
[114] Statute of the International Criminal Court, arts 6(d), 7(1)(g), 8(2)(b)(xxii).
[115] Geneva Convention III, arts 25, 29, 97, 108; Geneva Convention IV, arts 76, 85, 97, 124; Additional Protocol I, art 75(5); Additional Protocol II, art 5(2)(a).
[116] Geneva Convention IV, arts 16–18, 21–23, 38, 70, 89, 91, 127; Additional Protocol I, arts 70, 76(2) and (3); Additional Protocol II, art 6(4).

death penalty, special medical treatment and all other benefits given to nationals of the protecting power who are in the same circumstances.

Protections for Children

Special protections for children are afforded by international humanitarian law by virtue of children's physical weakness and the importance of their preservation to future generations. Some of these protections are shared with pregnant women and mothers of young children, including the provision of additional food for internees, special priority in the hearing of cases, immunity from the death penalty and the benefit of preferential treatment afforded to children who are nationals of the protecting power.[117] Children are to be afforded special respect and protected against any form of indecent assault.

Different types of protections under international humanitarian law set different standards for who is regarded as a child. Children under the age of 18 years who find themselves in the hands of an occupying power should not be forced to work and, if charged with an offence, should be treated in a way that respects their status as minors.[118] They shall not be made subject to the death penalty.[119] Children under the age of 15 years should not be separated from their families or left on their own and their education and religious observance must be facilitated.[120] They are also to be afforded preferential measures in relation to food, medical care and protection.[121] Children who are under 12 years of age should be visibly identified by identity discs or other means.[122]

Article 78 of Additional Protocol I further provides that evacuation of children, other than nationals of the country arranging the evacuation, is only to occur in circumstances where their health, medical treatment or (except in occupied territory) safety requires it. Evacuation is only to take place with the consent of parents or those responsible for the care of the children. All parties to the conflict are to take all feasible precautions to avoid endangering the evacuation. The child is to be educated with the greatest possible continuity while away from home. The child's details are

---

[117] Geneva Convention IV, arts 38, 68, 89; Additional Protocol II, art 6(4).
[118] Geneva Convention IV, arts 51, 76.
[119] Geneva Convention IV, art 68; Additional Protocol I, art 77; Additional Protocol II, art 6.
[120] Geneva Convention IV, art 24.
[121] Geneva Convention IV, arts 23, 50, 89; Additional Protocol I, art 70.
[122] Geneva Convention IV, art 24.

to be recorded and sent to the Central Tracing Agency of the ICRC to facilitate reunification with her or his family.

The two Additional Protocols both provide that children under the age of 15 must not be recruited into the armed forces or take part in hostilities.[123] Additional Protocol I further provides that, in the case of children aged between 15 and 18, the oldest must be recruited first.[124] Combatants under the age of 15 are to be housed separately from other prisoners of war if captured, except where family accommodation is provided. The prohibition on recruiting children under the age of 15 is recognised as a norm of customary international law applying in all conflicts[125] and there is growing international support for recognising a minimum age of 18.[126]

The Convention on the Rights of the Child, which has gained near universal support from the international community since being opened for signature in 1989,[127] reinforces many of the protections for children provided by the law of armed conflict and also adds its own standards. It provides that the 'best interests of the child' are to be a primary consideration in all actions concerning children under the age of 18, whether those actions are taken by public or private institutions.[128] States parties must provide children with the protection and care necessary for their wellbeing. The Convention recognises a child's right to know and be cared for by her or his parents and to preserve her or his national and other identity. A child permanently or temporarily deprived of her or his family environment is entitled to special protection and assistance from the state.[129]

The Convention on the Rights of the Child pays particular regard to the rights of children in armed conflict. State parties undertake to respect and to ensure respect for the norms of international humanitarian law and

---

[123] Additional Protocol I, art 77(2); Additional Protocol II, art 4(3)(c).

[124] Additional Protocol I, art 77(2).

[125] Jean-Marie Henckaerts and Louise Doswald-Beck, *Customary International Humanitarian Law* (CUP 2005) rules 136–7. See also *Prosecutor v Sam Hinga Norman*, Special Court for Sierra Leone Appeals Chamber Decision on Jurisdiction, 31 May 2004.

[126] For discussion, see Jean-Marie Henckaerts and Louise Doswald-Beck, *Customary International Humanitarian Law* (CUP 2005) 484–5, 488.

[127] The United States, Somalia and South Sudan were the only recognised states not to have ratified the Convention at the time of writing.

[128] The term 'best interests of the child' is widely used in both international and domestic legal contexts. For discussion of the ethical issues raised by the term, see Jonathan Crowe and Lisa Toohey, 'From Good Intentions to Ethical Outcomes: The Paramountcy of Children's Interests in the *Family Law Act*' (2009) 33 *Melbourne University Law Review* 391.

[129] Convention on the Rights of the Child, arts 3, 7(1), 8(1), 20(1).

are required to take all feasible measures to ensure protection and care of children who are affected by armed conflict. The Convention contains the same rules with regard to the recruitment of children into the armed forces as are contained in Additional Protocol I.[130] It further provides that states must take all appropriate measures to promote physical and psychological recovery of children who have been the victims of neglect, mistreatment or armed conflict.[131]

An Optional Protocol to the Convention dealing specifically with the involvement of children in armed conflict currently has 150 state parties. The Optional Protocol recognises the harmful and widespread impact that armed conflict has on children. It requires states not to conscript persons under 18 years of age into their armed forces and to take all feasible measures to ensure that members of their forces under that age are not directly involved in hostilities.[132] State parties must also raise the minimum age for voluntary recruitment into national forces from 15 (as provided for in the Convention) and deposit a binding declaration that states the minimum age at which voluntary recruitment will be permitted.[133] Non-state armed groups are not to recruit or use in hostilities persons under 18 years of age in any circumstances.[134]

Protections for Journalists

Journalists play an important role in armed conflicts, risking their lives to provide coverage of events to the outside world. The perilous nature of the war correspondent's role has been brought home by the fate of journalists such as Daniel Pearl, who was kidnapped and beheaded in 2002 while covering the armed conflict in Pakistan.[135] Journalists are covered by the protections afforded to civilians under international humanitarian law, but they are also the subject of special provisions recognising the risks of their investigative role. Journalists, like civilians, may be injured through being

---

[130] Convention on the Rights of the Child, art 38.
[131] Convention on the Rights of the Child, art 39.
[132] Optional Protocol to the Convention on the Rights of the Child on the Involvement of Children in Armed Conflict, arts 1–2.
[133] Optional Protocol to the Convention on the Rights of the Child on the Involvement of Children in Armed Conflict, art 3.
[134] Optional Protocol to the Convention on the Rights of the Child on the Involvement of Children in Armed Conflict, art 4.
[135] For discussion of historical attempts to protect journalists in wartime, see Dylan Howard, 'Remaking the Pen Mightier than the Sword: An Evaluation of the Growing Need for the International Protection of Journalists' (2002) 30 *Georgia Journal of International and Comparative Law* 505.

caught up in hostilities or bombardment of towns and cities. However, they may also be targeted for political reasons or because of their work in exposing those guilty of violence or corruption.

Geneva Convention III provides that accredited war correspondents are entitled to prisoner of war status where they fall into the hands of the enemy.[136] Journalists who are not accredited war correspondents are covered by Article 79 of Additional Protocol I, which reiterates that a journalist engaged in professional activities is to be considered a civilian provided that she or he takes no action adversely affecting her or his civilian status, such as playing a direct role in hostilities. A card confirming the journalist's status may be issued by her or his state of nationality. This provision does not add substantially to the protections enjoyed by journalists due to their civilian status, but it reinforces the principle that they must not be targeted because of their profession.

CIVIL DEFENCE ORGANISATIONS

The general protections extended under international humanitarian law to civilian populations and objects are supplemented by principles concerning civil defence organisations whose role is to assist the civilian population in times of conflict. 'Civil defence' is defined in Additional Protocol I as 'humanitarian tasks intended to protect the civilian population against the dangers, and to help it to recover from the immediate effects, of hostilities or disasters and also to provide the conditions necessary for its survival.'[137] The definition encompasses a range of possible functions including, but not limited to, warning, evacuation, management of shelters and blackouts, rescue, fire fighting and first aid. This reflects the diverse roles such organisations have played in different conflicts.[138]

During the Second World War, civil defence organisations were highly effective in minimising civilian casualties.[139] Additional Protocol I therefore provides that civil defence organisations should be respected and protected.[140] This protection may cease if such organisations are used to commit acts harmful to the enemy outside their proper tasks, but warning

---

[136] Geneva Convention III, art 4A(4). See also Additional Protocol I, art 79(2). The protections afforded to prisoners of war are discussed in depth in Chapter 5.
[137] Additional Protocol I, art 61(a).
[138] Yves Sandoz, Christophe Swinarski and Bruno Zimmermann (eds), *Commentary on the Additional Protocols* (Martinus Nijhoff 1987) 719.
[139] Ibid 713.
[140] Additional Protocol I, art 62(1).

to cease the improper role must be given and disregarded before any hostile action is taken.[141] Civil defence organisations will not be deprived of protection under this principle merely because they cooperate with military authorities or carry out functions with incidental benefits for combatants *hors de combat*.[142]

---

[141] Additional Protocol I, art 65(1).
[142] Additional Protocol I, art 65(2).

5. Protection of combatants *hors de combat*

Combatants are protected by the law of armed conflict in a number of different ways. Combatants engaged in active hostilities are protected by the restrictions on means and methods of warfare discussed in Chapter 3. The prohibition against inflicting superfluous injury, for example, exists primarily for the protection of combatants. Combatants also benefit from the restrictions on means and methods of warfare imposed by the doctrine of military necessity, the prohibitions on specific types of weapons deemed to cause unnecessary suffering and the rules concerning perfidy and forbidden orders.

This chapter, by contrast, is concerned with the protections afforded to combatants placed *hors de combat* (outside the fight) through capture, injury or other forms of incapacitation. Article 41 of Additional Protocol I provides that a person shall be regarded as *hors de combat* if she or he is in the power of an adverse party, has clearly indicated an intention to surrender or has been rendered unconscious or incapacitated by wounds or sickness and is therefore incapable of defending her- or himself. The provision further stipulates that persons *hors de combat* are not to be attacked.

Captured combatants benefit from the protections afforded to prisoners of war under Geneva Convention III, Additional Protocol I and other treaties. We will therefore begin this chapter by looking in detail at the guarantees attached to prisoner of war status. Combatants injured on the battlefield benefit from the protections afforded to the sick and wounded. Some of these are shared with civilians; for example, combatants benefit from the protections afforded to medical personnel and objects examined in Chapter 4. Other guarantees, however, are specifically aimed at protecting sick and wounded belligerents. We will examine those protections at the end of this chapter. We will also briefly consider the principles of the law of war concerning respect for the dead.

PRISONER OF WAR STATUS

The main treaty governing the treatment of prisoners of war is Geneva Convention III. Prisoners of war received rudimentary protection under the 1864 Geneva Convention for the Amelioration of the Condition of the Wounded in Armies in the Field. They also received some protection under the Hague Regulations. Their position was then greatly improved following the adoption of the 1929 Geneva Convention Relative to the Treatment of Prisoners of War, which was the first treaty focusing solely on this issue.

The 1929 Convention was superseded in 1949 by Geneva Convention III, which continues to be the main treaty governing this area, although it is supplemented in some respects by Additional Protocol I. We will see shortly that the protections afforded to prisoners of war under Geneva Convention III are extremely detailed (although they are rarely, if ever, perfectly fulfilled). Geneva Convention III and Additional Protocol I only operate in international armed conflicts. However, prisoners of war also enjoy protections in non-international conflicts, as we will see in more detail below.

Who is a Prisoner of War?

Article 4 of Geneva Convention III provides an extensive definition of prisoner of war status. A prisoner of war is defined as a person belonging to any of a number of enumerated categories, who has 'fallen into the power of the enemy'. The first category listed in the provision covers members of the regular armed forces of a party to the conflict. The second category includes members of other armed groups who:

- are under responsible command;
- bear a fixed, distinctive sign recognisable at a distance;
- carry arms openly; and
- respect the requirements of international humanitarian law.

These first two categories, then, correspond to the categories of legally recognised combatants discussed previously in Chapter 3. Anyone who is recognised under Geneva Convention III as a combatant is therefore entitled to prisoner of war status if captured by the enemy. Article 4 then goes on to list several additional categories of prisoners of war who may not be covered by the definition of a combatant. These include:

- persons who typically accompany armed forces, but are not members of the forces themselves, such as civilian members of aircraft crews, war correspondents, supply contractors and so on;

- members of crews of merchant marine and civil aircraft of a party to the conflict;
- inhabitants of a particular region who spontaneously take up arms;
- former members of armed forces who are caught in an attempt to rejoin the forces of which they used to be members.

Article 5 of Geneva Convention III governs the duration of prisoner of war status. The provision states that the protections of Geneva Convention III apply to prisoners of war from the time they fall into the power of the enemy until their final release and repatriation. It also provides that if there is any doubt as to whether a person qualifies as a prisoner of war, she or he should be afforded all the protections of Geneva Convention III until her or his status can be determined by a competent tribunal.

The definition of prisoner of war status in Geneva Convention III has now been supplemented by Additional Protocol I. According to Article 44 of Additional Protocol I, '[a]ny combatant, as defined in Article 43, who falls into the power of an adverse Party shall be a prisoner of war'. We previously encountered the Article 43 definition of a combatant in Chapter 3. The definition covers all armed forces or groups under the command of a party to the conflict who are subject to an internal disciplinary system and distinguish themselves from the civilian population or, in situations where this is not possible, carry arms openly whenever engaging in or preparing to engage in an attack.

The effect of Additional Protocol I is to slightly widen the definition of prisoner of war status set out in Geneva Convention III (at least among those states that are parties to the Additional Protocol). The main difference between the regimes is that whereas Geneva Convention III requires combatants to distinguish themselves from civilians through a uniform or other distinctive sign, Additional Protocol I recognises that this is sometimes too demanding. Members of resistance groups and volunteer militia should be recognised as combatants and afforded prisoner of war protections even if they do not wear uniforms, provided that they carry arms openly during attacks.

Spies and Mercenaries

Anyone falling within the categories of combatants and associated persons listed in Geneva Convention III and Additional Protocol I who falls into the hands of the enemy is entitled to prisoner of war status. The next question that arises concerns who is *not* entitled to prisoner of war status. Detained civilians are, of course, not prisoners of war, but we saw in Chapter 4 that they will often be entitled to broadly similar guarantees as protected persons under Geneva Convention IV. There are also some detainees who will not qualify as prisoners of war despite playing an active role in the armed conflict. The three main categories are spies, mercenaries and unprivileged belligerents.

Spies and mercenaries have traditionally been excluded from prisoner of war status under the law of armed conflict. Parties may grant members of these classes prisoner of war status if they wish, but they are not obliged to do so. The position of spies is covered in Article 46 of Additional Protocol I. Spies are defined in that provision as military personnel engaged in espionage (information gathering, sabotage and the like) who are acting clandestinely and are not in uniform. The covert nature of spying operations is central to this definition. A member of the armed forces who gathers information in uniform or who does so without deception or false pretences will not be considered a spy.[1]

Article 46(1) stipulates that any person falling within the above definition is not entitled to prisoner of war status when captured and 'may be treated as a spy'. The provision does not specify what being 'treated as a spy' means. Traditionally, spies have risked summary execution, but this is now clearly prohibited.[2] The answer therefore seems to be that spies, unlike combatants, are not immune from punishment for their hostile acts under the laws of the detaining power. Article 5 of Geneva Convention IV stipulates that captured spies should be treated humanely and are entitled to a fair trial before being subjected to any form of punishment.[3] They should be treated as 'protected persons' under the Convention insofar as this is consistent with the security of the detaining power. However, they are regarded as having forfeited their rights of communication.

Mercenaries are defined under Article 47 of Additional Protocol I as persons who are not nationals of a party to the conflict or members of the regular armed forces of a state and are specifically recruited to fight in the conflict for a substantial material reward. The provision states that mercenaries 'shall not have the right to be a combatant or a prisoner of war'.[4] This means that mercenaries, like spies, are liable to punishment in accordance with the laws of the detaining power.[5] They are, however,

---

[1] Additional Protocol I, art 46(2), (3).
[2] Geneva Convention IV, art 5; Additional Protocol I, art 75(4).
[3] See also Additional Protocol I, art 75(4).
[4] Additional Protocol I, art 47(1).
[5] Yves Sandoz, Christophe Swinarski and Bruno Zimmermann (eds), *Commentary on the Additional Protocols* (Martinus Nijhoff 1987) 575.

entitled to be treated humanely and afforded a fair trial before any punishment is imposed.[6]

It is debatable whether spies and mercenaries should continue to be excluded from prisoner of war status. The exclusion of spies from prisoner of war protection seems intended to strike a balance between protecting spies from summary punishment and allowing parties to defend themselves robustly against the threat posed by covert operations.[7] However, it is arguable that the current position yields more ground than necessary to the concern of warring parties to protect classified information. In the case of mercenaries, the rationale seems to be that, historically, such fighters have obtained a reputation for poor discipline and disregard for the laws of war. However, it is hard to see why mercenaries should not be entitled to be regarded as prisoners of war, provided that they are adequately trained and respect international humanitarian law.

Two further points fall to be made about spies and mercenaries. First, Additional Protocol I makes it clear that if there is any doubt as to whether a detainee is a spy or a mercenary, she or he should be assumed to be entitled to prisoner of war status until the matter is assessed by a competent tribunal.[8] Second, it is worth emphasising that spies and mercenaries are far from unprotected by international humanitarian law, despite not being entitled to prisoner of war status. They are entitled to the protections of Geneva Convention IV except as required by the security of the detaining power.[9] Furthermore, they are entitled at all times to the fundamental guarantees listed in Article 75 of Additional Protocol I, including humane treatment and procedural justice.

Unprivileged Belligerents

There is a third class of active participants in armed conflict, apart from spies and mercenaries, who are not entitled to prisoner of war status. These are persons who are actively engaged in fighting, but for one reason or another do not satisfy the definition of a combatant under Geneva Convention III or Additional Protocol I. This may be because the armed group within which they operate is not sufficiently well organised to count as being under responsible command or having an internal disciplinary system. Alternatively, it may be because they do not distinguish

---

[6] Geneva Convention IV, art 5; Additional Protocol I, art 75(4).
[7] Yves Sandoz, Christophe Swinarski and Bruno Zimmermann (eds), *Commentary on the Additional Protocols* (Martinus Nijhoff 1987) 563.
[8] Additional Protocol I, art 45(1).
[9] Geneva Convention IV, art 5.

themselves from the civilian population. We saw in Chapter 3 that persons within this category are often referred to as 'unprivileged belligerents'.

One of the prerequisites for combatant status under Geneva Convention III is respect for the rules of international humanitarian law.[10] However, Article 44(2) of Additional Protocol I clarifies that violating the law of armed conflict does not deprive a combatant of her or his right to be considered a prisoner of war. The exception to this rule is a combatant who does not carry arms openly when launching an attack. Additional Protocol I provides that a person falling into this category is not a prisoner of war, but is nonetheless entitled to protections 'equivalent in all respects' to those afforded to prisoners of war.[11] It is unclear whether such a person is liable to punishment under the law of the detaining power in the same way as spies and mercenaries.[12] The wording of the provision suggests she or he is not, since such treatment would not be 'equivalent in all respects' to prisoner of war status.

We saw in Chapter 3 that unprivileged belligerents, although they are not prisoners of war, still enjoy robust protections. The guarantees available to them are similar to those enjoyed by spies and mercenaries. They will typically be entitled to the protections of Geneva Convention IV, unless this is inconsistent with the security of the detaining power[13] or they are detained by their own state or its allies.[14] They are further protected by the fundamental guarantees in Article 75 of Additional Protocol I. Unprivileged belligerents, like spies and mercenaries, are vulnerable to prosecution for their hostile acts under the law of the detaining power, but they enjoy robust procedural safeguards.[15] The provisions mentioned above ensure that nobody detained as a result of armed conflict, even a spy, mercenary or unprivileged belligerent, is entirely outside the reach of international humanitarian law. Everyone enjoys at least a basic level of protection.

TREATMENT OF PRISONERS OF WAR

Geneva Convention III sets out a number of basic principles governing the treatment of prisoners of war. According to Article 13 of Geneva

---

[10] Geneva Convention III, art 4A(2)(d).
[11] Additional Protocol I, art 44(4).
[12] Yves Sandoz, Christophe Swinarski and Bruno Zimmermann (eds), *Commentary on the Additional Protocols* (Martinus Nijhoff 1987) 539–40.
[13] Geneva Convention IV, art 5, 42.
[14] Geneva Convention IV, art 4.
[15] Geneva Convention IV, arts 71–76, 126; Additional Protocol I, art 75(4).

Convention III, '[p]risoners of war must at all times be humanely treated'. Article 14 provides that '[p]risoners of war are entitled in all circumstances to respect for their persons and their honour'. Article 16 contains a guarantee of equal treatment, stating that '[a]ll prisoners of war shall be treated alike [. . .] without any adverse distinction based on race, nationality, religious belief or political opinions'. Reprisals against prisoners of war are absolutely prohibited.[16] No mental or physical torture, or any form of coercion or disadvantageous treatment, may be inflicted on prisoners of war to secure any type of information whatsoever.[17]

The underlying rationale for the protections in Geneva Convention III is that keeping enemy combatants prisoner is not a form of punishment or reprisal, but merely a temporary security measure. It is a basic principle of international humanitarian law that combatants are not to be punished for taking part in the conflict. We saw in Chapter 3 that this is the primary meaning of the statement in Article 43(2) of Additional Protocol I that combatants 'have the right to participate directly in hostilities'. Combatants, unlike spies, mercenaries and unprivileged belligerents, are not liable to prosecution under the law of the detaining power merely for engaging in hostile conduct.

It follows from this fundamental principle that prisoners of war should not be housed under punitive conditions, but should always be treated humanely. They should, as far as possible, be detained in a way that protects their health, security and general welfare. They are also entitled, as we will see, to communicate with the outside world and maintain the basic components of meaningful community life. Captured combatants no longer pose an active threat to the lives or objectives of detaining forces. As such, they cease to be legitimate military targets and should be treated with respect.

Capture of Prisoners of War

Prisoners of war enjoy significant protections from the moment they are captured. According to Article 17 of Geneva Convention III, a captured combatant is required to divulge only her or his full name, rank, date of birth and any serial number. Article 17 further provides that the detaining party must issue prisoners of war with an identity card bearing this information. The card must be shown to detaining authorities upon demand, but may not be confiscated. The principle that captured soldiers need

---

[16] Geneva Convention III, art 13.
[17] Geneva Convention III, art 17.

only reveal their 'name, rank and serial number' has become well known through popular culture. Military forces may impose a duty on their members to avoid providing further information.[18]

Article 17 stipulates that prisoners of war who cannot identify themselves due to physical or mental incapacity should be handed to the medical service. A prisoner who refuses to provide identifying information may not be coerced or threatened. According to Article 18, captured combatants are entitled to retain their personal effects, including protective articles (such as gas masks), clothing and food, even if military issue. However, arms, horses, military equipment and military documents may be confiscated. If money is taken from a prisoner, it must be recorded on a register and a receipt issued. The money must then be held in the prisoner's name until she or he is repatriated.

Article 19 of Geneva Convention III provides that prisoners of war must be evacuated as soon as possible to an area far enough from the combat zone to keep them out of danger. Until this is done, they must not be needlessly exposed to military activities. The communication rights of captured combatants are dealt with under Article 70. Immediately after capture, prisoners of war must be allowed to write to their families and the Central Prisoners of War Agency advising their capture, address and state of health. Delivery of these communications must not be unreasonably delayed.

The Central Prisoners of War Agency is an administrative body provided for under Article 123 of Geneva Convention III. It is to be established in a neutral country in collaboration with the International Committee of the Red Cross (ICRC). The Agency's role is to collect information concerning prisoners of war and transmit this information to prisoners' families. Each party to the conflict is also obliged to establish an Information Bureau to keep records of prisoners of war and communicate their status to their home state. The Information Bureau is also responsible for collecting the personal valuables of deceased, escaped or released prisoners of war and returning these to their families.[19]

Prisoner of War Camps

Article 21 of Geneva Convention III states that prisoners of war may be confined in a camp. However, the internees may not be held in close confinement except where necessary to safeguard their health. Prisoners

---

[18] See, for example, United States Military Code of Conduct, art 5.
[19] Geneva Convention III, art 122.

of war may only be detained on land, in premises allowing hygiene and good health.[20] They must not be stationed near a combat zone and must not be used to shield military objectives from attack.[21] Living quarters for prisoners of war should be adequately heated and lit, with bedding and blankets. Male and female prisoners of war should be housed in separate quarters.[22]

Article 26 of Geneva Convention III stipulates that food and water for prisoners of war shall be of sufficient quantity, quality and variety to keep the internees in good health and avoid excessive loss of weight. Prisoners undertaking strenuous labour should be provided with extra rations where needed. Detainees are entitled to be involved with the preparation of their meals and the use of tobacco shall be permitted. It is prohibited to withdraw food from detainees as a means of collective punishment. According to Article 27, prisoners of war must be provided with clothing, underwear and footwear suitable for the climate. Detainees undertaking work should be clothed appropriately.

Article 28 provides that prisoner of war camps should include a canteen where detainees can buy food, tobacco, soap and other everyday items at or below the market price. Any profits shall be used to benefit the prisoners. The exercise needs of prisoners of war are considered in Article 36. Detainees should be able to exercise outdoors and open spaces are to be provided for this purpose. Prisoners should be allowed premises and equipment to engage in sports, games and other recreational pursuits.

The detaining power must take all necessary measures to ensure the cleanliness and health of prisoners of war. There should be adequate washing and sanitation facilities. Sufficient baths, showers, water, soap and laundry facilities must be available, including separate facilities for women.[23] Every prisoner of war camp must have an infirmary, with suitable facilities for contagious and mental diseases and for the physically impaired.[24] Prisoners of war should have medical examinations at least once a month.[25] Decisions to transfer prisoners between camps should take into account their interests. Sick and wounded detainees should not be transferred if it would endanger their health.[26]

---

[20] Geneva Convention III, art 22.
[21] Geneva Convention III, art 23.
[22] Geneva Convention III, art 23.
[23] Geneva Convention III, art 29.
[24] Geneva Convention III, art 30.
[25] Geneva Convention III, art 31.
[26] Geneva Convention III, arts 46–47.

Medical and Religious Personnel

Medical personnel and chaplains associated with the armed forces are dealt with under Article 33 of Geneva Convention III. Persons falling within these categories are not considered prisoners of war, since they are not combatants. However, they may nonetheless be detained to provide assistance to prisoners of war during their captivity. Medical personnel and chaplains detained under this provision are then entitled to protections equivalent in all respects to those given to prisoners of war. They are also entitled to be provided with the necessary facilities for fulfilling their medical and spiritual duties.

Article 34 of Geneva Convention III stipulates that prisoners of war shall enjoy complete latitude in their religious activities. There should be adequate facilities for religious observance. Chaplains who are detained to minister to detainees should be allowed to follow their religious conscience and maintain contact with ecclesiastical authorities.[27] Captured combatants who are ministers should be afforded similar conditions and exempted from other work.[28] Detainees who have medical qualifications may be required to tend to other prisoners, but shall likewise be exempted from other employment.[29]

Disciplinary Procedures

Article 39 of Geneva Convention III provides that each prisoner of war camp shall be put under the command of an officer of the detaining power. The commander is responsible for ensuring compliance with the rules of Geneva Convention III. Prisoners of war should salute the commanding officer, as well as other officers of the detaining power who are of a higher rank than themselves. The text of Geneva Convention III should be made available to prisoners in a language they can understand.[30] Commands, notices and questioning of prisoners should also be in a comprehensible language.[31]

Prisoners of war should be subject to the same rules of conduct as the armed forces of the detaining power. Any rule imposed on prisoners of war that does not also apply to detaining forces shall be enforced with

---

[27] Geneva Convention III, art 35.
[28] Geneva Convention III, art 36.
[29] Geneva Convention III, art 32.
[30] Geneva Convention III, art 41.
[31] Geneva Convention III, arts 17, 41.

disciplinary measures only.[32] A trial of a prisoner of war for a judicial offence (that is, an offence too serious to be met simply with disciplinary action) shall be carried out by a military court, except in certain exceptional circumstances. In all cases, the court must be impartial and independent.[33] Penalties must be the same as for the forces of the detaining power. Collective punishments, corporal punishment, imprisonment without daylight and other forms of cruelty are forbidden.[34]

Articles 89 and 90 of Geneva Convention III set out the allowable disciplinary punishments for prisoners of war. They include fines, suspension of privileges (other than the rights guaranteed by the Geneva Conventions), fatigue duties not exceeding two hours daily and solitary or other forms of confinement. Punishments may never be inhuman, brutal or dangerous. No disciplinary punishment, including confinement, may last longer than 30 days. Any offence that involves punishment exceeding this limit is deemed to be a judicial offence and must be tried accordingly. Article 42 makes it clear that the use of weapons against prisoners of war is an extreme measure. It must be preceded by appropriate warnings, especially when prisoners are attempting to escape.

Escape Attempts

Traditionally, it has been recognised that prisoners of war may feel a duty to attempt to escape. This duty is explicitly contained in the codes of conduct of some military forces.[35] Escape attempts by prisoners of war tend to be valorised in public discourse and popular culture, as in the 1963 American film, *The Great Escape*, featuring Steve McQueen. The rules of Geneva Convention III relating to escape attempts strike a balance between the duty prisoners may feel to escape and the legitimate interest of detaining powers in keeping prisoners confined and maintaining orderly conditions in detention.

According to Article 91 of Geneva Convention III, a prisoner of war who successfully escapes and is later recaptured shall not be punished. An escape is deemed successful when the prisoner rejoins the armed forces of her or his own state or its allies or, alternatively, leaves the territory controlled by enemy forces. Article 92 provides that a prisoner who unsuc-

---

[32] Geneva Convention III, art 82.
[33] Geneva Convention III, art 84; Additional Protocol I, art 75(4).
[34] Geneva Convention III, art 87; Additional Protocol I, art 75(2).
[35] See, for example, United States Military Code of Conduct, art 3.

cessfully attempts to escape may be liable to disciplinary punishment, but no more serious measures may be taken, even for repeat offences.

Article 93 stipulates that attempts to escape shall not be an aggravating circumstance if a prisoner of war is subject to judicial proceedings for a more serious offence committed during the escape. Furthermore, offences committed in the course of an escape attempt that do not involve physical violence shall be punished by disciplinary measures only. It is possible, however, that a prisoner of war who commits a violent offence during an escape attempt could be subject to judicial punishment following a trial. This would potentially cover offences such as murder or assault against civilians.

Article 93 does not make it clear whether a prisoner of war may be judicially punished for killing or injuring an enemy combatant during an escape attempt. The better view seems to be that attacks made on enemy combatants in the course of escape attempts are not liable to judicial prosecution, although they may be met with disciplinary measures.[36] This follows from the basic principle that combatants are entitled to take an active part in armed hostilities and may not be punished for doing so.[37] At the same time, however, a prisoner of war who attempts to kill or injure her or his captors during an escape attempt will become a legitimate military target while engaging in the attack.[38]

Labour of Prisoners of War

According to Article 49 of Geneva Convention III, the detaining power may utilise the labour of prisoners of war who are physically fit. Officers shall not be required to work, but they may request work if they wish. Non-commissioned officers may only be required to do supervisory work, unless they request otherwise. Article 50 then sets out the types of work other prisoners may legally be required to do, including:

- camp administration or maintenance;
- agricultural work;
- mineral and manufacturing work;
- public works with no military character or purpose;
- transport and stores work with no military character or purpose;

---

[36] Disciplinary measures against prisoners of war are subject to the limitations set out in Geneva Convention III, arts 89–90, as discussed above.
[37] Additional Protocol I, art 43(2).
[38] Additional Protocol I, art 41(2). See also art 51(3).

- commercial business;
- arts and crafts;
- domestic service; and
- public utility services with no military character or purpose.

The wording of Article 50 gives effect to the general principle that prisoners of war may not be required to undertake work with a military character. This is a corollary of the basic requirement to respect prisoners' honour.[39]

Prisoners of war must be granted suitable working conditions, especially regarding accommodation, food, clothing and equipment.[40] The conditions should be equivalent to those of local workers. Prisoners undertaking labour should be given additional food rations if required.[41] No prisoner of war may be forced to do labour which is unhealthy, dangerous (such as removing landmines) or humiliating.[42] Working hours must not be excessive by local standards; appropriate breaks and holidays must be provided.[43] Prisoners of war engaged in labour shall be paid a fair working wage.[44]

Communication

Prisoners of war enjoy robust communication rights under Geneva Convention III. Combatants are entitled to write to their families upon capture to provide details of their address and state of health.[45] According to Article 71, prisoners of war must be allowed to send and receive letters and cards, which should be conveyed without delay. Article 72 extends this protection to cover parcels containing food, clothing, medical supplies, and recreational, educational and religious items.[46] Correspondence to and from prisoners of war may be censored by the authorities, but this must be done as swiftly as possible.[47]

Communication among detainees and between prisoners and camp authorities is also protected. Article 78 grants prisoners of war the right

---

[39] Geneva Convention III, art 14. See also art 52.
[40] Geneva Convention III, art 51.
[41] Geneva Convention III, art 26.
[42] Geneva Convention III, art 52.
[43] Geneva Convention III, art 53.
[44] Geneva Convention III, arts 54, 62.
[45] Geneva Convention III, art 70.
[46] Geneva Convention III, art 72.
[47] Geneva Convention III, art 76.

to make requests and complaints to the detaining authorities. Article 79 provides that prisoners' representatives shall be appointed within each camp to represent the detainees' interests to camp authorities, the detaining power and the ICRC. The prisoners' representative in camps for officers shall be the senior officer; in other camps, representatives are to be elected every six months by secret ballot. In camps containing prisoners of different nationalities, multiple representatives shall be appointed. The role of the representatives is to 'further the physical, spiritual and intellectual well-being' of the prisoners.[48] They should be provided the assistance and facilities necessary for their role and exempted from other work if required.[49]

Release of Prisoners of War

Articles 109 and 110 of Geneva Convention III state that prisoners of war who are seriously sick or wounded should be repatriated to their home country. Prisoners are defined as being seriously sick or wounded if their physical or mental fitness is gravely diminished and they are not likely to recover within a year.[50] Prisoners of war repatriated for poor health may not later be redeployed on active military duties.[51] All other prisoners of war are to be repatriated without delay after the cessation of hostilities.[52]

A prisoner of war who is entitled to be repatriated may not be kept back by the detaining power merely because she or he has not fulfilled a disciplinary punishment.[53] However, prisoners facing serious criminal charges may be kept back to face trial.[54] Upon repatriation, all personal articles of value taken from prisoners of war must be returned.[55] The remaining balance of accounts kept in the names of prisoners, containing wages and money taken from them upon capture, must be communicated to their home nation with a view to settling the account following repatriation.[56]

---

[48] Geneva Convention III, art 80.
[49] Geneva Convention III, art 81.
[50] Geneva Convention III, art 110.
[51] Geneva Convention III, art 117.
[52] Geneva Convention III, art 118.
[53] Geneva Convention III, art 115.
[54] Geneva Convention III, art 119.
[55] Geneva Convention III, art 119.
[56] Geneva Convention III, art 66. See also art 64.

Death of Prisoners of War

Special procedures apply with respect to the death of prisoners of war. These are set out in Article 120 of Geneva Convention III. Wills of prisoners of war should be drawn up so as to be valid in their home countries. After death, the will must be sent back to the home country without delay. A death certificate shall be issued for every death of a prisoner of war, noting the date, place and cause of death, along with the date and place of burial and the information necessary to identify the prisoner's grave. Burial or cremation shall be preceded by a medical examination to determine the cause of death.

Prisoners of war are entitled to an honourable burial, in accordance with their religious beliefs and traditions. Graves should be marked and maintained. Prisoners should have individual graves unless unavoidable circumstances dictate otherwise. Bodies may be cremated only for imperative reasons of hygiene or on account of the deceased's religion or express wishes. Every death or serious injury of a prisoner suspected to be caused by another person, including detaining officials and other internees, shall be the subject of an immediate enquiry, with a report to be sent to her or his home state.[57]

PRISONERS OF WAR IN NON-INTERNATIONAL CONFLICTS

Geneva Convention III, like the other Geneva Conventions of 1949, only applies in international armed conflicts.[58] For this reason, it is commonly stated that prisoner of war status does not exist in non-international conflicts.[59] This is technically true, if prisoner of war status is understood strictly in terms of the protections afforded by Geneva Convention III. However, it reflects a narrow understanding of what prisoner of war status means. Prisoners of war are belligerents placed *hors de combat* by reason of capture. These persons enjoy special protections in armed conflicts of all kinds.

---

[57] Geneva Convention III, art 121.
[58] Geneva Convention III, art 2.
[59] See, for example, Gary Solis, *The Law of Armed Conflict* (CUP 2010) 99, 191; John Cerone, 'Status of Detainees in Non-International Armed Conflict' (2006) 10 *American Society of International Law Insights* 17. Compare Jean-Marie Henckaerts and Louise Doswald-Beck, *Customary International Humanitarian Law* (CUP 2005) 395.

Prisoners of war in the broader sense outlined above are protected under Common Article 3 of the Geneva Conventions. Common Article 3 makes explicit mention of persons 'placed *hors de combat* by [. . .] detention, or any other cause'. It guarantees such persons humane treatment and freedom from violence, outrages against personal dignity and punishment without due process. Captured fighters in non-international conflicts are also protected by the fundamental guarantees in Articles 4 and 5 of Additional Protocol II. The protections in Article 4 apply to 'all persons who [. . .] have ceased to take part in hostilities, whether or not their liberty has been restricted'. Article 5 then provides further protections for 'persons deprived of their liberty for reasons related to the armed conflict'.

According to Article 5, persons detained in non-international armed conflicts are entitled to food and drinking water, healthy conditions and protection from the elements.[60] They are entitled to religious freedom and assistance from chaplains.[61] If made to work, their working conditions should be comparable to the local population.[62] There should be separate quarters for men and women.[63] Detainees should be permitted to send and receive letters and cards.[64] They should not be interned close to the combat zone and should be allowed to benefit from regular medical examinations.[65] Their physical and mental health and integrity should not be endangered by act or omission.[66]

Detainees in non-international conflicts are further protected by the guarantees of due process set out in Article 6 of Additional Protocol II. Many of the provisions of Articles 5 and 6 reproduce guarantees afforded to prisoners of war under Geneva Convention III. The regime of protection for captured fighters under Additional Protocol II is obviously far less detailed than that contained in Geneva Convention III. However, it is detailed enough to support the claim that a form of prisoner of war status also exists in non-international conflicts. Captured fighters are protected in conflicts of both kinds.

There is, however, one important difference between prisoner of war status under Geneva Convention III and the position of captured fighters under Common Article 3 and Additional Protocol II. Combatants in international armed conflicts have the right to take part in warfare and

---

[60] Additional Protocol II, art 5(1)(b).
[61] Additional Protocol II, art 5(1)(d).
[62] Additional Protocol II, art 5(1)(e).
[63] Additional Protocol II, art 5(2)(a).
[64] Additional Protocol II, art 5(2)(b).
[65] Additional Protocol II, art 5(2)(c), (d).
[66] Additional Protocol II, art 5(2)(e).

may not be punished for doing so.[67] Belligerents in non-international conflicts, on the other hand, are liable to prosecution under domestic law for their hostile actions. However, any such prosecution is required to abide by the due process guarantees expressed in Common Article 3 and Additional Protocol II.[68]

SICK AND WOUNDED COMBATANTS

The protection of sick and wounded combatants was one of the original objectives of the Geneva law. The suffering of injured combatants left behind on the battlefield was one of the features of the Battle of Solferino that inspired Henri Dunant to found the ICRC.[69] The duty to care for injured combatants then formed one of the main emphases of the original 1864 Geneva Convention. Sick and wounded combatants on land are currently protected by Geneva Convention I, which is supplemented by Additional Protocol I. Sick, wounded and shipwrecked combatants at sea are likewise covered by Geneva Convention II. Its provisions largely mirror those set out in Geneva Convention I.[70]

Article 13 of Geneva Convention I states that the Convention applies to sick and wounded persons who fall into a number of listed categories. The categories listed in that provision parallel those used to define prisoner of war status under Article 4 of Geneva Convention III.[71] Article 14 of Geneva Convention I reiterates that sick and wounded combatants who fall into the hands of enemy forces are entitled to the protections afforded to prisoners of war under Geneva Convention III.

Article 10 of Additional Protocol I provides a clear statement of the underlying principles of this area of international humanitarian law. The provision states that combatants who are injured or sick must be respected and protected in all circumstances and must receive the fullest possible medical attention. Article 12 of Geneva Convention I likewise provides that wounded and sick military and associated personnel must be treated humanely and with care. They shall not wilfully be left without medical

---

[67] Additional Protocol I, art 43(2).
[68] Geneva Conventions, art 3(1)(d); Additional Protocol II, art 6.
[69] Henri Dunant, *A Memory of Solferino* (ICRC 1986).
[70] For the relevant principles of customary international humanitarian law, see Jean-Marie Henckaerts and Louise Doswald-Beck, *Customary International Humanitarian Law* (CUP 2005) rules 109–111.
[71] See also Geneva Convention II, art 13.

assistance and it is prohibited to commit violence against their lives and persons.

Article 15 of Geneva Convention I stipulates that parties shall take all possible measures to search for and collect wounded and sick combatants at all times and particularly after a battle. Article 11 provides that sick and wounded combatants must be treated in accordance with accepted medical standards. Medical records must be kept and an injured combatant has the right to refuse any surgical operation.

We saw in Chapter 3 that any attempt to feign protected status in order to obtain the confidence of the enemy amounts to perfidy and is therefore prohibited. Article 37(1) of Additional Protocol I lists a number of specific examples of perfidious conduct, including feigning incapacitation by wounds or sickness. It is therefore prohibited for combatants to use their actual or purported injuries as a cover for committing hostile acts. Article 8 of Geneva Convention I makes it clear that the special protections for sick and wounded combatants cease to apply if they commit any hostile action. Sick and wounded fighters who continue to target the enemy may themselves be attacked in turn.

Medical Units

We saw in Chapter 4 that all medical personnel, whether military or civilian, enjoy special protection under the Geneva law. Article 12 of Additional Protocol I provides that medical units are not to be the object of attack. These protections extend to both military and civilian medical units.[72] Similar protections apply to medical vehicles.[73] Articles 19 and 24 of Geneva Convention I likewise state that medical units shall not be attacked, but must be respected and protected in all circumstances.[74] This principle is recognised as holding customary law status in both international and non-international conflicts.[75]

Medical personnel are defined in Article 8 of Additional Protocol I as those whose function is exclusively to search for, collect, transport, diagnose or treat the wounded, sick and shipwrecked, or to administer medical units or medical transports.[76] Medical units, like sick and wounded combatants, cease to be protected if they commit, outside their humanitarian function,

---

[72] Additional Protocol I, arts 12(2), 15.
[73] Additional Protocol I, art 21.
[74] See also Geneva Convention II, arts 22, 36.
[75] Jean-Marie Henckaerts and Louise Doswald-Beck, *Customary International Humanitarian Law* (CUP 2005) rules 25–30.
[76] See also Geneva Convention I, art 24.

acts hostile to the enemy. However, a warning must be given and ignored before protection is lifted.[77] Any use of the protected status of medical units as cover for hostile acts is a clear violation of the prohibition on perfidy.[78]

Medical personnel can carry 'light individual weapons' for their own protection without losing their protected status. They may also be guarded by sentries or an escort.[79] The term 'light individual weapons' in this context is open to interpretation, but would seem to cover standard issue service rifles, such as the M16 assault rifle used by the United States military, as well as lighter sidearms. Medical personnel enjoy immunity against any kind of punishment for administering treatments compatible with medical ethics.[80] We saw above that combatants cannot be punished merely for taking part in hostilities; likewise, medical personnel cannot be punished for carrying out their duties.

RESPECT FOR THE DEAD

It is an important principle of international humanitarian law that combatants and other persons killed as a result of armed conflict should be treated with respect. Article 15 of Geneva Convention I provides that the dead should not be left on the battlefield, but searched for and collected. Their bodies should not be abused. Article 17 further states that bodies should be examined to confirm death and, if possible, establish identity. The results of this investigation should be recorded in a report.[81]

The dead should be honourably interred in individual graves with any appropriate religious rites wherever possible.[82] Cremation should only be carried out if imperative for hygiene purposes. The graves of deceased combatants should be grouped according to nationality if possible and 'properly marked and maintained so that they may always be found'.[83] Article 8 of Additional Protocol II recognises a duty to search for and respect the dead in non-international conflicts. The basic principles in this area constitute customary law in armed conflicts of all kinds.[84]

---

[77] Additional Protocol I, art 13; Geneva Convention I, art 21.
[78] Additional Protocol I, art 37(1). See the discussion of perfidy in Chapter 3.
[79] Additional Protocol I, art 13(2); Geneva Convention I, art 22.
[80] Additional Protocol I, art 16(1).
[81] See also Geneva Convention II, arts 18–19.
[82] Compare Geneva Convention II, art 20.
[83] Geneva Convention I, art 17. See also Additional Protocol I, art 34.
[84] Jean-Marie Henckaerts and Louise Doswald-Beck, *Customary International Humanitarian Law* (CUP 2005) rules 112–16.

6. Humanitarianism and human rights

International humanitarian law and international human rights law have much in common. Both fields of law emphasise the basic values of humanity. Both also assume a cosmopolitan moral outlook of the type discussed in Chapter 1 in relation to limits on armed conflict. However, there are also some important distinctions between the two fields. First, international humanitarian law only operates in the context of an armed conflict, whereas international human rights law is more general in scope.

Second, international humanitarian law is much older than international human rights law. The former can be traced to Ancient Greek and Roman times and was first formalised during the Middle Ages.[1] The latter, by contrast, has largely arisen only since 1945. A third difference is that international human rights law tends to be significantly more aspirational than international humanitarian law. We saw in Chapter 1 that humanitarianism is primarily concerned with curbing the slide into absolute warfare. International humanitarian law therefore focuses on only the most basic components of human welfare, rather than aiming at a fuller conception of human flourishing.

This chapter begins by introducing the concept of a right, in order to clarify the basic structure of international human rights discourse. We will then turn to the more specific concept of a human right, examining the sense in which human rights claim universality and considering different possible categories of human rights standards. The chapter then briefly discusses the history, sources and institutional machinery of international human rights law, before returning to the relationship between humanitarianism and human rights. We will examine the various kinds of tensions that exist between these bodies of law and explore the prospects for systemic integration.

---

[1] See the discussion in Chapter 1.

THE CONCEPT OF A RIGHT

In order to understand the notion of a *right*, which is central to international human rights law, it is useful to begin with the concept of an *interest*. Let us say that a person has an interest in something if it makes her or his life better in some way or other. It will be apparent from this definition that people have all sorts of interests. You have an interest in this book being interesting and informative, getting a pay rise at work, having an attractive person sit next to you when you ride the bus and so on.

It would be nice if all our interests were always satisfied. However, we often have no legitimate expectation that this be the case. For example, if you are a lazy and unmotivated employee, you probably have no legitimate expectation of a pay rise. Likewise, nobody is entitled to have an attractive person sit next to them on the bus; that depends substantially on the luck of the draw. We might capture this idea by saying that people do not always have a *right* to everything that is in their interest.

A right, then, is a normatively protected interest. If you have a right to something, you have both an interest in that thing *and* a legitimate expectation that your interest be realised. For example, if you own this book, you have an interest in its not being stolen. You also have a legitimate expectation that your book not be stolen; that is, you have a *right* not to be treated in that way. Compare this with the case of the lazy and unmotivated employee: she or he still has an interest in getting a pay rise, but has no legitimate expectation of that occurring. That is, she or he has no right to the desired outcome.

Another way of expressing the idea that rights are normatively protected interests is to say that rights give rise to *duties* in others.[2] Your legitimate expectation that your book not be stolen means that others have a duty not to steal it. A duty, in this context, is a normative requirement. It gives someone a reason to do or not do an action. In the context of rights talk, we can describe duties as supplying other-regarding reasons for action. They are reasons we have because of what we owe to other people.

---

[2] The idea that rights strictly so called necessarily give rise to correlative duties was famously emphasised by the American legal theorist, Wesley Newcomb Hohfeld. For an overview, see Jonathan Crowe, *Legal Theory* (Thomson Reuters 2009) ch 8.

The Strength of Rights

People often talk about their rights as if they are absolute. That is, the statement 'I have a right to X' is often used as a way of settling a person's entitlement to X. An absolute right is an inviolable constraint that can never be overridden. It gives other people decisive reasons to act or not act in the required way. If all rights were absolute, then the fact that a person has a right to X would, indeed, settle the question of whether she or he is entitled to X. Other people would then be obliged to act in ways that respect this right.

Are all rights absolute? There is reason to doubt it. In fact, it is hard to think of many (or perhaps any) rights that are truly absolute. Take your right that other people not steal your book. This looks like a fairly robust right. However, what if your ruthless enemy credibly threatens to kill five innocent people unless we steal your book? It seems that, in such a case, it is permissible for us to steal your book. It might even be wrong for us not to do so. It therefore appears that your right is less than absolute.

Most rights seem to be less than absolute when examined in this way. That is, it is typically possible to imagine a case where even fairly robust rights should plausibly give way to competing claims. This suggests that the rights have a certain weight, but do not apply absolutely in all circumstances. We might say that your right that we not steal your book gives us a weighty, but not absolute reason not to do so. Normally, we should not steal your book, but that duty can sometimes be overridden.

If all rights were absolute, then all rights would be equally strong. However, if at least some rights are non-absolute, then this raises the possibility that some rights are more stringent than others. It seems clearly to be the case that some rights are more easily overridden than other rights. For example, your right that we not kill you is stronger than your right that we not pinch your arm. However, both these rights are arguably less than absolute, since they could be overridden by other claims in extreme cases.

Consider, for example, the following case:

Hostage: Tim, a ruthless criminal, is holding twenty innocent people hostage. He tells Lisa, an innocent bystander, that he intends to kill all twenty. However, if Lisa agrees to kill one hostage, Tim will let the others go free. There is no other way of saving the hostages. Lisa reluctantly accepts the proposal.[3]

---

[3] For discussion, see Jonathan Crowe, 'Does Control Make a Difference? The Moral Foundations of Shareholder Liability for Corporate Wrongs' (2012) 75 *Modern Law Review* 159, 168 et seq. See also Bernard Williams, 'A Critique of

The hostage in this example has a right to life. However, it may be permissible or even obligatory for Lisa to kill the hostage. If this is correct, then it shows that the hostage's right to life, although very stringent, is not absolute.

Prima Facie Rights

Does the fact that most or all everyday rights can sometimes be overridden refute the existence of absolute rights? Not necessarily. Some theorists seek to defend absolute rights by specifying the content of the rights more completely. This strategy is known as *specificationism*.[4] For example, we might say you have an absolute right that we not steal your book *except* in circumstances *A*, *B*, *C* and so forth. Alternatively, we could say you have an absolute right that we not steal your book *unjustly*. In either case, when the content of your right is fully specified, taking account of all possible circumstances, it turns out that what seemed like justified infringements are really part of the right itself.

One criticism of specificationism, though, is that it robs rights talk of its explanatory power. The point of rights talk is to help us discover what we ought to do. That is, people rely on statements such as 'I have a right to *X*' to establish how other people ought to treat them. However, specificationism means that rights claims tell us little unless we know all the details of the rights being cited. That is, we need to know what we ought to do in given circumstances in order to know what our rights are. This seems to suggest that rights claims cannot help us to work out how we should behave.

Is this a decisive objection to specificationism? Not necessarily. Specificationism can still give non-absolute rights an explanatory role by treating them as prima facie standards. A prima facie right *tends* to tell us what we ought to do, but upon closer examination it may turn out to be an inaccurate or incomplete account. For example, your claim that we not steal your book is not an absolute right, but it is still a prima facie right, because it tells us what to do in most cases. In other words, if we are aware of your prima facie right that we not steal your book, we will normally know how to behave where that question is concerned. This shows that rights talk can be helpful without claiming absolute force.

Utilitarianism' in JJC Smart and Bernard Williams, *Utilitarianism: For and Against* (CUP 1973) 98 et seq.

[4] For a defence of the specificationist understanding of rights, see Jonathan Crowe, 'Explaining Natural Rights: Ontological Freedom and the Foundations of Political Discourse' (2009) 4 *New York University Journal of Law and Liberty* 70.

Reasoning with Rights

We have seen that everyday talk about rights often turns out to be less than absolute. How, then, should we incorporate rights into our reasoning about how to act? We have already seen that rights claims typically give us a reason for action with a certain amount of weight. However, they can be overridden. A right, then, can be seen as creating a presumption in favour of a certain type of action. However, where it clashes with another right or leads to serious negative consequences, it might not prevail.

Reasoning with rights can be difficult, because sometimes it will not be clear exactly what weight to give to different factors. There will be easy cases and hard cases. For example, if your ruthless enemy credibly threatens to kill five innocent people unless we steal your book, then we should steal your book. However, what if, instead, your enemy credibly threatens to punch five people in the nose? Or pinch 30 people on the arm? Everyone can form intuitions and considered views about what ought to happen in such cases, but it is difficult to weigh the competing claims in a systematic way.

The examples posed above may seem outlandish. However, international courts and other bodies carry out far more complex weighing exercises on a regular basis. For example, international human rights law recognises a right to freedom of expression.[5] This right is clearly non-absolute, but how stringent is it? What if a person denies the Holocaust? Does the social damage caused by anti-Semitic ideas outweigh the right to freedom of expression?[6] What if a person publishes a memoir giving details of intelligence operations? Does the threat posed to national security outweigh the right?[7]

THE CONCEPT OF A HUMAN RIGHT

International human rights law posits universal rights enjoyed by all humans. In this respect, it has strong affinities to the natural rights tradition. A natural right is a right that certain creatures have simply by virtue of their natural characteristics. Discussions of natural rights have

---

[5] Universal Declaration of Human Rights, art 19; International Covenant on Civil and Political Rights, art 19; European Convention on Human Rights, art 10.

[6] Compare *Faurisson v France*, United Nations Human Rights Committee Decision, 8 November 1996 (answering 'yes').

[7] Compare *Observer and Guardian v United Kingdom*, European Court of Human Rights Judgment, 26 November 1991 (answering 'no').

historically focused mainly on human rights. Human rights, then, are rights all human beings have simply by virtue of being human. They are a species of natural rights, because being human is a natural characteristic of certain creatures.

The notion of human rights has significant intuitive appeal. However, what rights fall into this category and where do they come from? International documents like the Universal Declaration of Human Rights, the International Covenant on Civil and Political Rights and the International Covenant on Economic, Social and Cultural Rights represent an attempt to sketch out answers to the first of these questions.

The second question posed above has been a matter of great debate among philosophers. The most common approach has been to identify human capacities, such as the capacity to feel pain, to reason and communicate, or to form a plan of one's life, in virtue of which humans have natural rights.[8] However, this approach raises difficult questions about how to regard human beings who lack, or have permanently or temporarily lost, the relevant capacities. It also raises the precise connection between those capacities and the different kinds of rights humans are taken to have.

Increasing attention has been given over the last few decades to whether non-human animals have natural rights. The influential work of philosophers such as Peter Singer and Tom Regan has contributed to this trend.[9] If one of the capacities that gives humans natural rights is the capacity to feel pain, then there seems good reason to extend at least some rights to other animals. As Jeremy Bentham famously argued:

> The French have already discovered that the blackness of the skin is no reason why a human being should be abandoned without redress to the caprice of a tormentor. It may come one day to be recognized, that the number of legs [and other superficial differences between humans and non-humans] are reasons equally insufficient for abandoning a sensitive being to the same fate. What else is it that should trace the insuperable line? Is it the faculty of reason, or, perhaps, the faculty for discourse? [. . .] The question is not, Can they *reason*? nor, Can they *talk*? but, Can they *suffer*?[10]

---

[8] For further discussion, see Jonathan Crowe, 'Explaining Natural Rights: Ontological Freedom and the Foundations of Political Discourse' (2009) 4 *New York University Journal of Law and Liberty* 70.

[9] See, for example, Peter Singer, *Animal Liberation* (Random House 1975); Tom Regan, *The Case for Animal Rights* (University of California Press 1983). See also Jonathan Crowe, 'Levinasian Ethics and Animal Rights' (2008) 26 *Windsor Yearbook of Access to Justice* 313.

[10] Jeremy Bentham, *An Introduction to the Principles of Morals and Legislation* (Hafner Press 1948) 311 n [ch XVII, §1].

The Concept of Universality

Human rights are supposed to be universal: they extend to all humans at all times and in all places. However, questions are sometimes raised about the cultural specificity of the concept. This issue arises in both temporal and geographical senses. If human rights apply *at all times*, then any natural rights humans have now they had in the past. This means that if there is now a human right not to be enslaved, then communities in the past that thought slavery was permissible were gravely wrong. In such communities, it seems, human rights violations were rampant.[11] However, people sometimes hesitate to make such sweeping normative claims about the cultural practices of past societies.

Similarly, doubts have sometimes been raised about the claim that the same human rights apply to humans *in all places*. International human rights law aspires to apply throughout the globe. However, this area of law is sometimes accused of having a bias towards the perspectives and values of Western nations and the developed world. This criticism takes various forms. For example, it is sometimes said that international human rights law reflects an individualist perspective characteristic of Western societies, rather than the family- and community-oriented viewpoint more common in Eastern nations. It is also argued that international human rights law elevates formal rights over economic development, contrary to the interests of the developing world.[12]

There is no scope here for a full consideration of these criticisms. However, there are some structural features of the concept of human rights that are worth noting in this context. First, even if human rights are universal, this does not mean that their implementation must be identical in all places. Human rights set out a framework for how humans may be treated. They stipulate baselines of permissible behaviour, so that certain types of treatment (such as slavery) are ruled out. However, this framework falls far short of completely stipulating how societies should be run.

---

[11] We do not mean to imply that slavery does not still occur today. For a discussion of contemporary forms of slavery, see David K Androff, 'The Problem of Contemporary Slavery: An International Human Rights Challenge for Social Work' (2010) 54 *International Social Work* 209.

[12] For a helpful overview, see Yash Ghai, 'Human Rights and Asian Values' (1998) 9 *Public Law Review* 168. For a discussion of the relevance of this debate to international humanitarian law, see René Provost, 'The International Committee of the Red Widget? The Diversity Debate and International Humanitarian Law' (2007) 40 *Israel Law Review* 614.

It leaves open a rich and diverse range of social and legal structures that are compatible with the baseline rules.

The non-absolute nature of human rights is also relevant here. If human rights are less than absolute, they may potentially be overridden if social and economic circumstances demand. This prospect must be approached with caution if the universal aspirations of human rights are not to be negated. Nonetheless, international human rights law recognises that most rights are subject to exceptions or derogations in exceptional circumstances. It also recognises that competing rights may need to be weighed against one another, as in the cases mentioned above. This represents another way in which the framework of universal human rights is more flexible than it might at first appear.

Categories of Human Rights

Another important conceptual distinction relevant to human rights concerns negative and positive rights. Negative rights are rights that other people not do something. Your right that we not steal your book is of this type. Positive rights, on the other hand, are rights that other people take some form of positive action to assist you in achieving a particular goal. Your right to health care, for example, is generally taken to imply that other people have a duty to assist you in obtaining health care if necessary.

Generally speaking, negative rights tend to be both more common and less controversial than positive rights. Some philosophers have argued that all human rights are negative.[13] However, there are good reasons to think that we have at least some positive rights. A famous argument for this conclusion is made by Singer.[14] He poses the example of a small child drowning in a shallow pond. You are walking past the pond and have the ability, at little risk to yourself, to save the child's life. Are you obliged to do so? It seems highly plausible that the child in this case has a positive right to your assistance.[15]

Singer's pond case is one thing. A more complex question, however, is

---

[13] See, for example, James Otteson, *Actual Ethics* (CUP 2006) 22–4; Jan Narveson, *The Libertarian Idea* (Broadview Press 2001) ch 5.
[14] Peter Singer, 'Famine, Affluence and Morality' (1971) 1 *Philosophy and Public Affairs* 229; Peter Singer, *Practical Ethics* (CUP 1993) 229.
[15] Some commentators resist this conclusion. James Otteson, for example, argues that you are not *obliged* to save the child's life, even though it is a *praiseworthy* thing to do. See James Otteson, *Actual Ethics* (CUP 2006) 29, 148–9. For criticism of this view, see Jonathan Crowe, 'Review of *Actual Ethics* by James R Otteson' (2007) 23(2) *Policy* 55.

how far our positive obligations extend. Do we have a positive duty to help others access food, medical care, education, access to arts and culture and so on? The issue of the extent of positive rights intersects at this point with a debate among international human rights law commentators about what are often called *generations* of rights. First-generation rights include individual civil and political rights. These are mostly negative rights, but cover a few positive civil rights such as voting rights and the right to a fair trial.

Second-generation rights include social, economic and cultural rights. They cover a greater range of substantive positive rights, such as rights to employment, housing and health care. Finally, third-generation rights go beyond the previous categories, covering such topics as self-determination, economic and social development and protection of the environment and natural resources. Each of these successive generations of rights has proved increasingly controversial. This partly reflects the fact that each generation is more demanding in terms of the positive duties it places on other parties.

ORIGINS OF INTERNATIONAL HUMAN RIGHTS LAW

Traditionally, international law has focused on relations between states. International human rights law, by contrast, concerns the rights of individual persons. The primary focus of this field of law is on protecting individuals from rights violations by states, rather than other individuals, but the emphasis on individuals as the bearers of rights is nonetheless highly significant. Where, then, did this focus come from? A number of historical influences can be identified, some of which are discussed briefly below.

The Law of Aliens

The emphasis of international human rights law on individual entitlements can be traced to some extent to the international law of aliens. International law did not traditionally concern itself with relations between a state and its own citizens. However, states have long been obliged to accord certain protections to foreign officials (under diplomatic law) and foreign nationals more generally. Under the law of aliens, an injury to a citizen of a state by another state was viewed as an injury to the first state.[16] It follows that states can pursue claims against other states on behalf of their nationals.

---

[16] Ian Brownlie, *Principles of Public International Law* (OUP 2003) 497–8.

The law of aliens therefore fitted within the traditional model of international law, insofar as it relied on states to take action on behalf of their nationals. Individual aliens could not necessarily compel their state to act on their behalf. Nonetheless, some of the underlying ideas in this area of law hinted towards the aspirations that would be more explicitly enshrined in international human rights law.

A central question in the law of aliens concerned what standard of protection aliens should be afforded under international law. There have long been two schools of thought on this issue.[17] One view held that aliens should be entitled to the same rights as citizens of the host state. This effectively meant that if the host state oppressed its own citizens, it could do the same to aliens. The second view was that aliens are entitled to minimum standards of treatment anywhere in the world. In other words, there were uniform international guarantees protecting foreigners against state actions.

The second of these views was endorsed to some extent by the Permanent Court of International Justice (PCIJ) in the *Case Concerning German Interests in Polish Upper Silesia*,[18] which concerned the confiscation of German private estates by the Polish government. The PCIJ confirmed in that case that there are international minimum standards protecting the vested property rights of foreigners. The idea that individuals could rely on international law to protect their rights against foreign states, albeit only by convincing their own state to intercede on their behalf, can be seen as an important first step towards the uniform individual rights enshrined in international human rights law.

International Humanitarian Law

Another key influence on international human rights law was provided by the development of international humanitarian law. We have seen throughout this book that international humanitarian law sets out minimum standards for the treatment of various groups during wartime. These include a range of standards akin to individual rights. We have considered the detailed protections afforded to civilians and disabled combatants under international humanitarian law in previous chapters.

International humanitarian law, like the law of aliens, has traditionally been mainly concerned with protecting individuals against the actions of

---

[17] For a helpful overview, see ibid 501–3.
[18] *Case Concerning German Interests in Polish Upper Silesia (Merits)*, Permanent Court of International Justice (PCIJ) Judgment, 25 May 1926.

foreign nations. We have seen throughout this book that international humanitarian law has been primarily concerned with armed conflicts between two or more states, although the body of principles dealing with non-international conflicts continues to grow. International humanitarian law generally presumes that individuals affected by armed conflict are most at risk when they fall into the hands of a party of which they are not nationals. The 'protected persons' regime under Geneva Convention IV is designed to be of broad application, but it does not cover persons who find themselves in the hands of their own state or its allies.[19]

Some aspects of international humanitarian law, however, do more than protect individuals against foreign entities. The law of non-international armed conflict, for example, protects those affected by civil warfare against their own states. Common Article 3 of the Geneva Conventions recognised for the first time that there were limits on how states could treat their own citizens in internal conflicts. The text of that provision reads like a guarantee of individual rights. A similar point applies to the more extensive list of guarantees contained in Articles 4–6 of Additional Protocol II.

The Second World War

International law prior to the Second World War contained other scattered rules and documents protecting specific human rights. Statements by the international community condemning slavery, for example, date to the Declaration Relative to the Universal Abolition of the Slave Trade adopted at the Congress of Vienna in 1815. These ideas then found expression in the 1926 Convention to Suppress the Slave Trade and Slavery and the 1956 Supplementary Convention on the Abolition of Slavery. Parties to these treaties undertook concrete obligations to prevent and repress slavery in all its forms.

Peace negotiations following the First World War also gave attention to minority rights. The PCIJ recognised in its Advisory Opinion on *Minority Schools in Albania* in 1935 that international law aims at equal rights for minorities.[20] The case concerned an attempt by the Albanian government to close private schools run by racial and cultural minorities in favour of a universal public education system. The PCIJ expressed the view that equality for minority groups required that they be able to maintain separate institutions for preserving their traditions, language and other characteristics.

It was not until after the Second World War, however, that the impetus

---

[19] Geneva Convention IV, art 4.
[20] *Minority Schools in Albania*, PCIJ Advisory Opinion, 6 April 1935.

began to grow for a body of international law directly enshrining the rights of individuals against abuse by their own and allied states. Events before, during and after the Second World War presented clear and obvious challenges to the rights of minorities. The German genocides against Jews, Gypsies, homosexuals and other groups received international attention. After the Second World War, Europe was awash with refugees and displaced persons who found themselves at the mercy of foreign governments.

THE ROLE OF THE UNITED NATIONS

The foundation of the United Nations (UN) in 1945 signalled a new era for international protection of human rights. The primary aim of the organisation was to preserve global peace in the aftermath of the Second World War, but a concern with individual rights was also evident from the outset. The UN Charter was adopted on 24 October 1945. The Preamble expresses the following aims of the world community:

> We the peoples of the United Nations determined to save succeeding generations from the scourge of war, which twice in our lifetime has brought untold sorrow to mankind, and to reaffirm faith in fundamental human rights, in the dignity and worth of the human person, in the equal rights of men and women and of nations large and small [. . .] have resolved to combine our efforts to accomplish these aims [. . .].

According to Article 1(1) of the UN Charter, the function of the organisation is to 'maintain international peace and security'. Article 1(2) adds that the objective is to 'develop friendly relations among nations based on respect for the principle of equal rights and self-determination of peoples'. Article 1(3) then extends this principle to include respect for individual rights, stating that the UN aims to: 'achieve international co-operation in solving international problems of an economic, social, cultural, or humanitarian character, and in promoting and encouraging respect for human rights and for fundamental freedoms for all without distinction as to race, sex, language, or religion [. . .]'. The UN Charter itself does not make detailed provision for human rights protection. However, the UN has since developed an extensive framework of human rights conventions and associated organisational machinery.

The Universal Declaration

The most important initial step by the UN in the area of human rights was the adoption of the Universal Declaration of Human Rights (UDHR) in 1948. The UDHR is not a treaty. It was adopted by a vote of the UN General Assembly, rather than being ratified individually by member states. There were no dissenting votes, although eight states abstained. The UDHR is therefore a persuasive statement of the aspirations of the international community, rather than a binding legal document. However, there is no doubt that it has enormous symbolic force, regardless of its precise legal status.

The general tenor of the UDHR is aspirational. It sets out goals for the international community. Chief among these aspirations is the vision of a set of minimum guarantees applying to all people everywhere. This aspiration to universality is evident throughout the document. According to Article 1 of the UDHR, '[a]ll humans are born free and equal in dignity and rights'. Article 2 immediately goes on to provide that '[e]veryone is entitled to all the rights and freedoms set out in this Declaration, without distinction of any kind'. Some of the specific rights contained in the Declaration include:

- freedom from slavery;[21]
- freedom from torture and cruel, inhuman and degrading treatment;[22]
- recognition and equality before the law;[23]
- the right to a fair trial;[24]
- the right to privacy;[25]
- freedom of movement;[26]
- the right to marry and have a family;[27]
- the right to private property;[28]
- freedom of thought, conscience, expression and assembly;[29]
- the right to vote and seek public office;[30]
- the right to social security;[31]
- the right to work and leisure time;[32]

---

[21] Universal Declaration of Human Rights, art 4.
[22] Universal Declaration of Human Rights, art 5.
[23] Universal Declaration of Human Rights, arts 6–7.
[24] Universal Declaration of Human Rights, arts 8–11.
[25] Universal Declaration of Human Rights, art 12.
[26] Universal Declaration of Human Rights, arts 13–14.
[27] Universal Declaration of Human Rights, art 16.
[28] Universal Declaration of Human Rights, art 17.
[29] Universal Declaration of Human Rights, arts 18–20.
[30] Universal Declaration of Human Rights, art 21.
[31] Universal Declaration of Human Rights, art 22.
[32] Universal Declaration of Human Rights, arts 23–24.

- the right to sustenance and education;[33]
- the right to participate in culture and the arts.[34]

Article 29 adds that people also have duties to support their community, 'in which alone the free and full development of [human] personality is possible'. A person's rights may be restricted by law, but only 'for the purpose of securing due recognition and respect for the rights and freedoms of others and of meeting the just requirements of morality, public order and the general welfare in a democratic society'.

The International Covenants

The UDHR is one part of what is sometimes called the International Bill of Rights. The other parts are the International Covenant on Civil and Political Rights (ICCPR) and the International Covenant on Economic, Social and Cultural Rights (ICESCR) of 1966. The Covenants were designed to give more clout to the UDHR. Unlike the UDHR, they are binding treaties. Both took about ten years to gain enough parties to enter into force, but they now have widespread support. The ICCPR currently has 167 state parties, while the ICESCR has 160.

The ICCPR obliges parties to 'respect and ensure' the rights enumerated in the document.[35] Where necessary, legislation should be enacted to bring this about.[36] The Covenant essentially covers the same rights as Articles 1–21 of the UDHR. It contains its own administrative machinery, providing for a Human Rights Committee, which receives periodic reports from states on implementation.[37] States may also opt to allow other states to bring complaints about them.[38] The First Optional Protocol to the ICCPR, ratified by 114 states at the time of writing, allows for complaints by individuals. A Second Optional Protocol, adopted in 1989 and ratified by 75 states, abolishes the death penalty.

The ICESCR is less definite and demanding in its language. It obliges each state party to 'take steps' to 'progressively' realise the rights contained in the document 'to the maximum of its available resources'.[39] The Covenant elaborates on Articles 22–27 of the UDHR. It provides

---

[33] Universal Declaration of Human Rights, arts 25–26.
[34] Universal Declaration of Human Rights, art 27.
[35] International Covenant on Civil and Political Rights, art 2(1).
[36] International Covenant on Civil and Political Rights, art 2(2).
[37] International Covenant on Civil and Political Rights, arts 28, 40.
[38] International Covenant on Civil and Political Rights, art 41.
[39] International Covenant on Economic, Social and Cultural Rights, art 2.

for a reporting system like that under the ICCPR, administered by the UN Economic and Social Council.[40] The reports are now received by the Committee on Economic, Social and Cultural Rights, established in 1985. There is now also an Optional Protocol, dating from 2008, allowing for individual complaints to be made under the ICESCR. However, it currently only has eight state parties and is yet to enter into force.

Human Rights Machinery

The UN has evolved into a highly complex and bureaucratic organisation. There are a number of key UN bodies relevant to international human rights law. The UN effectively has a legislative body (the General Assembly), an executive body (the Security Council) and a judiciary (the International Court of Justice, the International Criminal Court and other UN tribunals). The General Assembly and the Security Council are both sometimes called upon to make declarations on human rights. The Security Council also has the power to impose sanctions. There is also, as mentioned above, an extensive UN bureaucracy concerned with various kinds of issues relating to human rights.

Various UN committees exist to monitor compliance with human rights treaties. We have already mentioned the Human Rights Committee established under Article 28 of the ICCPR. The Committee comprises members of 'high moral character and recognised competence' from throughout the world.[41] As mentioned above, it receives state reports and also considers complaints from both states and individuals with the consent of the states involved. We saw above that the ICESCR also provides for a reporting system, now administered through a dedicated UN committee.

A number of other human rights treaties have their own monitoring bodies established under the auspices of the UN. These include the International Convention on the Elimination of All Forms of Racial Discrimination of 1965 (Committee on the Elimination of Racial Discrimination),[42] the Convention on the Elimination of All Forms of Discrimination against Women of 1979 (Committee on the Elimination of Discrimination Against Women)[43] and the Convention against Torture

---

[40] International Covenant on Economic, Social and Cultural Rights, art 16.
[41] International Covenant on Civil and Political Rights, art 28(2).
[42] International Convention on the Elimination of All Forms of Racial Discrimination, art 8.
[43] Convention on the Elimination of All Forms of Discrimination against Women, art 17.

and Other Cruel, Inhuman or Degrading Treatment or Punishment of 1984 (Committee against Torture).[44]

The Economic and Social Council (ECOSOC) is another key organ of the UN. It has 54 members elected by the General Assembly. Its mission is to initiate studies and reports on economic, social, cultural, health and education issues.[45] It also plays a role in promoting human rights. ECOSOC has spawned a range of subsidiary bodies, including the Commission on Human Rights, which was succeeded in 2006 by the more broadly based Human Rights Council. The Council's functions include advising states on the implementation of human rights and periodically reviewing compliance. It has jurisdiction to report on individual complaints, but only with the consent of the state involved. The Office of the High Commissioner for Human Rights also serves as a focal point for human rights promotion and has a general mandate to advise nations and treaty-monitoring bodies.

REGIONAL HUMAN RIGHTS SYSTEMS

The UN continues to play a key role in international human rights law. However, regional human rights systems are increasingly prominent. Regional systems for disseminating and enforcing human rights standards have some clear advantages over UN mechanisms. They are more responsive to local needs and are capable of generating greater political pressure at a regional level. On the other hand, regional systems have been blamed for fuelling the fragmentation of international human rights law. Different legal standards may develop in different regions, leading to confusion and undermining the aspiration to universality that undergirds the notion of human rights.

Europe has by far the most developed regional human rights system. The Council of Europe was first established in 1948. It now has 47 member states. The European Convention on the Protection of Human Rights and Fundamental Freedoms (ECHR) entered into force in 1953. All Council of Europe member states are parties. The ECHR focuses primarily on civil and political rights. It is augmented by a series of Protocols making additions and amendments to the original document.

The European Commissioner of Human Rights plays a promotional

---

[44] Convention against Torture and Other Cruel, Inhuman or Degrading Treatment or Punishment, art 17.
[45] United Nations Charter, art 62.

and advisory role within the European system, similar to the role of the UN High Commissioner mentioned above. The system also features a specialised European Court of Human Rights, established under the ECHR.[46] The Court is unusual among international tribunals in allowing standing to individuals.[47] This individual jurisdiction became universal and compulsory for member states in 1998, under Protocol 11 to the ECHR. The European Union has its own judicial body, the Court of Justice of the European Union (CJEU), which is occasionally called upon to decide human rights issues that arise under European Union law.

The American human rights system revolves around the Organization of American States (OAS). The OAS dates from 1948 and has 35 member states. The associated American Convention on Human Rights, adopted in 1969, currently has 25 parties. The United States and Canada, two prominent OAS members, have not ratified it. The Convention focuses mainly on civil and political rights. It has two Protocols dealing with economic, social and cultural rights and the death penalty.

The responsibility for overseeing the American Convention on Human Rights rests with an administrative body, the Inter-American Commission on Human Rights, and a judicial body, the Inter-American Court of Human Rights.[48] The Commission plays an advisory and monitoring role. It is also empowered to look into complaints brought by states, non-governmental organisations and individuals.[49] The Court, by contrast, only has jurisdiction over matters brought before it by states or the Commission.[50]

The African Charter on Human and Peoples' Rights dates from 1986. It was created under the auspices of the Organisation of African Unity, which has since been supplanted by the African Union. The Charter is distinctive in the focus it places on economic, social and cultural rights, as well as rights of peoples. It also contains provisions on individual and peoples' duties. The Charter currently has 53 state parties. There is an Optional Protocol on the Rights of Women in Africa. The African Commission on Human and Peoples' Rights plays a monitoring role under the Charter and is empowered to receive state and individual complaints.[51]

---

[46] European Convention on the Protection of Human Rights and Fundamental Freedoms, art 19.
[47] European Convention on the Protection of Human Rights and Fundamental Freedoms, art 34.
[48] American Convention on Human Rights, art 33.
[49] American Convention on Human Rights, arts 44–45.
[50] American Convention on Human Rights, art 61.
[51] African Charter on Human and Peoples' Rights, arts 47, 55.

The African Court on Human and Peoples' Rights was established in 2006 under a Protocol to the Charter. Standing before the Court is normally limited to states and the Commission, which can present cases on behalf of individuals.[52]

Other regional systems are currently less developed. The Arab Charter of Human Rights was adopted by the League of Arab States in 2004. There is a monitoring system associated with the Charter,[53] but no state or individual complaints mechanism. The Commonwealth of Independent States in the former Soviet Union adopted a Convention on Human Rights and Fundamental Freedoms in 1995. Compliance is monitored by a Human Rights Commission. Asia and the Pacific currently lack a uniform system, although some aspirations are expressed in the 1997 Asian Charter of Human Rights.

CLASHES OF HUMAN RIGHTS

We saw earlier in this chapter that most, if not all, everyday rights are most plausibly regarded as less than absolute. How does international human rights law recognise and accommodate the non-absolute nature of rights? Clashes of rights under international human rights law tend to be resolved on a case-by-case basis, using the type of reasoning process described earlier. Earlier cases can then help with later decisions. There is a resistance to recognising any general hierarchy of international human rights. However, as we will see shortly, some rights have come to be viewed as particularly stringent.

Derogations

International human rights law recognises the non-absolute character of many rights through the notion of derogations, examined briefly above. These are basically exceptions to human rights norms allowed in extreme circumstances. According to Article 4(1) of the ICCPR, for example, states may derogate from their human rights obligations under the Covenant in times of 'public emergency threatening the life of the nation', but only to 'the extent strictly required by the exigencies of the situation'.

---

[52] Protocol to the African Charter on Human and Peoples' Rights on the Establishment of the African Court on Human and Peoples' Rights, art 5.
[53] Arab Charter of Human Rights, arts 40–41.

Similar provisions appear in the European and American human rights conventions.[54]

The scope for derogations in international human rights law does not extend to norms of *jus cogens*. These are peremptory norms of international law from which no derogation is permitted.[55] The exact list of such norms is disputed, but it is generally recognised as including the prohibitions on torture, genocide and slavery. The basic rules of international humanitarian law are also widely viewed as *jus cogens* norms.[56] The recognition of *jus cogens* norms within international human rights law shows that some human rights standards are more stringent than others. Indeed, norms of *jus cogens* are effectively treated as absolute rights. This makes intuitive sense: even if most rights are non-absolute, the rights against torture, genocide and slavery seem like plausible exceptions.[57]

Margins of Appreciation

A further way that international human rights law alleviates the problem posed by clashes of rights is to give states a certain amount of discretion in deciding how to interpret and apply international human rights standards, taking account of local circumstances, needs, values and policy considerations. This is also one way that international human rights law accommodates regional and cultural differences of the type that sometimes give rise to human rights scepticism, as discussed above.

The jurisprudence of the European Court of Human Rights recognises that states enjoy a margin of appreciation in implementing human rights standards. The rationale for this is that states are often best placed to decide how to implement human rights in light of regional needs and values. In the case of *Handyside v United Kingdom*, for example, the Court held that states have some leeway to set obscenity standards by reference

---

[54] See European Convention on the Protection of Human Rights and Fundamental Freedoms, art 15(1); American Convention on Human Rights, art 27.

[55] Vienna Convention on the Law of Treaties, art 53.

[56] International Law Commission, *Fragmentation of International Law: Difficulties Arising from the Diversification and Expansion of International Law* (ILC 2006) 189.

[57] The issue of whether torture can ever be morally justified is hotly debated. For some illuminating perspectives on the moral status of torture, see John Kleinig, 'Ticking Bombs and Torture Warrants' (2005) 10 *Deakin Law Review* 614; David Sussman, 'What's Wrong With Torture?' (2005) 33 *Philosophy and Public Affairs* 1; Emmanuel Levinas, 'Useless Suffering' in *Entre Nous* (Michael B Smith and Barbara Harshav tr, Columbia University Press 1998).

to local norms.[58] The principle was later used to uphold United Kingdom laws allowing the detention of suspected terrorists for up to seven days without judicial review, taking into account the challenges posed by terrorist groups operating in Northern Ireland.[59]

Modification of Treaty Obligations

There are other ways that states can modify their obligations under international human rights law. For example, states ratifying human rights law treaties often make reservations and declarations. A reservation is a unilateral statement by a state that purports to alter the legal effect of a treaty as it applies to that state.[60] International law prohibits reservations that are incompatible with a treaty's object and purpose.[61] Reservations to *jus cogens* norms are also generally viewed as unenforceable.

Declarations are similar to reservations, except that they concern the interpretation of a treaty, rather than the applicability of specific obligations. Again, declarations cannot be inconsistent with the object and purpose of the treaty. Finally, it should be noted that a state that has ratified a treaty may often denounce its obligations under the convention. Many treaties contain express provision for denunciation and set out the procedure to be followed, but some are silent on the issue. This includes a number of important human rights treaties, such as the ICCPR, the ICESCR and the Convention on the Elimination of All Forms of Discrimination against Women.[62]

HUMAN RIGHTS IN ARMED CONFLICT

What, then, is the relationship between international human rights law and the norms of international humanitarian law discussed throughout this book? We saw in earlier chapters that international humanitarian law

---

[58] *Handyside v United Kingdom*, European Court of Human Rights Judgment, 7 December 1976.
[59] *Brannigan and McBride v United Kingdom*, European Court of Human Rights Judgment, 26 March 1993. For critical discussion, see Susan Marks, 'Civil Liberties at the Margin: The UK Derogation and the European Court of Human Rights' (1995) 15 *Oxford Journal of Legal Studies* 69.
[60] Vienna Convention on the Law of Treaties, art 2.
[61] Vienna Convention on the Law of Treaties, art 19.
[62] For a detailed overview, see Yogesh Tyagi, 'The Denunciation of Human Rights Treaties' (2008) 79 *British Yearbook of International Law* 86.

only applies in the context of armed conflict. International human rights law, by contrast, aspires to general application. Does this mean that international human rights law applies in wartime? What happens when its requirements are in tension with international humanitarian law?

The following discussion will focus particularly on the challenges posed by tensions between international humanitarian law and international human rights law. However, it bears noting at the outset that although these two bodies of law sometimes conflict, in many ways they are mutually supporting.[63] The lists of fundamental guarantees found in the Geneva Conventions and the Additional Protocols, which apply to everyone affected by armed conflict, enshrine many of the basic protections of human rights law on issues ranging from freedom from torture to equality before the law.[64]

Conflicts of Norms

There are a number of distinct ways in which international humanitarian law and international human rights law might be in tension. The most obvious way this might happen would be through a direct clash of norms: for example, if international humanitarian law *requires* an action that international human rights law *prohibits*. However, it is hard to think of examples of direct clashes of this sort. It is not generally the case that either body of law requires actions that would be precluded under the other. It is generally possible to follow both sets of rules by respecting the more demanding standard.

A second way that international humanitarian law and international human rights law might be in tension is if one field of law *permits* an action that the other *prohibits*. This comes closer to capturing the essence of the problem, although we will see later in this chapter that there are broader issues at stake. An obvious example of this kind of tension concerns the right to life under international human rights law, as enshrined for example in Article 6 of the ICCPR. This right would seem, if it prevents anything, to restrain states from launching deadly attacks on individuals within their territories. However, international humanitarian law permits

---

[63] Compare Jean-Marie Henckaerts and Louise Doswald-Beck, *Customary International Humanitarian Law* (CUP 2005) 299–305.
[64] Geneva Conventions, art 3; Additional Protocol I, art 75; Additional Protocol II, arts 4–5. For discussion of the customary law position, see Jean-Marie Henckaerts and Louise Doswald-Beck, *Customary International Humanitarian Law* (CUP 2005) ch 32.

such attacks against combatants, provided that the rules relating to proportionality, prohibited weapons and so forth are respected.[65]

A case can be made that even this kind of tension can be reconciled through existing legal mechanisms. There are two related strategies that might be pursued in this context. The first strategy makes use of provisions in human rights treaties allowing for derogations in emergency situations. We saw previously that international human rights law contains a number of mechanisms for acknowledging the non-absolute nature of rights. Some rights are clearly more stringent than others, but even the right to life is generally thought to have exceptions in cases such as self-defence. It might therefore be argued that those aspects of international humanitarian law that initially seem to license human rights violations really just reflect the non-absolute character of the rights in question. Armed conflict, it might be said, is an exceptional situation in which derogations from the normal requirements of international human rights law are necessary.

This view of armed conflict as a situation where derogations from human rights norms are permissible is explicitly enshrined in some human rights conventions. Article 15(1) of the ECHR, for example, provides that:

> In time of war or other public emergency threatening the life of the nation any High Contracting Party may take measures derogating from its obligations under this Convention to the extent strictly required by the exigencies of the situation, provided that such measures are not inconsistent with its other obligations under international law.

Article 15(2) of the ECHR allows derogations from the right to life under Article 2 'in respect of deaths resulting from lawful acts of war'.[66] The American Convention on Human Rights contains a similar provision to Article 15(1).[67] Derogations from international human rights standards based on wartime exigencies cannot extend to violations of *jus cogens* norms, but it is hard to see how international humanitarian law could reasonably be construed as permitting acts such as torture, genocide and slavery.[68]

A more difficult issue arises in relation to the right to life under Article 6

---

[65] See, for example, Additional Protocol I, arts 48, 57.
[66] See also European Convention on the Protection of Human Rights and Fundamental Freedoms, art 2(2).
[67] American Convention on Human Rights, art 27.
[68] Compare Geneva Conventions, art 3; Additional Protocol I, art 75; Additional Protocol II, arts 4–5. For discussion of whether the law of war can be construed as permitting genocide, see *Legality of the Threat or Use of Nuclear Weapons*, ICJ Advisory Opinion, 8 July 1996 [26].

of the ICCPR. We saw previously that Article 4(1) of the Covenant allows for derogations in emergency situations, but that provision is expressly made inapplicable to Article 6.[69] The International Court of Justice (ICJ) has therefore relied on a second strategy to reconcile Article 6 with international humanitarian law. This strategy relies on the malleability of the human rights standards themselves. The application of human rights norms, on this view, differs with the context. The demands of human rights law in wartime might therefore prove significantly different from those in peacetime. This approach to Article 6 was developed by the ICJ in the *Nuclear Weapons Advisory Opinion*:

> [T]he protection of the International Covenant of Civil and Political Rights does not cease in times of war, except by operation of Article 4 of the Covenant whereby certain provisions may be derogated from in a time of national emergency. Respect for the right to life is not, however, such a provision. In principle, the right not arbitrarily to be deprived of one's life applies also in hostilities. The test of what is an arbitrary deprivation of life, however, then falls to be determined by the applicable *lex specialis*, namely, the law applicable in armed conflict, which is designed to regulate the conduct of hostilities. Thus whether a particular loss of life [. . .] is to be considered an arbitrary deprivation of life contrary to Article 6 of the Covenant, can only be decided by reference to the law applicable in armed conflict and not deduced from the terms of the Covenant itself.[70]

This analysis suggests that wartime modifies the requirements of international human rights law, while the nature and extent of this modification is governed by international humanitarian law. In other words, during armed conflicts, the former set of norms is amended by the latter to the extent that they are in tension. In wartime, then, international human rights law is the *lex generalis* (general law); it gives way to the *lex specialis* (specialised law) of international humanitarian law, in accordance with the maxim *lex specialis derogat legi generali* (the specialised law overrides the general law).

The ICJ further clarified its understanding of the relationship between international humanitarian and international human rights law in the *Israeli Wall Advisory Opinion*, summarising its position as follows:

> The protection offered by human rights conventions does not cease in case of armed conflict, save through the effect of provisions for derogation [. . .] As

---

[69] International Covenant on Civil and Political Rights, art 4(2).
[70] *Legality of the Threat or Use of Nuclear Weapons*, International Court of Justice (ICJ) Advisory Opinion, 8 July 1996 [25].

138   *Principles of international humanitarian law*

regards the relationship between international humanitarian law and human rights law, there are thus three possible situations: some rights may be exclusively matters of international humanitarian law; others may be exclusively matters of human rights law; yet others may be matters of both these branches of international law. In order to answer the question put to it, the Court will have to take into consideration both these branches of international law, namely human rights law and, as *lex specialis*, international humanitarian law.[71]

This passage, read with the excerpt from the *Nuclear Weapons Advisory Opinion* discussed previously, suggests that the ICJ's approach effectively combines the two strategies mentioned above. Any tension between human rights and humanitarian norms in the context of armed conflict is resolved in favour of the latter. This is accomplished by either relying on the notion of derogations or using international humanitarian law to determine the contours of the rights themselves. The analysis set out in the *Israeli Wall Advisory Opinion* was later reiterated by the ICJ in *Democratic Republic of the Congo v Uganda*.[72]

Monism and Dualism

It will be useful at this point to introduce two competing views that might be taken on the question of whether international human rights law applies in wartime. The *dualist* view holds that international humanitarian law applies only in wartime and international human rights law applies only in peacetime. There is no overlap between the two legal regimes. The *monist* view, on the other hand, holds that international human rights law applies in both wartime and peacetime. This view entails that during an armed conflict international humanitarian law and international human rights law coexist.

The dualist view was defended in an early article on humanitarian law and human rights by the distinguished military lawyer and scholar, Colonel GIAD Draper.[73] However, it has few supporters today. Dualism removes the prospect of conflicts between international humanitarian law and international human rights law, but it is very difficult to reconcile with human rights treaties that specifically envisage that their provisions will

---

[71] *Legal Consequences of the Construction of a Wall in the Occupied Palestinian Territory*, ICJ Advisory Opinion, 9 July 2004 [106].
[72] *Armed Activities on the Territory of the Congo (Democratic Republic of the Congo v Uganda)*, ICJ Judgment, 19 December 2005 [216]–[217].
[73] GIAD Draper, 'Humanitarian Law and Human Rights' [1979] *Acta Juridica* 193.

apply in wartime.[74] It is also clearly inconsistent with the ICJ judgments considered above. The monist view, by contrast, is now generally accepted, partly but certainly not only as a result of its adoption by the ICJ. The authors of the International Committee of the Red Cross study on customary international humanitarian law note that '[t]here is extensive state practice to the effect that human rights law must be applied during armed conflicts'.[75] They also cite numerous UN resolutions and investigations where the applicability of human rights norms during armed conflict has been noted and violations condemned.

A more complete understanding of the motivations for the monist view can be gained by considering recent debates on the fragmentation of international law. The proliferation of different bodies of rules within international law, differentiated by subject matter, region or forum, creates possible inconsistencies and prevents states and individuals from readily knowing their obligations. The issue of fragmentation in international law was deemed sufficiently important to be discussed in depth in a report issued by a high-profile study group of the International Law Commission (ILC).[76] The study group was chaired by Martti Koskenniemi, an eminent international law scholar and legal theorist, who had explored the issue previously in a number of academic publications.[77]

The ILC study group placed particular emphasis in its report on the need for what it termed 'systemic integration' of different fields of international law.[78] Decision makers in international law have a responsibility to seek coherence between the various norms that are relevant to a dispute that comes before them. This aspiration reflects the nature and normative aims of law as an institution:

---

[74] See, for example, Convention on the Rights of the Child, art 38; European Convention on the Protection of Human Rights and Fundamental Freedoms, arts 2(2), 15(2).

[75] Jean-Marie Henckaerts and Louise Doswald-Beck, *Customary International Humanitarian Law* (CUP 2005) 303.

[76] International Law Commission, *Fragmentation of International Law: Difficulties Arising from the Diversification and Expansion of International Law* (ILC 2006). For a helpful overview, see Anthony Cassimatis, 'International Humanitarian Law, International Human Rights Law and Fragmentation of International Law' (2007) 56 *International and Comparative Law Quarterly* 623.

[77] See, for example, Martti Koskenniemi, 'The Politics of International Law' (1990) 1 *European Journal of International Law* 4; Martti Koskenniemi and Païvi Leino, 'Fragmentation of International Law? Postmodern Anxieties' (2002) *Leiden Journal of International Law* 553.

[78] International Law Commission, *Fragmentation of International Law: Difficulties Arising from the Diversification and Expansion of International Law* (ILC 2006) 25–8.

Law is also about protecting rights and enforcing obligations, above all rights and obligations that have a backing in something like a general, public interest. Without the principle of 'systemic integration' it would be impossible to give expression to and to keep alive any sense of the common good of humankind, not reducible to the good of any particular institution or 'regime'.[79]

The monist view discussed above reflects this wider aspiration to achieve integration and coherence between different facets of international law. It aspires to a unified body of international law operating in situations of armed conflict that incorporates standards from both international humanitarian law and international human rights law as appropriate. This project inescapably raises difficult questions about precisely how the two sets of norms are to be integrated. The notion of international humanitarian law as the *lex specialis* represents a useful device for analysing these types of conflicts, but it does not automatically resolve all the questions that may arise on specific issues.

The general presumption under the *lex specialis* principle is that international humanitarian law will prevail during armed conflicts. However, the framework also entails that human rights standards will generally still operate, even though international humanitarian law does not provide for them. The difficulty, then, is to decide which human rights norms continue unaltered in armed conflict and which do not. This will involve assessing whether the norms are in tension with humanitarian law and, if so, to what extent. It may be that this question can only be fully resolved on a case-by-case basis.

A Deeper Tension?

We saw above that at least some of the tensions between international humanitarian law and international human rights law can potentially be resolved by either interpreting human rights standards through reference to humanitarian norms or treating armed conflict as an exceptional situation in which derogations from human rights are necessary. There is, however, arguably a deeper source of tension between these two fields of law: they rest on fundamentally different and perhaps opposed motivations and theories.[80] We have seen throughout this book that international humanitarian law aims primarily at universal acceptance

---

[79] Ibid 244.
[80] Compare Louise Doswald-Beck and Sylvain Vité, 'International Humanitarian Law and Human Rights Law' (1993) 293 *International Review of the Red Cross* 94.

of a common set of rules to moderate the harmful effects of armed conflicts. International human rights law, by contrast, seeks to recognise the fundamental components of human flourishing in civil, political, social, economic and cultural contexts.

It is useful in this context to recall the distinction drawn in Chapter 1 between two aspirations that often guide the development of legal principles. The first aspiration is to create a body of norms that coheres with underlying ethical principles. This is what the ILC study group describes as the goal of systemic integration. The second aspiration is to achieve general acceptance of the norms that comprise the legal system. Many legal systems will place significant emphasis on both coherence and acceptance. A case can be made, however, that international human rights law places particularly high value on coherence, due to its aspirational character and its reliance on the underlying concepts of human dignity and natural rights. The normative force of human rights norms, in other words, rests substantially on their claim to embody shared human goals.

International humanitarian law, by contrast, might be said to lie at the other end of the spectrum. We saw in Chapter 1 that humanitarian norms often prioritise simplicity and clarity over coherence with underlying ethical principles, since the primary aim of this body of law is to secure recognition and respect from all participants in armed conflict. If the legitimacy of human rights law stems from its coherence with its underlying narrative of human flourishing, the legitimacy of humanitarian law might perhaps be said to stem from its general acceptance by the international community.

There is a sense, then, in which the claims to legitimacy of international humanitarian law and international human rights law rest on conflicting theories. Human rights scholars sometimes complain that the pragmatism of humanitarian law is inconsistent with the lofty aspirations of human rights norms.[81] However, the opposite charge can also be made: allowing the relatively vague and aspirational demands of human rights law to apply in wartime risks undermining humanitarian law's central quest for a clear and transparent set of rules that all parties to a conflict can agree upon.

The monist vision of international law endorsed by the ICJ and the ILC study group assumes that this tension can be overcome and that

---

[81] See, for example, Vera Gowlland-Debbas, 'The Right to Life and Genocide: The Court and an International Public Policy' in Laurence Boisson de Chazournes and Philippe Sands (eds), *International Law, the International Court of Justice and Nuclear Weapons* (CUP 1999) 335.

humanitarian and human rights law can be integrated. However, neither body provides a detailed road map for how this can be accomplished while still upholding the claims to legitimacy associated with both fields of law. The monist view, as we have seen, is now widely endorsed and it is doubtful that dualism provides a desirable alternative, given that it entails a general suspension of human rights norms in wartime. However, the challenges involved in integrating humanitarianism and human rights should not be underestimated.

7. Liability of states and non-state groups

International law has traditionally been viewed as the body of law governing relations between states. For this reason, it commonly used to be called the law of nations. Nowadays, by contrast, there is an increasing emphasis on the place of individuals in international law. This shift in emphasis takes two main forms. First, as we saw in the previous chapter, international law increasingly places direct limits on how states can treat individuals and gives individuals standing to complain about breaches of their rights. Second, international law now imposes criminal liability upon individuals for violations of certain norms. We will examine this issue in greater depth in Chapter 8.

The increasing focus that international law places on individuals is particularly evident in international humanitarian law (as well as its counterpart, international human rights law, which we examined in the last chapter). Contemporary international humanitarian law gives a significant place to individual criminal liability. Much publicity has been given in recent decades to the work of international criminal tribunals, such as the International Criminal Tribunal for the Former Yugoslavia (ICTY) and the International Criminal Court, in pursuing violations of the international law of armed conflict.

We will see in the next chapter that criminal proceedings against individuals have historically played a significant role in the development of international humanitarian law. However, it is important not to overemphasise these proceedings, as it can create a misleading picture. Individual criminal responsibility in humanitarian law is still a fairly recent phenomenon. Furthermore, it is far from being the main mechanism through which this field of law is enforced. The effectiveness of the law of armed conflict still depends centrally on whether states recognise and respect its rules.

It is also important in this context to recognise the role played by non-state groups in armed conflicts. The vast majority of contemporary armed conflicts are fought within the boundaries of a single state. These internal conflicts may involve state forces, but in some cases they may be fought solely between non-state groups. The question of whether and to what extent non-state armed groups can be considered bound by international humanitarian law is therefore crucial to the effectiveness of this body of rules. We will consider this issue in further detail at the end of the present chapter.

WHAT IS A STATE?

We turn first to the liability of states for violations of international law. It is useful to begin by exploring the legal definition of a state. For many purposes, the term 'state' is synonymous with 'country' or 'nation'. However, sometimes further clarification is needed. It is worth noting in this context that the term 'state' is not synonymous with 'government'. Different governments may come and go within a state, while the state and its international obligations stay the same. There can also be a government without a state, as we will see below. Governance arrangements alone therefore do not settle the question.

Taiwan provides a current example of how the issue of statehood under international law is not necessarily settled by stable borders or governance arrangements. The Republic of China (ROC), which governs Taiwan and nearby islands, was recognised as the government of China by the United Nations (UN) from 1949 until 1971, when the UN seat was assumed by the People's Republic of China (PRC). The PRC does not recognise the ROC. Only a small minority of recognised states maintain official diplomatic relations with the ROC, although many more have unofficial relations. Taiwan, then, has a defined territory and stable government by the ROC, but is nonetheless not identified as a state by most of the international community. Does this mean it is not a state under international law?

A related set of issues arises in relation to Palestine. The Gaza Strip and West Bank, which comprise the Palestinian territories, were part of the British mandate approved by the League of Nations following the First World War. Following the creation of Israel in 1948, they were first occupied by Israel, then Egypt and Jordan, then Israel again. Since the early 1990s, they have been governed de facto by the Palestinian Authority, which has official diplomatic relations with around half the international community. Since mid 2007, however, different factions effectively control the two regions. Palestine, then, enjoys greater diplomatic recognition than Taiwan, but its territory and governance arrangements are less stable. How does this bear on the question of statehood?

The Montevideo Convention on the Rights and Duties of States of 1933 is often cited as setting out the legal position on statehood. The Convention was a regional treaty that was signed by only 16 American states, but it is widely regarded as codifying customary international law.

Article 1 of the Montevideo Convention sets out the four characteristics a state should possess. These are:

- a permanent population;
- a defined territory;
- some form of government; and
- the capacity to enter into relations with other states.

Each of these criteria demands some level of stability in the composition of the state in question. The requirement of a permanent population, for example, does not seem to require any minimum number.[1] However, the population must be somewhat stable and not purely transient. The criterion of a defined territory does not mean the borders must be undisputed, but some part of the territory must be stable and defined. The requirement of a form of government likewise requires a relatively stable civil organisation wielding some effective control over the territory.[2] Governments may come and go, but there must be some stability in the overall system of government.

Once a state is recognised by the international community, however, even prolonged bouts of unrest or anarchy will not necessarily see it lose that status. Somalia provides a striking illustration, since it has effectively been without a centralised government since 1991. It remains to be seen whether the newly created Federal Government of Somalia, established in August 2012, will succeed in wielding genuine national authority. The relatively stable northern region of Somaliland unilaterally seceded from Somalia in 1991 and claims independent statehood. A UN report published in 1999 concluded that Somalia lacked the traditional attributes of statehood. However, it continued to be recognised by the international community. Somaliland, although comparatively stable in borders and governance, is not generally recognised by other states.

The final requirement of statehood prescribed in the Montevideo Convention is the capacity to enter into relations with other states. This criterion implies that the putative state in question must not be subordinated to another state's effective authority. In other words, a prerequisite for entering into diplomatic relations as a state is that you have the ability to speak on your own behalf. A further practical requirement for entering into formal relations with other states might seem to be that those states are willing to deal with you. It is on this basis that it is sometimes said

---

[1] Ian Brownlie, *Principles of Public International Law* (OUP 2003) 82–3.
[2] Ibid 71.

there is an additional requirement for statehood beyond those explicitly set out in the Montevideo Convention: namely, that the putative state be recognised by members of the international community.

Article 3 of the Montevideo Convention contradicts this idea, providing that 'the political existence of the state is independent of recognition by the other states'. However, this statement is controversial. There are effectively two schools of thought on this issue. Those who deny the recognition requirement support what is called the *declarative theory* of statehood. According to this theory, statehood is determined by the four indicators listed in the Montevideo Convention. It is an objective test and does not depend on international opinion. This is probably the dominant view among commentators.[3]

Those who endorse the recognition requirement, by contrast, subscribe to the *constitutive theory* of statehood. This theory notes that having certain characteristics does a state no practical good unless it is recognised by other states. Recognition is therefore a prerequisite for truly joining the international community. Proponents of this view differ on whether recognition can dispense with the need for the de facto criteria listed in the Montevideo Convention or is an additional requirement. This issue becomes crucial when assessing the legal status of an entity such as Somalia.

STATE RESPONSIBILITY

When is a state responsible for violations of international law? For a long time, the law in this area was contested. However, some important basic principles can now be found in the International Law Commission's Draft Articles on State Responsibility (DASR). The latest version of the Articles dates from 2001. They were formally endorsed by the UN General Assembly in Resolution 56/83 of 2002.

Article 4(1) of the DASR provides that '[t]he conduct of any State organ shall be considered an act of that State under international law.' The Articles then go on to clarify that '[a]n organ includes any person or entity who has that status in accordance with the internal law of the State.'[4] This will include, for example, the state's official armed forces.[5] States are

---

[3] James Crawford, *The Creation of States in International Law* (OUP 2006) 25.
[4] Draft Articles on State Responsibility, art 4(2).
[5] Jean-Marie Henckaerts and Louise Doswald-Beck, *Customary International Humanitarian Law* (CUP 2005) 530–32.

similarly responsible for the conduct of a person or entity who 'is empowered by the law of that State to exercise elements of the governmental authority' and is acting in that capacity at the relevant time.[6] According to Article 7 of the DASR, the conduct of a state organ or a person or entity empowered by the state will be regarded as an act of the state if the person or entity is acting in an official capacity at the time, even if the specific act under consideration exceeds authority or contravenes instructions.

State responsibility under the DASR is not confined to official state organs or persons granted governmental authority under law. Article 8 of the DASR provides that a state is also responsible for the conduct of any person or group acting under the instructions of, or under the direction or control of, that state. A state can even be responsible in some circumstances for an act committed by another state. This will occur if the first state knowingly aids and assists, directs and controls, or coerces the second state to commit the relevant act.[7] These provisions evidently call for careful interpretation.

The Test of Control

The question of when a state will be deemed responsible for the actions of another individual, group or state under international law has been considered in a number of important decisions by international tribunals. We encountered some of these decisions previously in Chapter 1, where we discussed the test of control in the context of determining whether an armed conflict is international or non-international for legal purposes. We saw there that a non-international conflict may sometimes become internationalised where a third-party state is supporting one or more of the parties. The question then becomes whether the parties should be deemed to be acting 'on behalf of' the third-party state.

We saw in Chapter 1 that two tests have been developed for resolving this issue. The first standard, known as the 'effective control' test, derives from the International Court of Justice (ICJ) decision in *Nicaragua v United States*.[8] The ICJ held there that a group is acting on behalf of a state if the state has 'effective control' over it.[9] This requires the state to issue the group with instructions to commit specific acts, rather than merely providing technical support or financial assistance. The *Nicaragua*

---

[6] Draft Articles on State Responsibility, art 5.
[7] Draft Articles on State Responsibility, arts 16–18.
[8] *Nicaragua v United States (Merits)*, International Court of Justice (ICJ) Judgment, 27 June 1986.
[9] Ibid [115].

case arose from a civil war between the Nicaraguan government and a coalition of rebel guerrillas, known as the Contras. Nicaragua alleged that the United States government was training and funding the Contras and that its operatives were responsible for placing mines in Nicaraguan harbours.

The ICJ found in *Nicaragua* that these allegations were supported on the facts. The United States was therefore held liable to make reparations for illegal use of force against Nicaragua based on the acts carried out by its agents. The United States was not held responsible, however, for violations of international law committed by the Contras. The ICJ found that the United States had provided extensive technical and material support and assistance to the rebel group, but this ultimately fell short of the high standard imposed by the effective control test.[10] The ICJ's ruling therefore illustrates the high bar for attribution of responsibility articulated in the case.[11]

The second test in this area comes from the ICTY Appeals Chamber decision in *Prosecutor v Tadić*. The Appeals Chamber ruled in that case that the test articulated by the ICJ in *Nicaragua* only applies to the control of individuals and disorganised groups.[12] Control of organised groups, on the other hand, is more appropriately assessed using the weaker 'overall control' test.[13] The overall control standard does not require that the state issues directions to perform specific acts. Rather, it asks whether the state 'wields general control over the group, not only by equipping and financing [it], but also by coordinating or helping in the general planning of its military activity'.[14]

The position emerging from these two decisions is therefore as follows. A state is responsible for the acts of a non-state actor if the actor is acting 'on behalf of' the state.[15] An individual or disorganised group will be deemed to be acting 'on behalf of' a state for these purposes where the state exercises 'effective control' over the individual or group, as defined by the ICJ in *Nicaragua*. An organised group, on the other hand, will be deemed

---

[10] Ibid [116].
[11] For critical discussion of the ICJ's reliance on the effective control test, see Antonio Cassese, 'The *Nicaragua* and *Tadić* Tests Revisited in Light of the ICJ Judgment on Genocide in Bosnia' (2007) 18 *European Journal of International Law* 649, 653–5.
[12] *Prosecutor v Tadić*, International Criminal Tribunal for the Former Yugoslavia (ICTY) Appeals Chamber Judgment, 15 July 1999 [99]–[100].
[13] Ibid [120].
[14] Ibid [131].
[15] Ibid [88]–[97].

to be acting 'on behalf of' a state where the state exercises 'overall control' over the group, as defined by the ICTY Appeals Chamber in *Tadić*.

It should be noted, however, that the legal position is not uncontested. The *Bosnian Genocide* case decided by the ICJ in 2007 raised the question of whether the Federal Republic of Yugoslavia was responsible for acts of genocide carried out by Bosnian Serb armed forces.[16] The ICJ declined to apply the overall control test set out in the *Tadić* decision, preferring to rely on the effective control test articulated in *Nicaragua*. The Court reasoned that the effective control test had been developed by the ICTY only to determine whether the Yugoslavian conflict was international or non-international in character and applying it to issues of state responsibility would overly broaden the concept.

Antonio Cassese, the inaugural President of the ICTY and a distinguished international law scholar, has argued that the ICJ was incorrect to reject the overall control test in the *Bosnian Genocide* case.[17] Cassese contends, persuasively in our view, that the application of that test to the issue of state responsibility for organised groups is supported by both international case law and state practice. A strong argument can also be made that applying the effective control test to organised groups sets the bar for state responsibility too high. It remains to be seen whether the ICJ will be prepared to reconsider its stance in the *Bosnian Genocide* decision when the issue arises in future cases.

Acknowledgment and Adoption

The exercise of effective or overall control is not the only way that a state may become responsible for a non-state group's actions. A state that plays no part initially in the behaviour of non-state actors may nonetheless be held responsible in some cases if it subsequently acknowledges and adopts the actions as its own. The test of acknowledgement and adoption was recognised by the ICJ in the *Tehran Hostages* case.[18] The case concerned an incident where a group of Iranian students seized control of the United States embassy in Tehran and took a number of embassy staff hostage.

---

[16] *Case Concerning the Application of the Convention on the Prevention and Punishment of the Crime of Genocide (Bosnia and Herzegovina v Serbia and Montenegro)*, ICJ Judgment, 26 February 2007.

[17] Antonio Cassese, 'The *Nicaragua* and *Tadić* Tests Revisited in Light of the ICJ Judgment on Genocide in Bosnia' (2007) 18 *European Journal of International Law* 649.

[18] *Case Concerning United States Diplomatic and Consular Staff in Tehran*, ICJ Judgment, 24 May 1980.

The Iranian government, led by the Ayatollah Khomeini, played no part in the initial occupation of the embassy. However, the Ayatollah did not call on police to remove the students, but publicly endorsed and encouraged their actions. The ICJ held that the Ayatollah's endorsement transformed the actions of the students into the actions of Iran.[19] It is important to note that the responsibility of Iran was based on its continuation of the activities of the students. That is, at some point during the occupation, the actions ceased to be merely those of private individuals and became those of the state.

State responsibility under this heading may not be so easily established in respect of actions by private individuals that are too short in duration to be continued by the state. It may be possible for a state to retrospectively adopt the actions of individuals as its own, but this will likely occur only where the adoption is unequivocal and unqualified. An example of such conduct may be where a representative of the state makes a statement indicating that the conduct of individuals is conduct of the state. However, it seems likely that such clear examples of state adoption will be rare in practice. States will be wary of making public statements adopting potentially illegal acts as their own.

The Relevance of Common Article 1

A further issue relevant to state responsibility for breaches of international humanitarian law relates to Common Article 1 of the Geneva Conventions. This provision, which appears identically in all four Geneva Conventions of 1949, states that '[t]he High Contracting Parties undertake to respect and ensure respect for the present Convention in all circumstances'. The same wording is also found in Article 1(1) of Additional Protocol I.[20] The interpretation of Common Article 1 has been the subject of some debate. The terms of the provision could be construed in at least three different ways.

The narrowest possible interpretation of Common Article 1 would read it as simply reiterating the duty of state parties and their organs to abide by the rules of the Geneva Conventions. However, it is generally accepted that the provision has a broader meaning. At the very least, it is thought to oblige state parties to take all necessary steps to ensure

---

[19] Ibid [74]. Compare Draft Articles on State Responsibility, art 11.
[20] See also Additional Protocol III, art 1(1). The wording does not appear in Additional Protocol II, although Common Article 1 itself applies to Common Article 3 of the Geneva Conventions and therefore has application in non-international armed conflicts.

respect for humanitarian norms by private individuals and groups within their jurisdiction.[21] The provision therefore imposes a duty upon states to incorporate and enforce the laws of armed conflict through their domestic legal systems.

It is widely thought that Common Article 1 goes even further than this, obliging states to take steps to ensure respect for the Geneva Conventions not only by their own organs and private entities, but also by other state parties.[22] In other words, the provision entreats state parties to 'do everything in their power to ensure that the humanitarian principles underlying the Conventions are *applied universally*'.[23] The ICJ took the view in the *Nuclear Weapons Advisory Opinion* that Common Article 1 obliges every state party to the Geneva Conventions, 'whether or not it is a party to a specific conflict, [. . .] to ensure that the requirements of the instruments in question are complied with'.[24] It has been argued that the collective responsibility the provision creates for ensuring respect for humanitarian rules gives it a 'quasi-constitutional' status in international law.[25]

The relevance of Common Article 1 for state responsibility arises from the duty it creates to ensure respect for international humanitarian law within a state's domestic jurisdiction. A state may be in breach of its Common Article 1 obligations if it fails to take measures to prevent a non-state group from breaching humanitarian rules within its territory, even though the state does not exercise control over the group or endorse its actions. The actions of the non-state group will not be attributable to the state in this scenario, but the state may still be at fault for failing to prevent them.

It is also relevant to note in this context the general duty of states under international law to prevent and remedy injuries to foreign nationals within their jurisdiction. Under the doctrine of denial of justice, when a person suffers injury in a foreign country, the state in which the person

---

[21] Jean S Pictet et al (eds), *Commentary on the Geneva Conventions* (ICRC 1960) vol 1, 25–6.
[22] Ibid vol 1, 26; Carlo Focarelli, 'Common Article 1 of the Geneva Conventions: A Soap Bubble?' (2010) 21 *European Journal of International Law* 125, 127.
[23] Jean S Pictet et al (eds), *Commentary on the Geneva Conventions* (ICRC 1960) vol 4, 16.
[24] *Legality of the Threat or Use of Nuclear Weapons*, ICJ Advisory Opinion, 8 July 1996 [158].
[25] Laurence Boisson de Chazournes and Luigi Condorelli, 'Common Article 1 of the Geneva Conventions Revisited: Protecting Collective Interests' (2000) 837 *International Review of the Red Cross* 67, 85–6.

was injured has an obligation to take reasonable measures to apprehend and prosecute the person responsible.[26] A state that fails in this duty is not thereby rendered responsible for the actions of the wrongdoer, but rather breaches its own independent obligation to bring the perpetrator to justice.[27] A similar analysis applies to a state that fails in its obligations under Common Article 1.

Serious Breaches

The DASR contains special provisions relating to serious breaches of international law. These provisions apply only to gross or systematic breaches of peremptory norms, also known as norms of *jus cogens*.[28] We saw in Chapter 6 that *jus cogens* norms are standards of international law from which no derogation is permitted.[29] The obligations conferred by these norms are so important that they are seen as being owed to the international community as a whole (*erga omnes* or towards all), rather than merely to individual states. The list of peremptory norms is generally viewed as including the prohibitions on torture, genocide, slavery and apartheid, as well as the basic principles of the law of war.[30]

Article 41 of the DASR provides that states have an obligation to cooperate to bring any serious breach of international law to an end through lawful means. Additionally, states are prohibited from recognising as lawful any situation created through a serious breach or from rendering aid or assistance in maintaining the situation. The obligation on states to take measures to bring the serious breach to an end extends to all states, regardless of whether they are individually affected by the violation. The relatively small number of principles recognised as peremptory norms means that Article 41 has limited application. It is arguable, however, that this obligation was contravened by members of the international community in failing to take coordinated action against the genocides that occurred in Rwanda during the 1990s and the Darfur region of Sudan during the 2000s.

---

[26] See, for example, *Laura MB Janes et al (USA) v United Mexican States*, American-Mexican Claims Commission Award, 16 November 1925.
[27] Ibid [20].
[28] Draft Articles on State Responsibility, art 40.
[29] Vienna Convention on the Law of Treaties, art 53.
[30] International Law Commission, *Fragmentation of International Law: Difficulties Arising from the Diversification and Expansion of International Law* (ILC 2006) 189.

CONSEQUENCES OF RESPONSIBILITY

A wrong committed by one state against another results in, first, responsibilities of cessation and non-repetition and, second, a duty to make reparations.[31] Article 33(1) of the DASR provides that these obligations are owed both to the wronged state and to the international community as a whole. The responsibilities of cessation and non-repetition need little explanation. A state found to be acting wrongfully incurs obligations to stop behaving in that way and refrain from doing so again.

The duty to make reparations is more complex. Articles 34–37 of the DASR state that the duty to make reparations involves obligations of restitution, compensation and satisfaction. Restitution consists in re-establishing the situation that existed before the wrongful act, if at all possible. Compensation involves financial reimbursement for any wrong not made good by restitution. Satisfaction comprises acknowledging the breach, expressing regret, formally apologising or making another appropriate communication. Each of these components is part of the state's duty to make good on its wrong.

If a state fails to meet its obligation to make reparations, the wronged state has a limited right to take countermeasures. Countermeasures involve suspending the wronged state's normal obligations towards the other state.[32] The notion of countermeasures is evidently open to abuse by states who may seek to rely on perceived wrongs to justify their own violations of international law. Countermeasures may also escalate a dispute. The DASR therefore stipulates that countermeasures must be proportionate to the breach and are to be terminated as soon as the wrong is remedied.[33] Furthermore, some international obligations, such as the prohibition on the use of force and respect for fundamental human rights, cannot be suspended.[34] The blanket prohibition on reprisals in response to violations of international humanitarian law is also reiterated in this context.[35]

---

[31] Draft Articles on State Responsibility, arts 30–31. See also Jean-Marie Henckaerts and Louise Doswald-Beck, *Customary International Humanitarian Law* (CUP 2005) rule 150.
[32] Draft Articles on State Responsibility, arts 49–53.
[33] Draft Articles on State Responsibility, arts 51, 53.
[34] Draft Articles on State Responsibility, art 50.
[35] Draft Articles on State Responsibility, art 50(1)(c). See also Geneva Convention I, art 46; Geneva Convention II, art 47; Geneva Convention III, art 13; Geneva Convention IV, art 33; Additional Protocol I, arts 20, 51(6).

MODES OF ENFORCEMENT

It is one thing to establish that a state is responsible for a wrongful act under international law. It is another thing to enforce that responsibility and secure cessation and reparations. International law depends on a wide range of different methods for implementing and enforcing state obligations, including:

- diplomatic negotiation and pressure;
- monitoring and reporting processes;
- arbitration and mediation;
- complaints mechanisms;
- litigation in courts and tribunals;
- embargoes, sanctions and other countermeasures;
- as a last resort, the threat or use of military force.

Roughly speaking, the methods at the top of the list are the most widespread and important, but the ones further down on the list tend to get the most attention. The following sections examine some of these mechanisms in more detail.

Monitoring, Reporting and Complaints

It is useful to begin by looking at some of the less overtly coercive methods of holding states to their international law obligations. It is important to recognise the central role of diplomatic pressure in enforcing international norms. States are subject to ongoing monitoring of their international obligations. This process occurs in a range of diverse ways. Some international conventions establish dedicated committees with a monitoring role. We saw in Chapter 6 that a number of prominent international human rights treaties have this feature.[36] Some of these bodies, such as the Committee against Torture, have the power to initiate investigations based on information about possible breaches.[37]

Various other UN bodies hold formal monitoring roles. For example, there are Special Rapporteurs and Commissioners for a range of topics. These formal institutions, however, only scratch the surface of the

---

[36] See, for example, International Covenant on Civil and Political Rights, art 40; International Covenant on Economic, Social and Cultural Rights, art 16; International Convention on the Elimination of All Forms of Racial Discrimination, art 8.

[37] Convention against Torture and Other Cruel, Inhuman or Degrading Treatment or Punishment, art 20.

monitoring that takes place on a practical level. Non-governmental organisations play a key role in bringing violations to international attention. Some seek to achieve their purpose by generating publicity, while others work behind the scenes. The work of the International Committee of the Red Cross is particularly crucial in ensuring compliance with the law of armed conflict. States also monitor one another and exert pressure on numerous levels to comply with international norms.

A range of international law treaties impose reporting requirements on state parties. This typically requires states to make regular reports to a committee established in connection with the treaty. Again, this type of reporting regime is a common feature of human rights conventions, as discussed in Chapter 6. These reporting systems are sometimes derided as toothless,[38] but they serve as an important locus of diplomatic and political pressure. States who fail to submit reports or who are seen to be failing in their obligations risk being named and shamed by the international community. Their failings may be aired at international gatherings or raised in diplomatic negotiations.

We saw in Chapter 6 that some international human rights treaties also incorporate complaints mechanisms.[39] These processes can be utilised by states or, in some cases, by individuals. The latter form is particularly significant, as individuals may have less compunction in airing complaints publicly. The complaints processes raise similar issues to reporting in relation to their effectiveness. On the one hand, the bodies that receive and hear the complaints typically lack the ability to impose enforceable remedies (although there are exceptions, such as the provision for individuals to appear before the European Court of Human Rights).[40] Nonetheless, an adverse finding may raise enough negative publicity and diplomatic pressure to cause states to change their practices.

The International Court of Justice

We turn now to international courts. The International Court of Justice (ICJ) is the principal judicial organ of the UN.[41] It comprises 15 judges

---

[38] See, for example, Hans-Joachim Heintze, 'On the Relationship between Human Rights Law Protection and International Humanitarian Law' (2004) 856 *International Review of the Red Cross* 789, 798–9.
[39] See, for example, International Covenant on Civil and Political Rights, art 41; American Convention on Human Rights, arts 44–45.
[40] European Convention on the Protection of Human Rights and Fundamental Freedoms, art 34.
[41] United Nations Charter, art 92.

drawn from around the globe. The ICJ's jurisdiction is limited to litigation between states.[42] It has no jurisdiction over matters involving individuals. The ICJ's jurisdiction over a particular dispute depends on the consent of the states involved. States may elect to recognise the ICJ's jurisdiction in general or only for specific matters.[43] The consent-based nature of the ICJ's authority is a serious barrier to its effectiveness as an arbiter of international legal disputes.

Article 94(1) of the UN Charter stipulates that member states of the UN undertake to respect ICJ decisions to which they are parties. However, ICJ decisions do not bind states that are not parties. This is made clear in Article 59 of the ICJ Statute, which states that '[t]he decision of the Court has no binding force except between the parties and in respect of that particular case'. As mentioned above, there are two ways in which a state may consent to the jurisdiction of the ICJ. First, under Article 36(1) of the ICJ Statute, states may agree to refer a particular dispute or type of dispute to the Court. Second, under Article 36(2) (known as the 'Optional Clause'), states may agree in advance to the Court having general jurisdiction over any matters that may concern them.

Sixty-seven states have agreed to accept the ICJ's jurisdiction under Article 36(2) at the time of writing. However, most of them have issued conditional declarations that create exceptions for particular types of disputes. Another factor limiting the ICJ's jurisdiction is that the Court will not hear a dispute between consenting states where determining the issue would involve passing judgment on the rights of a third state who has not consented. This principle was famously recognised by the ICJ in the *Monetary Gold* case,[44] which involved a dispute over gold removed from Rome by Germany during the Second World War. The ICJ declined to hear the case because it would have involved passing comment on a legal dispute involving Albania, which did not recognise its jurisdiction.

The consent-based nature of the ICJ's jurisdiction presents a problem partly because, in practice, states that violate international law are likely to seek to avoid being bound by ICJ rulings. An example is provided by the case of *Nicaragua v United States*,[45] discussed previously in this chapter. The United States was desperate to avoid having the case heard

---

[42] Statute of the International Court of Justice, art 34. The only exception lies in the Court's power to provide advisory opinions. See Statute of the International Court of Justice, art 65.
[43] Statute of the International Court of Justice, art 36.
[44] *Monetary Gold Removed from Rome in 1943*, ICJ Judgment, 15 June 1953.
[45] *Nicaragua v United States (Merits)*, ICJ Judgment, 27 June 1986.

by the ICJ and went so far as to withdraw its acceptance of jurisdiction under Article 36(2). When the ICJ elected to hear the matter, the United States took no part in proceedings and later vetoed a draft UN Security Council Resolution calling on it to respect the outcome. As a result, the finding for Nicaragua proved unenforceable.

It is worth briefly exploring the role given to the UN Security Council in enforcing ICJ decisions.[46] Article 94(2) of the UN Charter provides that a state that has succeeded in litigation before the ICJ may request the assistance of the Security Council in enforcing the Court's orders if the other parties fail to comply. This is a useful provision, but it has its limits. Evidently, a state that is a permanent member of the Security Council can veto any attempt by the Council to enforce a judgment against it. This was why the Security Council proved unable to assist Nicaragua in the case discussed above.

Regional Tribunals

The ICJ is the most prominent international tribunal that adjudicates disputes between states. However, there are also various regional bodies. Examples include the Court of Justice of the European Union, the European Court of Human Rights and the Inter-American Court of Human Rights. We encountered some of these bodies previously in Chapter 6. As a general rule, regional courts such as those listed above are more effective in establishing jurisdiction and enforcing orders than the ICJ. These bodies can draw on local political and economic networks. For example, the European Courts draw effectiveness from the economic and political significance of the Council of Europe and the European Union.

However, the influence of these regional bodies is obviously geographically limited. They do not help in resolving disputes between states located in different geographical regions. Indeed, it could be argued that the increasing prominence of regional tribunals hinders the resolution of such disputes, by encouraging the emergence of distinctive regional interpretations of international norms. States from different regions may then find they are unable to resolve differences of opinion because they disagree on either the standards themselves or how they should be applied.

---

[46] For helpful discussion, see Attila Tanzi, 'Problems of Enforcement of Decisions of the International Court of Justice and the Law of the United Nations' (1995) 6 *European Journal of International Law* 539.

A TOOTHLESS TIGER?

It is sometimes said that due to issues such as the problem of consent, international law is a toothless tiger. It issues impressive aspirations and claims to legitimacy, but fails to back them up with enforcement. This line of argument has sometimes been used to support the conclusion that international law is not 'law' in the full sense of the term. The English legal theorist John Austin, for example, famously argued that international law is not 'law' properly so called, but rather a form of 'political morality'.[47] It is merely a collection of informal standards that states try to persuade one another to follow.

This perspective on international law, like Austin's theory of law generally, seems to assume that a hallmark of a fully-fledged legal system is the existence of effective formal methods of enforcement. Law, according to Austin, is essentially the commands of an omnipotent sovereign, backed up by sanctions.[48] However, this conception of law raises a number of important questions. Do all legal systems depend on formal sanctions for their effectiveness? Could there be law without police and the courts?[49]

There is good reason to think that law does not depend solely on sanctions for its effectiveness. After all, the total proportion of the population who ever appears in court for a criminal offence is fairly low. Does this mean other people are not subject to the law? A possible response to this line of argument might be that it is the *threat* of legal consequences that keeps people in line and stops them from committing violations. However, there are plenty of opportunities in everyday life to commit crimes without much fear of being caught. Nonetheless, most people continue to obey legal rules.

The legal philosopher HLA Hart argued in his influential work, *The Concept of Law*, that law does not gain its effectiveness from the threat of punishment, so much as the sense of obligation it imposes. The failure to appreciate this point, according to Hart, was the central failing in Austin's

---

[47] John Austin, *The Province of Jurisprudence Determined* (Weidenfeld and Nicolson 1954) 140–41.

[48] For an overview, see Jonathan Crowe, *Legal Theory* (Thomson Reuters 2009) 33–6.

[49] For discussion, see Gary Chartier, *Anarchy and Legal Order: Law and Politics for a Stateless Society* (CUP 2012); David Friedman, 'Anarchy and Efficient Law' in John Sanders and Jan Narveson (eds), *For and Against the State* (Rowman and Littlefield 1996).

theory of law.⁵⁰ People generally obey the law not purely out of fear of punishment, but because they feel a sense of duty to comply with social norms. The real test for the effectiveness of international law, from this perspective, is therefore not the availability of formal enforcement mechanisms, but whether states and individuals generally feel bound to take its rules seriously in their actions.

The social pressure exerted by the international community is, ultimately, the main reason states respect international law. Hart points out that something similar is true of law in general. People do not obey domestic law primarily because they fear being caught, but rather due to the sense of obligation that accompanies legal rules. The international court system for states is no doubt relatively toothless compared to many domestic legal systems. Nonetheless, it is important not to understate the effectiveness of informal mechanisms like diplomatic pressure, political negotiations and the efforts of non-governmental organisations in ensuring general compliance with international norms.

THE LIABILITY OF NON-STATE GROUPS

A further challenge for the effectiveness of international law concerns violations of global norms carried out by non-state groups. This issue holds particular importance for international humanitarian law, due to the widespread involvement of such groups in armed conflicts. The vast majority of contemporary armed conflicts involve one or more non-state parties. The position of these armed groups under the international law of armed conflict has long been ambiguous. It is sometimes assumed without much discussion that non-state parties to warfare are bound by humanitarian norms.⁵¹ However, there are difficult questions involved in explaining how this might be the case.⁵²

The main problem that arises in this context is that non-state groups cannot be parties to the Geneva Conventions or Additional Protocols.

---

[50] HLA Hart, *The Concept of Law* (Clarendon Press 1994) 90–1. For further discussion, see Jonathan Crowe, *Legal Theory* (Thomson Reuters 2009) ch 3.

[51] See, for example, *Nicaragua v United States (Merits)*, ICJ Judgment, 27 June 1986 [218]–[219].

[52] For helpful discussion, see Antonio Cassese, 'The Status of Rebels Under the 1977 Geneva Protocol on Non-International Armed Conflicts' (1981) 30 *International and Comparative Law Quarterly* 416; Sandesh Sivakumaran, 'Binding Armed Opposition Groups' (2006) 55 *International and Comparative Law Quarterly* 369.

160   *Principles of international humanitarian law*

This is true even of Additional Protocol II relating to non-international armed conflicts. Non-state armed groups are therefore technically not bound by the terms of those treaties. A number of possible explanations have been advanced as to why non-state groups might nonetheless be bound by at least some principles of international humanitarian law. The main suggestions have involved appeals to customary law, general principles of international law or the capacity of treaties to bind third parties. Each of these proposals has strengths and weaknesses.

We saw in Chapter 2 that customary international law, unlike treaty law, does not depend on consent of states. It is presumed to bind all members of the international community. It has sometimes been suggested that the binding character of customary international law extends not only to states, but also to non-state groups. Versions of this argument have been endorsed by the ICJ[53] and the Special Court for Sierra Leone.[54] The main shortcoming of this approach is that it means that non-state armed groups are only bound by those norms of international humanitarian law that have attained customary status. It is now well accepted that Common Article 3 of the Geneva Conventions represents customary law, but the same cannot be said of all parts of Additional Protocol II.[55]

The argument that non-state groups are bound by customary international law is sometimes augmented by reference to general principles of international law. The notion that fundamental humanitarian norms should be regarded as having the status of general principles of international law and are therefore binding regardless of their inclusion in treaties has found support from the ICJ[56] and the ICTY.[57] However, the nature and basis of general principles of international law continues to be debated.[58] It is doubtful whether this argument would have wider application than the appeal to customary law discussed above. It would likely be limited to the most basic humanitarian principles.

Finally, Cassese argues in an influential article that non-state groups

---

[53] *Nicaragua v United States (Merits)*, ICJ Judgment, 27 June 1986 [218].
[54] *Prosecutor v Kallon*, Special Court for Sierra Leone Decision on Jurisdiction, 13 March 2004 [47].
[55] See, for example, *Prosecutor v Tadić*, ICTY Appeals Chamber Decision on Jurisdiction, 2 October 1995 [98]; *Prosecutor v Akayesu*, International Criminal Tribunal for Rwanda Trial Chamber Judgment, 2 September 1998 [608]; *Prosecutor v Kallon*, Special Court for Sierra Leone Decision on Jurisdiction, 13 March 2004 [47].
[56] *Corfu Channel Case (Merits)*, ICJ Judgment, 9 April 1949, 22.
[57] *Prosecutor v Tadić*, ICTY Appeals Chamber Decision on Jurisdiction, 2 October 1995 [117].
[58] Ian Brownlie, *Principles of Public International Law* (OUP 2003) 15–19.

may be bound by international humanitarian law by virtue of the capacity of treaties to bind third parties.[59] Articles 35 and 36 of the Vienna Convention on the Law of Treaties (VCLT) state that third parties may obtain rights and obligations under a treaty if the parties to the treaty intend the third party to be bound and the third party agrees. It is debatable whether these provisions, themselves contained in a treaty, can be applied to non-state groups.[60] However, if they can, there is good reason to think that state parties to Common Article 3 and Additional Protocol II intended third parties involved in non-international armed conflicts to gain rights and obligations under the provisions.

The main limitation on this argument is that the treaty provisions in question will only be binding on third parties under the VCLT if the third parties agree. Article 35 of the VCLT, for example, states that a third party will only incur obligations under a treaty if the party accepts the obligations in writing. A non-state armed group could therefore potentially become bound by treaty provisions such as Common Article 3 and Additional Protocol II through this mechanism, but only if the group assented to the applicable rules. If the non-state group does not agree to be bound by the principles of international humanitarian law, it cannot be brought within the reach of the relevant treaties.

There is, of course, another way that non-state groups can be bound by humanitarian norms. This is through the adoption of those norms as part of the domestic law of the state or states within whose territory the groups are operating. If the rules of international humanitarian law have been incorporated into the domestic law of a particular state, as seems to be envisaged by Common Article 1 of the Geneva Conventions, they will apply to activities carried out by armed groups within that state's territory. It has further been suggested that states who are party to the Geneva Conventions and other relevant treaties thereby bind their subjects to respect the relevant norms, regardless of whether they have been explicitly incorporated into domestic legislation.[61]

The notion that non-state armed groups are bound by humanitarian norms through the legislative competence of states carries its own problems. Suppose a non-state armed group is engaged in battle with state forces within that state's territory. If the rebel group is defeated, its

---

[59] Antonio Cassese, 'The Status of Rebels Under the 1977 Geneva Protocol on Non-International Armed Conflicts' (1981) 30 *International and Comparative Law Quarterly* 416.

[60] Sandesh Sivakumaran, 'Binding Armed Opposition Groups' (2006) 55 *International and Comparative Law Quarterly* 369, 377.

[61] Ibid 384–5.

members could be prosecuted under domestic law for violations of the law of armed conflict that are recognised by the domestic legal system. However, the members of the group may well also be prosecuted for other domestic offences, such as treason or sedition, given that they lack the privilege against prosecution for participation in warfare enjoyed by recognised combatants in international armed conflicts.[62]

If the rebel group succeeds in defeating the state forces and assumes control of all or part of the state's territory, it may become bound by the state's treaty obligations under the rules of succession.[63] However, this may not cover its actions during the earlier stages of the armed conflict. There is no barrier in principle to a successful rebel force later applying domestic law to hold its members to account for violations of international humanitarian law, but there are obvious disincentives to do so. The underlying problem here is that relying on domestic law to implement humanitarian norms potentially strips them of the universality and generality implied by international law status. The recognition and enforcement of the norms may seem to lie at the victor's discretion.

Cassese notes in this context that 'what is at stake [. . .] is not whether rebels are subjects of domestic law, but their legal standing in *international law* – their status vis-à-vis both the lawful Government and third States and the international community at large'.[64] Others have argued it does not matter whether non-state groups are bound by humanitarian norms as a matter of domestic law or international law, as long as they are bound.[65] However, we have seen throughout this book that the legitimacy of the law of armed conflict depends significantly on its general recognition and acceptance by the international community. The universality of humanitarian law is undermined if its applicability turns out to depend on the legislative competence of specific state regimes.

The application to non-state groups of fundamental norms of international humanitarian law, such as those enshrined in Common Article 3, is relatively unproblematic due to their customary law status. However, it is less obvious how and to what degree non-state groups might be bound by

---

[62] See the discussion in Chapters 3 and 5.

[63] Compare Jean S Pictet et al (eds), *Commentary on the Geneva Conventions* (ICRC 1960) vol 3, 37; Liesbeth Zegveld, *The Accountability of Armed Opposition Groups in International Law* (CUP 2002) 26.

[64] Antonio Cassese, 'The Status of Rebels Under the 1977 Geneva Protocol on Non-International Armed Conflicts' (1981) 30 *International and Comparative Law Quarterly* 416, 429.

[65] Sandesh Sivakumaran, 'Binding Armed Opposition Groups' (2006) 55 *International and Comparative Law Quarterly* 369, 385–6.

the more detailed rules contained in treaties such as Additional Protocol II. The issue of whether members of non-state groups can be held to account for breaches of the law of armed conflict also raises the further question of whether and to what extent individuals can be held criminally responsible under international law. We will explore that topic in detail in the next chapter.

8. Liability of individuals

The previous chapter examined the ways in which states and non-state groups may be held responsible for violations of international humanitarian law. This chapter, by contrast, is concerned with the criminal responsibility of individuals for breaches of the law of armed conflict. There are some important historical and conceptual connections between international humanitarian law and international criminal law, but the two fields are far from synonymous. International crimes are not limited to violations of international humanitarian law, but also include acts such as genocide and crimes against humanity, which can be committed in either wartime or peacetime. Furthermore, not all violations of international humanitarian law give rise to individual criminal responsibility.

This chapter begins by considering the historical evolution of international criminal law. We will see that important developments in international criminal law have often arisen in response to violations of international law committed during armed conflicts. International criminal law and international humanitarian law have therefore often developed in tandem. Notable examples include the tribunals established to try war criminals following the Second World War, as well as the ad hoc tribunals created in the wake of the Yugoslavian and Rwandan conflicts. We will then examine the various offences that give rise to individual responsibility under international law, before turning to the different forms of criminal responsibility and the rules governing criminal proceedings.

INTERNATIONAL CRIMINAL LAW

International humanitarian law has traditionally been viewed as imposing obligations upon states. We saw in Chapter 1 that the traditional conception of warfare treated armed conflicts as conducted between two or more nations following formal declarations of hostilities. A significant shift in this picture occurred following the Second World War with the adoption of Common Article 3 of the Geneva Conventions, which brought non-international armed conflicts within the reach of international humanitarian law for the first time. This shift was accompanied by a growing recognition that states were not the only entities that could be held liable for violating the law of armed conflict. We saw in the previous chapter how Common Article 3 raised the prospect that international humanitarian law could be directly binding on non-state armed groups. The war crimes tribunals established following the Second World War represented another type of shift, insofar as they treated individuals as directly responsible for violations of humanitarian norms.

International criminal law is only one mechanism by which international humanitarian law is enforced today. It is arguably much less important in ensuring widespread respect for the laws of armed conflict than many of the mechanisms discussed in the previous chapter. However, the idea that a person might be held personally responsible for a violation of humanitarian norms is obviously a powerful incentive to observe these rules in practice. International criminal proceedings help to convey the message that individuals cannot escape direct accountability for wartime atrocities. They also play an important role in raising public awareness of humanitarian principles.

Early Developments

The earliest recorded international trial of an individual for violating humanitarian norms occurred in 1474. The defendant was Peter von Hagenbach, who had been appointed by the Duke of Burgundy to administer the city of Breisach, on the Upper Rhine. Hagenbach had been instructed to assert control over the city's citizens, in anticipation of an attack by the Duke's enemies. He carried out this order by inflicting atrocities on the local population, encouraging murder, rape and confiscation of property by his subordinates. When Breisach was occupied by a coalition of principalities opposed to the Duke of Burgundy, Hagenbach was convicted and sentenced to death by an ad hoc tribunal consisting of judges from the various coalition parties for violating the laws of God and humanity.[1]

A further notable attempt to hold individuals accountable for acts committed during armed conflict occurred during the American Civil War. We saw in Chapter 2 that President Abraham Lincoln's Lieber Code was an early attempt to codify the humanitarian principles governing land-based warfare. The Lieber Code made punishable wanton violence, destruction of property, robbery, rape and other similar acts committed

---

[1] Edoardo Greppi, 'The Evolution of Individual Criminal Responsibility under International Law' (1999) 835 *International Review of the Red Cross* 531.

in enemy territory. Following the end of the war, the Confederate commander responsible for a prisoner of war camp was convicted of ordering and committing torture and killing of prisoners.[2] However, no consistent measures were taken to impose individual responsibility for breaches of international humanitarian law until after the First World War.

Initial attempts to hold individuals accountable for violations of humanitarian norms following the First World War were not encouraging. The Treaty of Versailles provided for individuals associated with the losing powers – including Kaiser Wilhelm II – to be placed on trial for violations of the laws and customs of war.[3] However, the Kaiser avoided trial by fleeing to the Netherlands, which refused to extradite him. Other attempts to pursue those alleged to have violated humanitarian standards were also largely abortive. The German government refused to hand over military personnel whom the Allied powers wished to place on trial for violating international norms, so the Allies agreed to a compromise whereby the defendants would be tried by a German court in Leipzig.

The Allies provided German authorities with documents naming 896 individuals accused of violating the law of war, but a mere 12 defendants were originally listed for trial at Leipzig and only six were convicted. The heaviest sentence imposed was four years' imprisonment and, to make matters worse, the two defendants given the harshest penalties were allowed to escape soon after sentencing. These developments led the Allied representatives at the trials to leave in protest. Further trials conducted without any Allied presence yielded very few convictions.

The Nuremberg Tribunal

Following the Second World War, the victorious nations were determined to bring individual perpetrators of wartime atrocities to justice, while avoiding the problems that characterised the Leipzig experience. With this in mind, representatives of the Allied nations gathered in London in 1945 to discuss the creation of an International Military Tribunal to conduct the trials of Nazi officials accused of violating the law of war. Preliminary discussions about establishing such an institution had been continuing since 1942.

The meeting culminated in an agreement formally establishing the

---

[2] Weston D Burnett, 'Command Responsibility and a Case Study of the Criminal Responsibility of Israeli Military Commanders for the Pogrom at Shatila and Sabra' (1985) 107 *Military Law Review* 71, 79.

[3] Treaty of Versailles, arts 227–9.

International Military Tribunal (IMT). Annexed to the agreement was a Charter describing the body's constitution, jurisdiction and principles of operation. The procedures provided for in the Charter represent a compromise between the inquisitorial legal frameworks of France and Russia and the adversarial legal systems of Britain and the United States, although some of the fundamental elements of the Anglo-American approach, such as the presumption of innocence, were adopted. Article 6 of the IMT Charter lists three categories of international crimes. The taxonomy reflected in that provision has been influential in the development of international criminal law. The crimes outlined in Article 6 are as follows:

- 'crimes against peace', constituted by involvement in the planning, initiation or waging of an illegal war of aggression;
- 'war crimes', constituted by violations of the laws and customs governing the conduct of armed conflicts; and
- 'crimes against humanity', involving inhuman acts against a civilian population, such as extermination, enslavement or political, racial or religious persecution.

It bears noting that only the second of these three categories is unambiguously concerned with international humanitarian law (or what we described in Chapter 1 as the *jus in bello*). The crimes of aggression envisaged in the first category relate to the *jus ad bellum* (the body of law outlining when an armed conflict may legitimately be commenced). In regard to the third category, although Article 6 of the IMT Charter requires crimes against humanity to be committed 'before or during the war', it has since become accepted that such offences may be committed in either wartime or peacetime.[4]

The IMT subsequently presided over the notorious trial of major German war criminals conducted between 1945 and 1946 in Nuremberg, Germany, although its mandate was not limited to those proceedings. Twenty-four Nazi leaders were ultimately charged at Nuremberg. Twenty-two of these stood trial, with 19 being convicted and 12 of those receiving the death sentence.[5] The Tribunal's judgment is notable for the emphasis placed on the idea that wars are ultimately conducted by individuals, not

---

[4] See, for example, *Prosecutor v Kunarac*, International Criminal Tribunal for the Former Yugoslavia (ICTY) Trial Chamber Judgment, 22 February 2001 [183]; *Prosecutor v Kunarac*, ICTY Appeals Chamber Judgment, 12 June 2002 [83].

[5] *Trial of Major German War Criminals*, International Military Tribunal Judgment, 1 October 1946.

merely by states. Article 7 of the IMT Charter emphasises that an individual cannot avoid responsibility for a crime on the basis that she or he held an official post and was pursuing state policy. Article 8, meanwhile, provides that it is not exculpatory that a defendant was following orders from her or his government or a superior officer (the so-called 'Nuremberg defence').

The Nuremberg trials were important in establishing the body of jurisprudence that developed over time into the contemporary principles of individual criminal responsibility under international law. The United Nations (UN) General Assembly adopted Resolution 95(I) of 1946 affirming the principles of international law recognised by the IMT Charter and the Nuremberg judgment. The General Assembly also committed to have those principles codified by the International Law Commission (ILC).[6] This resulted in a list of seven 'Nuremberg principles' formulated by the ILC in 1950.[7] The principles reiterated the three categories of crimes set out in Article 6 of the IMT Charter. They also emphasised that a person is not relieved of criminal responsibility by virtue of the fact that she or he is pursuing official state policy or acting in accordance with superior orders.

Post-Nuremberg Trials

The notion of individual criminal responsibility for violations of international humanitarian law was also considered in several other prosecutions of Axis officials for violations of humanitarian norms during the Second World War, although these trials received less publicity than the Nuremberg proceedings. Prominent examples include the trials conducted by the International Military Tribunal for the Far East, which was based in Tokyo between 1945 and 1948 and focused on charges against high-ranking Japanese officials, and United States military tribunals in locations such as Nuremberg and Manila.

These proceedings were perhaps most significant for their contribution to the development of principles governing the responsibility of military commanders for crimes committed by their subordinates. The proposition that military officials may be subject to criminal sanctions for failing to prevent personnel under their command from breaching international humanitarian law was first relied upon in the trial of the Japanese General

---

[6] See also United Nations General Assembly Resolution 177(II) of 1950.
[7] International Law Commission, *Principles of International Law Recognized in the Charter of the Nuremberg Tribunal and in the Judgment of the Tribunal* (ILC 1950).

Tomoyuki Yamashita before a United States Military Commission in Manila.[8] The Commission's finding that Yamashita must have known or had reason to know of the atrocities committed by troops under his control provided the basis for contemporary principles of command responsibility, discussed in detail below.

The principles relating to command responsibility for violations of international humanitarian law were subsequently elaborated by the United States Military Tribunal at Nuremberg.[9] In the *High Command* case, the Tribunal noted that a commander is not to be held automatically responsible for all acts performed by subordinates, but liability will arise where the commander either ordered violations or failed to properly supervise subordinates to the level of criminal negligence.[10]

Another significant judgment of the United States Military Tribunal was the *Hostage* case, which involved the prosecution of Field Marshal Wilhelm List and 11 other officers alleged to be responsible for crimes committed by subordinates in Albania, Greece, Norway and Yugoslavia.[11] It was argued during the trial that the defendants did not know about the atrocities, even though they had been covered in reports to headquarters. The Tribunal found that a commander will not ordinarily be allowed to deny knowledge of acts occurring within the territory for which she or he is responsible or reports received at headquarters. The *Hostage* case therefore established the principle that an operational commander cannot avoid responsibility by claiming not to have personal knowledge of systematic crimes occurring within the field of command.[12] The subsequent development of the doctrine of command responsibility is discussed later in this chapter.

A further notable criminal prosecution arising from the Second World War was the trial of Adolf Eichmann by Israel in 1961.[13] Eichmann, who

---

[8] *Trial of General Tomoyuki Yamashita*, United States Military Commission Judgment, 7 December 1945. See also *In re Yamashita* 327 US 1 (1946).

[9] For more detail on the development of command responsibility, see *Prosecutor v Delalic*, ICTY Trial Chamber Judgment, 16 November 1998 [333]–[342].

[10] *United States v Wilhelm Von Leeb*, United States Military Tribunal Judgment, 27 October 1948.

[11] *United States v Wilhelm List*, United States Military Tribunal Judgment, 19 February 1948.

[12] For discussion of this case see Weston D Burnett, 'Command Responsibility and a Case Study of the Criminal Responsibility of Israeli Military Commanders for the Pogrom at Shatila and Sabra' (1985) *Military Law Review* 71, 109–13.

[13] *Attorney-General of the Government of Israel v Eichmann*, District Court of Jerusalem Judgment, 11 December 1961; *Attorney-General of the Government of*

had been responsible for administering a programme of genocide against the Jewish people during the war, was kidnapped in Argentina and taken back to Israel to face trial for war crimes, crimes against humanity and crimes against the Jewish people (genocide). The Israeli court found that it was able to try Eichmann on the basis of the principle of *universal jurisdiction*, according to which all states are empowered to try serious violations of international norms, regardless of where the acts occurred and the nationality of the perpetrators. The court also followed the example of the IMT in rejecting Eichmann's argument that he was merely following orders. Eichmann was ultimately convicted on all charges and sentenced to death.

The *Eichmann* decision stands as an important affirmation of the capacity of states to prosecute foreign nationals for serious breaches of international law committed outside the prosecuting state's borders. The traditional bases for a state to claim jurisdiction over a criminal offence are where the crime occurs in the state's territory, the perpetrator or victim is a national of the state or the crime directly harms the state's national security or other fundamental interests.[14] The principle of universal jurisdiction affirms that some crimes are of such general concern to the international community that any state may exercise jurisdiction over them, even in the absence of these traditional connections.

It is now widely accepted that universal jurisdiction exists with respect to serious international offences such as crimes against humanity, war crimes and genocide.[15] However, the principle remains controversial in some quarters due to its implications for the sovereignty of other states that may have an interest in either the crime or the perpetrator.[16] It is worth noting in this context that each of the Geneva Conventions of 1949 places an obligation on state parties to criminalise certain grave breaches of international humanitarian law and bring the perpetrators of such violations, 'regardless of their nationality', before the domestic legal system.[17] These provisions provide a strong foundation for the exercise of universal jurisdiction where war crimes are concerned.

Israel v Eichmann, Supreme Court of Israel Judgment, 29 May 1962. For a famous report and reflection on the case, see Hannah Arendt, *Eichmann in Jerusalem: A Report on the Banality of Evil* (Penguin 1994).

[14] Ian Brownlie, *Principles of Public International Law* (OUP 2003) 299–305.
[15] Ibid 303–4.
[16] See, for example, Henry Kissinger, 'The Pitfalls of Universal Jurisdiction' (2001) 80 *Foreign Affairs* 86.
[17] Geneva Convention I, art 49; Geneva Convention II, art 50; Geneva Convention III, art 129; Geneva Convention IV, art 146. See also Convention

Contemporary Tribunals

More recently, international war crimes have been tried by the International Criminal Tribunal for the Former Yugoslavia (ICTY) and the International Criminal Tribunal for Rwanda (ICTR), which were established during the 1990s to deal with violations of international norms arising specifically from conflicts in those regions. Those bodies have made important contributions in developing the principles governing international criminal jurisdiction in relation to humanitarian standards. In particular, the ICTY has now firmly established that persons may be criminally responsible for violations of international humanitarian law perpetrated in the context of non-international armed conflicts.[18]

Both the ICTY and the ICTR were established by the UN Security Council relying on its powers under Chapter VII of the UN Charter 'to maintain or restore international peace and security'[19] and the jurisdiction of both bodies is prescribed by statute. The jurisdiction of the ICTY extends to crimes committed in both international and non-international conflicts, while the ICTR is confined to crimes committed in internal conflicts.[20] This reflects the purely internal character of the conflict in Rwanda, as opposed to the mixed nature of the conflict that was waged in the former Yugoslavia.[21]

A number of other ad hoc tribunals have been established cooperatively by national authorities and the UN to try persons charged with offences in specific contexts. An example is the Extraordinary Chambers in the Courts of Cambodia, established to try senior leaders and those most responsible for atrocities during the rule of the Khmer Rouge in Cambodia between 1975 and 1979. The constitution and rules of the tribunal were created by negotiation between Cambodian authorities and the UN and finalised in 2003. The Extraordinary Chambers have jurisdiction in relation to

---

against Torture and Other Cruel, Inhuman or Degrading Treatment or Punishment, arts 5–7.

[18] See *Prosecutor v Tadić*, ICTY Appeals Chamber Decision on Jurisdiction, 2 October 1995 [94]–[137].

[19] United Nations Charter, art 39.

[20] Statute of the International Criminal Tribunal for the Former Yugoslavia, arts 1–5; Statute of the International Criminal Tribunal for Rwanda, arts 1–4.

[21] The mixed character of the Yugoslavian conflict was discussed in Chapter 1. See *Prosecutor v Tadić*, ICTY Appeals Chamber Decision on Jurisdiction, 2 October 1995 [77].

genocide, crimes against humanity, grave breaches of the law of armed conflict and other war crimes.[22]

Similarly, the Special Court for Sierra Leone was established after negotiations between the Sierra Leone government and the UN to prosecute those most responsible for serious violations of both international humanitarian law and Sierra Leonean law committed in the country since November 1996. The Special Court was established by treaty in 2002 and commenced proceedings the following year. It has concurrent jurisdiction with domestic courts and is presided over by both national and foreign judges.[23] The Appeals Chamber of the Special Court handed down an important decision in 2004 finding that amnesties granted to persons responsible for criminal offences during the conflict were no bar to prosecution before the tribunal.[24] Former Liberian President Charles Taylor was convicted by the Special Court in 2012 for 11 counts of crimes against humanity and war crimes, including rape and sexual slavery as crimes against humanity.[25] Taylor was the first African head of state to be convicted of war crimes by an international criminal tribunal.

A third example of an ad hoc tribunal established cooperatively by national authorities and the UN is the Special Tribunal established by the UN Transitional Administration in East Timor (UNTAET) to try persons accused of committing crimes in East Timor in 1999. The Special Panels for Serious Crimes were established as part of the District Court of Dili; one East Timorese judge and two foreign judges were included on each panel. These Special Panels had jurisdiction in respect of genocide, crimes against humanity, war crimes, torture and specified violations of the Indonesian Penal Code. Following East Timorese independence in May 2002, the Special Panels initially continued to operate under the authority of the East Timorese government, but were suspended in 2005.

More recently, the Special Tribunal for Lebanon was inaugurated on 1 March 2009. It differs somewhat from the other tribunals discussed above in the specificity of its initial mandate: to try those accused of carrying out one specific attack in Beirut on 14 February 2005 that killed 23 people,

---

[22] Law on the Establishment of Extraordinary Chambers in the Courts of Cambodia, arts 4–8.

[23] Statute for the Special Court of Sierra Leone, arts 8, 12.

[24] *Prosecutor v Kallon and Kamara*, Special Court for Sierra Leone (SCSL) Appeals Chamber Decision on Jurisdiction, 13 March 2004. For discussion, see Simon M Meisenberg, 'Legality of Amnesties in International Humanitarian Law: The Lomé Amnesty Decision of the Special Court for Sierra Leone' (2004) 856 *International Review of the Red Cross* 837.

[25] *Prosecutor v Taylor*, SCSL Trial Chamber Judgment, 18 May 2012.

including the former Prime Minister of Lebanon, Rafiq Hariri. The Special Tribunal is established by agreement between the Lebanese government and the UN, but applies Lebanese criminal law.[26] The Appeals Chamber of the Special Tribunal recently rejected arguments from representatives for the four current defendants challenging the legality and jurisdiction of the body.[27]

The International Criminal Court

The most significant development in international criminal jurisdiction in recent years has been the establishment of a permanent International Criminal Court (ICC). The Court promises to play a central role in conducting future criminal trials for violations of international humanitarian law. The Rome Statute, the treaty that establishes the Court and governs its operation, represents an important attempt to capture many of the current principles relating to international criminal responsibility.

The Rome Statute was adopted in 1998. Article 126 requires 60 ratifications for the Statute to enter into force. This threshold was reached in early 2002. The ICC's structure, jurisdiction and functions are set out in the Rome Statute and regulations adopted by judges of the court, together with two other key legal documents: the Rules of Procedure and Evidence and the Elements of Crimes. Article 11 of the Rome Statute provides that the ICC only has jurisdiction over offences committed after it entered into force. This has obviously limited the cases tried by the body to date.

The Rome Statute has been ratified by 121 states at the time of writing. Notable states not to have ratified the Statute include the United States, China and Russia. The number of state ratifications is crucial to the ICC's effectiveness. Article 12 of the Rome Statute provides that the Court's jurisdiction extends only to cases where the accused is a national of a state that has ratified the Statute or which involve acts committed on the territory of such a state. The United States has been particularly vocal in its opposition to the ICC. Its main concern appears to be that politically motivated prosecutions may be commenced against United States nationals, although there are significant safeguards in the Rome Statute to prevent this from occurring. One such safeguard is the *principle of complementarity* enshrined in Article 17 of the Rome Statute, which gives domestic authorities priority in the exercise of jurisdiction. The ICC is

---

[26] Statute of the Special Tribunal for Lebanon, art 2.
[27] *Prosecutor v Ayyash*, Special Tribunal for Lebanon Appeals Chamber Decision on Jurisdiction, 24 October 2012.

barred from hearing cases that fall within the jurisdiction of a state, unless the state is genuinely unwilling or unable to prosecute.

The principle of complementarity represents a complex and delicate compromise between the demands of international justice and state sovereignty.[28] Its practical effect may be that states reluctant to have their nationals prosecuted by the ICC are able to head off proceedings by claiming that they are taking action against alleged perpetrators. Nonetheless, the United States appears unpersuaded that the principle affords sufficient protection against its nationals being brought before the ICC without its consent. Nationals of states who are not party to the Rome Statute may be prosecuted by the ICC if they commit crimes on the territory of a party state. However, the United States has lobbied a number of other states to sign bilateral agreements pledging not to refer cases involving its nationals to the ICC. These agreements are effective under Article 98 of the Rome Statute concerning obligations to third parties, but they clearly undermine the ICC's effectiveness.

INTERNATIONAL CRIMES

Article 5 of the Rome Statute sets out the crimes over which the ICC has jurisdiction. These are the crime of genocide, crimes against humanity, war crimes and the crime of aggression. The taxonomy of international criminal offences enumerated in the Rome Statute effectively incorporates the three categories outlined in Article 6 of the IMT Charter (namely, crimes of aggression, war crimes and crimes against humanity), although the nature and scope of those offences have evolved considerably since 1945.

The Rome Statute also recognises a fourth category of offences relating to genocide. The crime of genocide, like the category of crimes against humanity recognised in the IMT Charter, can be committed in either wartime or peacetime. The choice of crimes for inclusion in the Rome Statute was guided by the aim of selecting norms that were not only part of customary international law, but also accepted as giving rise to individual criminal responsibility.[29] Many provisions of the Rome Statute are there-

---

[28] For discussion, see John T Holmes, 'The Principle of Complementarity' in RS Lee (ed), *The International Criminal Court: The Making of the Rome Statute* (Kluwer 1999).

[29] H von Hebel and D Robinson, 'Crimes within the Jurisdiction of the Court' in RS Lee (ed), *The International Criminal Court: The Making of the Rome Statute* (Kluwer 1999).

fore viewed as codifying or crystallising the customary law position.[30] The following sections will consider each of the categories of crimes recognised in the Rome Statute in greater detail.

The Crime of Genocide

The IMT Charter did not include any reference to genocide. Many of the Nazi officials tried at Nuremberg were no doubt guilty of genocide, but were instead convicted of crimes against humanity. However, genocide was identified as a criminal act by the UN General Assembly in 1946[31] and this was followed by the adoption of the Convention on the Prevention and Punishment of the Crime of Genocide in 1948. The elements of the crime of genocide are outlined in Article 6 of the Rome Statute.

The definition of genocide in Article 6 has two main components. The first component involves an act of killing, causing serious physical or mental harm, inflicting adverse life conditions, preventing births or removing children from a population. This is the *actus reus* or physical element of the offence. The second component is that the act in question be carried out with the intent to destroy, in whole or in part, a national, ethnic, racial or religious group. This is the *mens rea* or fault element of the crime. Article 6 largely reflects the definition of genocide in Article 2 of the 1948 Genocide Convention.[32]

The ICC Elements of Crimes were adopted by the Assembly of States Parties to the Rome Statute in 2002 and subsequently amended at the 2010 Review Conference in Kampala, Uganda. This document seeks to supplement the Rome Statute by listing the elements of the distinct crimes detailed in its provisions. Elements are listed, for example, for the crimes of genocide by killing, genocide by causing serious bodily harm and genocide by imposing measures intended to prevent births. The Elements of Crimes require that each specific type of conduct that can constitute genocide be committed against persons belonging to a national, racial, ethnic or religious group and that the perpetrator carry out the conduct with the intent to destroy the group, in whole or in part. They also require

---

[30] For discussion of whether the Rome Statute's inclusion of the war crime of child recruitment codified customary international law, see *Prosecutor v Sam Hinga Norman*, Special Court for Sierra Leone Appeals Chamber Decision on Jurisdiction, 31 May 2004 [32]–[33].

[31] United Nations General Assembly Resolution 96(I) of 1946.

[32] See also Statute of the International Criminal Tribunal for the Former Yugoslavia, art 4; Statute of the International Criminal Tribunal for Rwanda, art 2; Draft Code of Crimes against the Peace and Security of Mankind, art 17.

that the conduct take place in the 'context of a manifest pattern of similar conduct directed against that group or was conduct that could itself effect' the required level of destruction.[33]

A central issue raised by the definition of genocide is how a national, racial, ethnic or religious group is to be defined. The ICC Pre-Trial Chamber considered in 2009 whether an arrest warrant should be issued for Sudanese President Omar Al Bashir on suspicion of involvement in genocide. The Chamber found that although the targeted groups – the Fur, Masalit and Zaghawa – were not national, racial or religious groups, there were reasonable grounds to believe that they were 'ethnic groups' as each had its own language, tribal customs and traditional links to land.[34] The Chamber initially held that there was insufficient evidence that the Sudanese government had acted with intention to destroy those groups in whole or in part and therefore refused a warrant for genocide, although a warrant was issued for crimes against humanity and war crimes. However, that decision was overturned on appeal[35] and a warrant for genocide has since been issued.

There is also a deeper question here as to why the offence of genocide should be limited to the destruction of national, ethnic, racial and religious groups, rather than other social, cultural or political clusters. For example, under the current definition, extermination of a group based on sexuality would not constitute genocide. A question also arises about the meaning to be given to the words 'in whole or in part'. Clearly, the harm inflicted upon the group must pass a certain threshold in order to be characterised as genocide: inflicting harm on an individual or small group within the population will not suffice. However, it is unclear how much of a group must be targeted before the threshold is reached. If members of a national or ethnic group are targeted only within a particular geographical region, is that sufficient to manifest intention to destroy the group 'in whole or in part'?

This issue was considered by the ICTY in *Prosecutor v Krstić*. The perpetrators in that case had implemented a policy of killing all Bosnian men in the Srebrenica area. They argued that this was not genocide, since they targeted only men from a specific region and not Bosnians in general. The ICTY Trial Chamber and Appeals Chamber both rejected this argument. The Appeals Chamber found that what is required is an intention to

---

[33] International Criminal Court, *Elements of Crimes* (ICC 2011) 2.
[34] *Prosecutor v Al Bashir*, ICC Pre-Trial Chamber Decision on the Prosecution's Application for a Warrant of Arrest, 4 March 2009 [135]–[136].
[35] *Prosecutor v Al Bashir*, ICC Appeals Chamber Judgment on the Appeal of the Prosecutor, 3 February 2010.

destroy 'a substantial part' of the group such as to impact on the group as a whole.[36] Targeting Bosnian men within a certain region was indicative of such an intention. It remains unclear, however, how far this principle might extend in other cases.

Crimes Against Humanity

A definition of crimes against humanity is found in Article 7 of the Rome Statute. Crimes against humanity include a variety of acts carried out on a widespread or systematic basis against a civilian population. The specific acts covered by the definition are murder or extermination; enslavement; deportation or forcible transfer; imprisonment or deprivation of liberty; torture; rape; sexual slavery; enforced prostitution; enforced pregnancy; enforced sterilisation or other serious sexual violence; persecution of particular groups; enforced disappearance; apartheid; and other inhumane acts intentionally causing great suffering or mental or physical injury. The conduct in question must take place in the context of an attack that is either *widespread* in terms of its scale and number of victims or *systematic* in terms of the degree of preparation, strategy and planning involved. The perpetrator of the act must also be shown to have knowledge of its widespread or systematic context.

An 'attack directed against any civilian population' is defined in the Rome Statute as 'a course of conduct involving the multiple commission of [any of the acts referred to above] against any civilian population, pursuant to or in furtherance of a State or organizational policy to commit such attack'.[37] This requires that the attack against the civilian population be actively promoted or encouraged by the state or organisation. The absence of governmental or organisational action to prevent the attack cannot, of itself, be used to infer the existence of such a policy.[38] An attack is widespread if there is 'massive, frequent, large scale action, carried out collectively with considerable seriousness and directed against a multiplicity of victims'.[39] It is systematic if it is 'thoroughly organised and following a regular pattern on the basis of a common policy involving substantial

---

[36] *Prosecutor v Krstic*, ICTY Appeals Chamber Judgment, 19 April 2004 [8]–[12]. See also *Prosecutor v Krstić*, ICTY Trial Chamber Judgment, 2 August 2001 [590].
[37] Statute of the International Criminal Court, art 7(2)(a).
[38] International Criminal Court, *Elements of Crimes* (ICC 2011) 5 n.
[39] *Prosecutor v Akayesu*, International Criminal Tribunal for Rwanda (ICTR) Trial Chamber Judgment, 2 September 1998 [580].

[. . .] resources'.⁴⁰ The existence of a political objective, use of public resources and involvement of high-level political or military officials are relevant in assessing whether an attack meets this threshold.⁴¹

Finally, the offender must have knowledge of the wider context for her or his actions and be carrying them out as part of the wider attack. This requirement therefore excludes isolated acts carried out for purely personal reasons.⁴² The jurisprudence of the ICTY suggests that it is not necessary that the attack be carried out pursuant to a policy or plan.⁴³ However, as noted above, the Rome Statute specifically defines an attack in this context to be a course of conduct pursuant to state or organisational policy. Crimes against humanity can only be prosecuted under the ICTY Statute if committed in the context of an armed conflict, but this is not a requirement under the Rome Statute.⁴⁴

An important recent development in international criminal law has been the recognition that sexual violence committed in the context of a widespread or systematic attack against the civilian population will amount to a crime against humanity. Rape or sexual violence may also amount to genocide if carried out with the intention of destroying a racial, religious or ethnic group.⁴⁵ In the ICTY case of *Prosecutor v Kunarac*,⁴⁶ an international criminal tribunal dealt for the first time with a series of charges dealing exclusively with crimes of sexual violence. The defendants were convicted of rape, torture and enslavement as crimes against humanity on the basis of a campaign of sexual violence carried out against Bosnian Muslim women in the context of the Yugoslavian conflict.⁴⁷ No charges of genocide were brought, although there was evidence of ethnic cleansing as a motive for the attacks.

---

⁴⁰ Ibid.
⁴¹ *Prosecutor v Blaskic*, ICTY Trial Chamber Judgment, 3 March 2000 [203].
⁴² *Prosecutor v Kayishema*, ICTR Trial Chamber Judgment, 21 May 1999 [133]–[134].
⁴³ *Prosecutor v Kunarac*, ICTY Appeals Chamber Judgment, 12 June 2002 [98].
⁴⁴ Statute of the International Criminal Tribunal for the Former Yugoslavia, art 5. See also *Prosecutor v Kunarac*, ICTY Appeals Chamber Judgment, 12 June 2002 [82]–[83].
⁴⁵ *Prosecutor v Furundzija*, ICTY Trial Chamber Judgment, 10 December 1998 [172].
⁴⁶ *Prosecutor v Kunarac*, ICTY Trial Chamber Judgment, 22 February 2001.
⁴⁷ For a more recent case involving rape and sexual slavery as crimes against humanity, see *Prosecutor v Taylor*, SCSL Trial Chamber Judgment, 18 May 2012.

War Crimes

War crimes can be generally defined as grave or serious breaches of humanitarian law.[48] We saw previously in this chapter that each of the Geneva Conventions confers on parties a duty to criminalise certain grave breaches of humanitarian norms and bring the perpetrators to justice.[49] It is well accepted that not every breach of international humanitarian law gives rise to individual criminal responsibility; the duty to criminalise breaches therefore only applies to serious violations. There is no requirement that war crimes be widespread or systematic as for crimes against humanity, although Article 8 of the Rome Statute envisages that prosecutions by the ICC will focus on war crimes committed 'as a part of a plan or policy or as part of a large-scale commission of such crimes'.

War crimes, unlike genocide and crimes against humanity, can only occur in the context of an armed conflict. We saw in Chapter 1 that this requirement entails not just that an armed conflict be in existence at the time the act was committed, but also that the conflict is connected with the act in the sense that it helps to provide the perpetrator with motive or opportunity. In the words of the ICTY Appeals Chamber: 'The existence of an armed conflict must, at a minimum, have played a substantial part in the perpetrator's ability to commit [the crime, the] decision to commit it, the manner in which it was committed or the purpose for which it was committed.'[50] The list of war crimes included in the Rome Statute significantly expands on the crimes recognised in Article 6 of the IMT Charter. Article 8 of the Rome Statute lists four distinct categories of war crimes:

- grave breaches of the Geneva Conventions;
- other serious violations of the laws and customs of international armed conflict;
- serious violations of Common Article 3 of the Geneva Conventions applicable in non-international armed conflicts;
- other serious violations of the laws and customs of non-international armed conflict.

The Rome Statute lists a number of war crimes as constituting grave breaches of the Geneva Conventions. These are wilful killing; torture or

---

[48] Compare Jean-Marie Henckaerts and Louise Doswald-Beck, *Customary International Humanitarian Law* (CUP 2005) rule 156.
[49] Geneva Convention I, arts 49–50; Geneva Convention II, arts 50–51; Geneva Convention III, arts 129–30; Geneva Convention IV, arts 146–147.
[50] *Prosecutor v Kunarac*, ICTY Appeals Chamber Judgment, 12 June 2002 [58].

inhuman treatment; wilfully causing great suffering or injury; extensive, wanton destruction of property not justified by military necessity; forced enlistment; depriving a prisoner of war or other protected person of the right to a fair trial; unlawful deportation or confinement; and taking hostages.[51] There is also a much longer list of serious violations of the laws and customs of international armed conflict. These include attacking civilian populations and objects; attacking humanitarian missions; indiscriminate and disproportionate attacks; attacking a combatant who is *hors de combat*; perfidy and forbidden orders; using prohibited weapons; outrages upon personal dignity, rape and sexual violence; attacking objects bearing a protected emblem; and enlisting or conscripting children under 15 years of age.

The remaining war crimes included in the Rome Statute are offences that occur in the context of non-international armed conflicts. Violations of Common Article 3 of the Geneva Conventions include violence to life and person, outrages upon personal dignity (including humiliating and degrading treatment), taking hostages and passing sentences without due process. The category of other serious violations of the law and customs of war in non-international conflicts includes some of the same offences as listed for international conflicts, but there is no mention of topics such as the obligations of occupying powers, perfidy or indiscriminate and disproportionate attacks. The list of serious violations in non-international conflicts also omits the specific references to prohibited weapons found in the list applicable in international conflicts. A proposal to add the use of poisonous weapons and bullets that expand or flatten easily in the body to the former list was adopted by state parties in 2010 but has so far been ratified by only two states.

Difficult issues may sometimes arise as to whether a war crime was committed in the context of an international or non-international armed conflict, particularly where a riot or other disturbance escalates to the status of an armed conflict or a non-international conflict becomes internationalised at a certain point in its history. It is not a prerequisite for a charge of war crimes that the perpetrator conduct an assessment as to the existence of an armed conflict or its character, but only that the perpetrator be aware of the factual circumstances that establish the existence of the conflict.[52] The legal consequences of those circumstances are a matter for the tribunal to determine.

---

[51] See also Statute of the International Criminal Tribunal for the Former Yugoslavia, art 2.

[52] International Criminal Court, *Elements of Crimes* (ICC 2011) 13.

Crimes of Aggression

Crimes of aggression are the fourth category of crimes recognised under the Rome Statute. The concept is similar to the crimes against peace mentioned in Article 6 of the IMT Charter. However, the Rome Statute leaves this category undefined. The challenge of formulating a generally acceptable definition of crimes of aggression proved too great for agreement to be reached prior to the adoption of the Rome Statute in 1998. A working group was therefore established in 2002 to agree on a definition for subsequent adoption by state parties. The outcome of this process was endorsed by state parties at the Review Conference in 2010, but so far only one state has ratified the provision.

The definition of crimes against aggression adopted at the Review Conference refers to 'the planning, preparation, initiation or execution, by a person in a position effectively to exercise control over or to direct the political or military action of a State, of an act of aggression which, by its character, gravity and scale, constitutes a manifest violation of the Charter of the United Nations'.[53] An 'act of aggression' is defined as 'the use of armed force by a State against the sovereignty, territorial integrity or political independence of another State, or in any other manner inconsistent with the Charter of the United Nations', including by armed invasion, military occupation, bombardment, blockade or attacks on military forces on land or at sea. The definition also covers a state that allows a second state to use its territory for perpetrating an act of aggression against a third state.

This definition goes some way towards clarifying the scope of crimes against aggression, but it leaves significant scope for interpretation. A great deal depends on whether a military intervention is determined to be consistent with the UN Charter. The scope of military action authorised by the UN Charter is itself controversial, as demonstrated by the complex debates over the legality of the United States-led invasion of Iraq in 2003.[54] The basic position under the UN Charter is that the use of force by states is prohibited, except in cases of self-defence or collective action authorised by the Security Council.[55] The apparent lack of any basis for humanitarian intervention under this framework has led to criticisms over

---

[53] Statute of the International Criminal Court, art 8 *bis*.
[54] See, for example, Sean D Murphy, 'Assessing the Legality of Invading Iraq' (2004) 92 *Georgetown Law Journal* 173; John Yoo, 'International Law and the War in Iraq' (2003) 97 *American Journal of International Law* 563.
[55] United Nations Charter, arts 2(4), 42, 51.

its lack of flexibility.[56] The continuing controversy over the UN Charter, along with worries by states about how the definition of crimes of aggression may be interpreted and applied, no doubt helps to explain the low number of ratifications to date.

Other Crimes

There are a handful of other international crimes recognised by segments of the international community that are not covered in the provisions of the Rome Statute. These include crimes such as piracy, slavery, drug trafficking and terrorism. There is, however, some overlap between these crimes and offences recognised in the Rome Statute. For example, slavery or terrorism would constitute crimes against humanity if committed in the context of a widespread or systematic attack upon a civilian population. The *Kunarac* case discussed above provides an example of enslavement as a crime against humanity.[57] These offences could also constitute war crimes if committed during an armed conflict.

CRIMINAL RESPONSIBILITY

There are three basic forms of criminal responsibility recognised under international law. *Individual responsibility* is the responsibility individuals bear for participating in a crime either as a principal offender or in a secondary capacity such as aiding and abetting. *Command responsibility* is the type of responsibility held by those in positions of command or authority in relation to acts committed by their subordinates. Finally, *inchoate responsibility* is a type of criminal responsibility common to a range of domestic legal systems. It concerns the situation where the defendant has incited, attempted or conspired with others to commit an offence, but the offence has not been fully completed.

Individual Responsibility

Individual responsibility in its simplest form covers the situation where a perpetrator personally commits an offence. Article 25(2) of the Rome

---

[56] For a useful discussion, see Jean-Pierre L Fonteyne, 'The Customary International Law Doctrine of Humanitarian Intervention: Its Current Validity under the UN Charter' (1974) 4 *California Western International Law Journal* 203.
[57] *Prosecutor v Kunarac*, ICTY Trial Chamber Judgment, 22 February 2001.

Statute provides that any person who commits a crime within the ICC's jurisdiction shall be individually responsible for the crime and liable to punishment. A person must have committed both the physical and fault elements of the crime to fall within this provision. As a general rule, a person is only criminally responsible for an act if she or he has intention or knowledge at the time of carrying out the physical elements of the offence. In other words, she or he must both mean to engage in the act and, if a consequence is an element of the crime, intend to cause that consequence or be aware that it will occur in the ordinary cause of events.[58]

A more complicated situation arises where multiple perpetrators are involved. Article 25(3)(a) of the Rome Statute creates criminal responsibility in situations where a person commits a crime as an individual, jointly with another or through another person. Joint responsibility in this context has been interpreted to apply in situations where one or more perpetrators have joint 'control over the crime'.[59] International criminal law also recognises the type of responsibility known in common law jurisdictions as 'common purpose' or 'joint enterprise'.[60] This means that an individual will be responsible if she or he has participated in an integral part of the crime and shared the underlying purpose. The common purpose need not be planned and may arise spontaneously.[61]

A military commander will be individually responsible for a crime if she or he orders its commission.[62] International criminal law also recognises secondary or ancillary liability.[63] One form of ancillary liability is aiding and abetting. A person may be responsible as an aider or abettor if she or he renders assistance to the offender or encourages the offender while present at the crime. The aider and abettor need not share a common purpose with the main offender; it is sufficient if she or he knows that her or his actions are providing assistance.[64] This contrasts with joint criminal responsibility, which requires that the perpetrators intend to take part in the crime or pursue a common criminal purpose.

---

[58] Statute of the International Criminal Court, art 30.
[59] *Prosecutor v Bemba Gombo*, ICC Pre-Trial Chamber Decision on the Confirmation of Charges, 15 June 2009 [346]–[350].
[60] Statute of the International Criminal Court, art 25(3)(d).
[61] *Prosecutor v Furundzija*, ICTY Appeals Chamber Judgment, 21 July 2000 [120]; *Prosecutor v Tadić*, ICTY Appeals Chamber Judgment, 1 July 1999 [227].
[62] Statute of the International Criminal Court, art 25(3)(b); Jean-Marie Henckaerts and Louise Doswald-Beck, *Customary International Humanitarian Law* (CUP 2005) rule 152.
[63] Statute of the International Criminal Court, art 25(3); Draft Code of Crimes against the Peace and Security of Mankind, art 2(3)(d).
[64] *Prosecutor v Tadić*, ICTY Appeals Chamber Judgment, 1 July 1999 [229].

Command Responsibility

A military commander or other superior will sometimes be responsible for crimes committed by a subordinate even though she or he did not directly order them. Article 28 of the Rome Statute lists two requirements for this form of responsibility. These are, first, that the commander either knew or, owing to the circumstances, should have known that the subordinates were committing or were about to commit the crimes; and, second, that she or he failed to take all reasonable and necessary measures within her or his power to prevent or repress the commission of the crimes or submit the matter to competent authorities for investigation. This test for command responsibility generally mirrors that established in the jurisprudence of the ICTY and ICTR.[65]

A person may hold a position of command for the purposes of command responsibility either *de jure* or *de facto*. A *de jure* commander holds a formal position within an organised chain of command, while a *de facto* commander is not formally in command of subordinates but exercises effective control over them in a practical sense.[66] The ICTY and ICTR jurisprudence effectively applies the same test for responsibility to both types of commanders. However, Article 28 of the Rome Statute sets out slightly different standards for *de jure* military commanders and their *de facto* counterparts.

The main difference between the standards lies in the degree of knowledge required. A *de jure* military commander will be responsible for the actions of subordinates if she or he knew or had reason to know what was taking place. A commander is considered to have had 'reason to know' if she or he has general information that would put her or him on notice of the possibility of unlawful acts by subordinates.[67] This standard reflects the findings of the United States Military Commission in the *Yamashita* case and was subsequently confirmed in the jurisprudence of the ICTY and ICTR.

A *de facto* commander, on the other hand, must either know or 'consciously disregard' information about crimes in order to be held

---

[65] See, for example, *Prosecutor v Blaskic*, ICTY Trial Chamber Judgment, 3 March 2000 [294]; *Prosecutor v Krstić*, ICTY Trial Chamber Judgment, 2 August 2001 [604]. See also Draft Code of Crimes against the Peace and Security of Mankind, art 6; Jean-Marie Henckaerts and Louise Doswald-Beck, *Customary International Humanitarian Law* (CUP 2005) rule 153.

[66] *Prosecutor v Delalic*, ICTY Appeals Chamber Judgment, 20 February 2001 [254]–[256].

[67] Ibid [238]–[239].

responsible for them under Article 28 of the Rome Statute. The crimes in question must also concern activities that are within the commander's effective responsibility and control. It makes sense that the threshold for knowledge should be higher in circumstances where a person occupies a less formal position of authority and where lines of command are less clearly defined than they are in a military hierarchy. Nonetheless, it is open to question whether Article 28 sets the bar for command responsibility too high in at least some case of *de facto* command.

A commander will only be responsible for crimes committed by subordinates if she or he fails to take reasonable and necessary steps to prevent and repress the acts and punish the perpetrators. The issue of what constitutes 'reasonable and necessary' measures must be assessed in light of all the circumstances prevailing at the time.[68] In cases where a commander exercises clear authority over subordinates in accordance with a defined chain of command, a simple failure to issue an order that would have prevented the offences may constitute a failure to take reasonable and necessary steps. The issue may be more complicated where the command relationship is less clearly defined.

Inchoate Responsibility

Inchoate responsibility is a form of responsibility that applies where the perpetrator has incited, attempted or conspired with others to commit an offence, but the offence has not been fully completed. The Rome Statute recognises inchoate responsibility in the form of incitement only in relation to genocide.[69] Attempts are covered by the Rome Statute in circumstances where an offender commences the execution of a crime by taking a substantial step, but the crime does not occur because of circumstances independent of the person's intentions. However, a person will not be liable for an attempt where she or he voluntarily abandons the effort to commit the crime or otherwise prevents it from occurring.[70]

An early example of a conviction for incitement under international law is provided by the trial of Julius Streicher by the IMT at Nuremberg. Streicher was a member of the Nazi Party who edited and distributed vile anti-Semitic propaganda through his racist newspaper, *Der Stürmer*. The IMT determined that 'Streicher's incitement to murder and extermination,

---

[68] *Prosecutor v Delalic*, ICTY Trial Chamber Judgment, 16 November 1998 [394].
[69] Statute of the International Criminal Court, art 25(3)(e).
[70] Statute of the International Criminal Court, art 25(3)(f).

at the time when Jews in the East were being killed under the most horrible conditions, clearly constitutes persecution on political and racial grounds in connection with War Crimes, as defined by the Charter, and constitutes a Crime against Humanity.'[71] As noted above, genocide was not covered by the IMT Charter. It is likely, however, that Streicher's crimes fall squarely within the offence of incitement to genocide, as well as constituting a crime against humanity. Article 2(3) of the ICTR Statute provides for the offences of conspiracy to commit genocide, direct and public incitement to commit genocide, attempting to commit genocide and complicity in genocide. The case of *Prosecutor v Akayesu* concerned a de facto local authority akin to a mayor who was convicted of inciting genocide by inflammatory statements made at a public gathering.[72]

Defences

A number of defences are recognised under Articles 31 and 32 of the Rome Statute. The defences listed in those provisions are:

- duress, including by a person or by circumstance;
- self-defence, defence of another or defence of essential property;
- mental disease or defect;
- intoxication; and
- mistake of fact, if it negates the mental element required for the crime.

Mental disease or defect and intoxication will only constitute defences where they destroy the person's capacity to either appreciate the unlawfulness of her or his conduct or control her or his actions.[73] Intoxication also cannot be relied upon where it is voluntary and the person knew or disregarded the risk that she or he was likely to engage in a crime as a result.[74] However, it seems that a person may still rely on voluntary intoxication as a defence where the circumstances of alcohol consumption were such that she or he could not foresee the risk of later engaging in criminal activity.

Self-defence applies in circumstances where the force the person is defending against is imminent and unlawful. The response must be

---

[71] *Trial of Major German War Criminals*, International Military Tribunal Judgment, 1 October 1946, 502.
[72] *Prosecutor v Akayesu*, ICTR Trial Chamber Judgment, 2 December 1998 [549]–[562].
[73] Statute of the International Criminal Court, art 31(1)(a), (b).
[74] Statute of the International Criminal Court, art 31(1)(b).

proportionate to the danger posed to the person or property being protected. The mere fact that a person is engaged in a defensive military operation does not allow her or him to rely on self-defence to escape liability for criminal acts.[75] The defence of duress requires a threat of imminent death or continuing or imminent serious bodily harm, made by other people or constituted by other circumstances beyond the defendant's control. The defendant must act necessarily and reasonably to avoid the duress, and not intend to cause a greater harm than the one they are avoiding.[76] The 'necessary and reasonable' requirement means that it is unlikely duress could be relied upon if an alternative means of avoiding the threat was available.

We saw earlier in this chapter that the IMT Charter and the Nuremberg principles drafted by the ILC both emphasise that it is not a defence that an offence was committed pursuant to superior orders.[77] This negates the so-called 'Nuremberg defence'. Peter von Hagenbach, the defendant in the first international criminal trial mentioned at the start of this chapter, sought unsuccessfully to argue that in allowing atrocities to occur under his command, he had simply followed the orders of the Duke of Burgundy. The international tribunal that tried Hagenbach refused his request for an adjournment to seek the Duke's confirmation that he had simply been following orders.[78]

The Rome Statute provides that the defence of superior orders can only be relied upon if the person was under a legal obligation to obey the orders, she or he did not know that the order was unlawful and the order was not manifestly unlawful.[79] Orders to commit genocide or crimes against humanity are deemed manifestly unlawful for the purposes of the provision. A person could not, therefore, rely on a defence of superior orders in relation to a charge of crimes against humanity or genocide, even

---

[75] Statute of the International Criminal Court, art 31(1)(c).

[76] Statute of the International Criminal Court, art 31(1)(d).

[77] Charter of the International Military Tribunal, art 8; International Law Commission, *Principles of International Law Recognized in the Charter of the Nuremberg Tribunal and in the Judgment of the Tribunal* (ILC 1950). See also Statute of the International Criminal Tribunal for the Former Yugoslavia, art 7(4); Statute of the International Criminal Tribunal for Rwanda, art 6(4); Draft Code of Crimes against the Peace and Security of Mankind, art 5.

[78] Edoardo Greppi, 'The Evolution of Individual Criminal Responsibility under International Law' (1999) 835 *International Review of the Red Cross* 531, 534.

[79] Statute of the International Criminal Court, art 33. See also Jean-Marie Henckaerts and Louise Doswald-Beck, *Customary International Humanitarian Law* (CUP 2005) rule 155.

if she or he did not know that the order was unlawful. The requirement that the defendant not know that the order is unlawful means that in situations where the laws of armed conflict have been disseminated through military manuals or other means, it is unlikely that a person could rely on the defence in relation to a war crime such as intentionally attacking a civilian population.

Sovereign Immunity

A significant historical impediment to holding persons in positions of responsibility accountable for violations of international humanitarian law has been the principle of sovereign immunity. Traditionally, heads of state and those in other positions of power and responsibility within government could not be held criminally responsible for actions carried out in their official capacities. This immunity applied not only while they held office, but also once they had ceased to occupy their government positions.

The traditional continuation of sovereign immunity once a person had left her or his official post was obviously unsatisfactory, as it resulted in permanent impunity for those bearing the greatest level of responsibility for serious violations of the laws of war. An important development in narrowing the scope of the doctrine of sovereign immunity occurred with the *Pinochet* case decided by the United Kingdom House of Lords in 1998. The House of Lords held that Augusto Pinochet, the former dictator of Chile who presided over serious human rights violations during his term of office, did not enjoy immunity from criminal prosecution for serious international crimes such as torture and conspiracy to commit torture.[80] Lord Nicholls observed that international law 'has made it plain that certain types of conduct [. . .] are not acceptable on the part of anyone' and to uphold sovereign immunity in such a case would 'make a mockery of international law'.[81]

---

[80] *R v Bow Street Metropolitan Stipendiary Magistrate; Ex parte Pinochet Ugarte* [1998] 3 WLR 1456. The decision was later set aside due to possible bias on the part of one of the judges, but a subsequent House of Lords decision reached the same conclusion as the initial ruling, albeit for somewhat different reasons. See *R v Bow Street Metropolitan Stipendiary Magistrate; Ex parte Pinochet Ugarte (No 3)* [1999] 2 WLR 827. For a useful summary, see Andrea Bianchi, 'Immunity versus Human Rights: The *Pinochet* Case' (1999) 10 *European Journal of International Law* 237.

[81] *R v Bow Street Metropolitan Stipendiary Magistrate; Ex parte Pinochet Ugarte* [1998] 3 WLR 1456, 1333.

The Statutes of the ICTY, ICTR and ICC expressly provide that a person's official position, whether as head of state or as a responsible government official, does not relieve them of criminal responsibility.[82] The concept of sovereign immunity was further eroded in June 2001 by the arrest of former Yugoslavian President Slobodan Milosevic. Milosevic was indicted by the ICTY for violations of the laws and customs of war and crimes against humanity. He was subsequently charged with grave breaches of the Geneva Conventions, genocide, complicity in genocide and other charges. The fact that he was the head of state at the time of committing the acts in question was not a barrier to his prosecution. Milosevic died in custody in 2005 before proceedings against him were finalised.

An exception to the trend against recognising sovereign immunity in cases involving serious violations of international law occurred in 2002 with the decision of the International Court of Justice (ICJ) in the *Arrest Warrant* case.[83] The case concerned an arrest warrant issued by Belgium for Abdulaye Yerodia Ndombasi, the then serving foreign minister of the Democratic Republic of the Congo, for war crimes and crimes against humanity. Belgium asserted the capacity to try Yerodia under the principle of universal jurisdiction discussed earlier in this chapter. However, the ICJ ordered Belgium to cancel the arrest warrant on the basis that state officials enjoy immunity from criminal prosecution during their term in office. The Court took the view that immunity was necessary to ensure that serving government officials could perform their duties effectively.

The doctrine of sovereign immunity is therefore still very much alive, at last so far as current state officials are concerned. Nonetheless, it continues to be gradually undermined.[84] We saw above that the Special Court for Sierra Leone recently convicted former Liberian President Charles Taylor for crimes against humanity and war crimes committed while in office.[85] The Prosecutor of the ICC has also issued charges against a number of individuals who currently hold or previously held positions of government responsibility. Arrest warrants have been issued for the current Sudanese

---

[82] Statute of the International Criminal Tribunal for the Former Yugoslavia, art 7(2); Statute of the International Criminal Tribunal for Rwanda, art 6(2); Statute of the International Criminal Court, art 27.

[83] *Case Concerning the Arrest Warrant of 11 April 2000 (Democratic Republic of the Congo v Belgium)*, International Court of Justice Judgment, 14 February 2002.

[84] For a useful discussion, see Jasper Finke, 'Sovereign Immunity: Rule, Principle or Something Else?' (2010) 21 *European Journal of International Law* 853.

[85] *Prosecutor v Taylor*, SCSL Trial Chamber Judgment, 18 May 2012.

President, Omar Al Bashir, the current Sudanese Minister of Defence, Abdel Raheem Muhammed Hussein, and former Sudanese Minister of State for the Interior, Ahmad Harun.[86] The three men are alleged to bear responsibility for crimes against humanity and war crimes committed during the conflict in the Darfur region in the Sudan. All three remain at large at the time of writing.

Procedural Guarantees

The ICC has no jurisdiction over any person who was below the age of 18 when an offence was committed.[87] The Rome Statute also adopts the well-recognised legal principle of double jeopardy or *ne bis in idem* (not twice in the same), which provides that no person can be tried twice for the same offence.[88] This principle entails that no person acquitted before the ICC can be tried again for the same crime. However, it also prevents the ICC from pursuing offenders who have been tried elsewhere for the same offence, except where the previous proceedings were a sham or lacked impartiality. A person may be charged with multiple international crimes in relation to the same conduct as long as the offences have different elements or the provisions creating them protect different interests.[89]

Persons accused of crimes under international law are entitled to the presumption of innocence. The prosecution must prove its case to beyond a reasonable doubt or the equivalent civil law standard.[90] International criminal law also establishes principles designed to ensure fairness to the accused, such as the right to be tried by an impartial tribunal, the right of accused persons to know the charges against them, the right to silence and the right to legal representation.[91] A person cannot be prosecuted by

---

[86] The ICJ in the *Arrest Warrant* case noted the possibility of sitting government officials being prosecuted before international tribunals, such as the ICC, that enjoy jurisdiction in such cases. See *Case Concerning the Arrest Warrant of 11 April 2000 (Democratic Republic of the Congo v Belgium)*, International Court of Justice Judgment, 14 February 2002 [61].

[87] Statute of the International Criminal Court, art 26.

[88] Statute of the International Criminal Court, art 20.

[89] See further *Prosecutor v Delalic*, ICTY Appeals Chamber Judgment, 20 February 2001 [412]–[413]; *Prosecutor v Akayesu*, ICTR Trial Chamber Judgment, 2 September 1998 [468].

[90] See, for example, *Prosecutor v Delalic*, ICTY Trial Chamber Judgment, 16 November 1998 [601]; *Prosecutor v Aleksovski*, ICTY Appeals Chamber Judgment, 24 March 2000 [57]; Statute of the International Criminal Court, art 67.

[91] Draft Code of Crimes against the Peace and Security of Mankind, arts 11–12.

the ICC for conduct that occurred prior to the Rome Statute coming into force.[92]

THE ROLE OF CRIMINAL LIABILITY

Significant advances in international criminal jurisdiction have almost always arisen in response to armed conflicts. Likewise, significant advances in international humanitarian law have regularly occurred as a result of criminal proceedings. The Nuremberg judgment and the *Tadić* decision of the ICTY are two important examples. Nonetheless, international humanitarian law and international criminal law are clearly distinct. We have seen in this chapter that some international crimes, such as genocide and crimes against humanity, can be committed in peacetime. Furthermore, only grave violations of international humanitarian law give rise to individual criminal responsibility.

What, then, is the role of criminal liability within international humanitarian law? There can be no doubt that high-profile prosecutions of war criminals such as Slobodan Milosevic and Charles Taylor have helped to increase global awareness of humanitarian norms. However, it should also be clear from the above discussion that individual liability is far from central to international respect for the law of armed conflict. Prosecutions under international criminal law are generally restricted to the 'most serious crimes of international concern'.[93] This means that criminal prosecution can only ever play a limited role in the enforcement of humanitarian norms, in a legal sense as well as a practical one.

International humanitarian law represents a broad collection of rules and customs that have come to be acknowledged throughout the world as desirable minimum standards for the conduct of warfare. The dissemination of those standards has been achieved primarily through collaboration between states and the efforts of international organisations such as the Red Cross Movement, rather than by imposing punishments upon individuals. The continuing rise of international criminal institutions undoubtedly represents a positive development in encouraging compliance with humanitarian principles, but the main force of international humanitarian law still lies in the diplomatic pressure and goodwill generated through the cooperation of the international community.

---

[92] Statute of the International Criminal Court, art 24.
[93] Statute of the International Criminal Court, art 1.

Index

absolute warfare 2, 9, 115
acceptance 9, 140–42
Additional Protocol I
  application of 21, 39–40
  development of 39–40
Additional Protocol II
  application of 18, 39–40, 159–63
  development of 39–40
  and civilian status 72–3
Additional Protocol III 41
Afghanistan 14, 46
African Charter on Human and
  Peoples' Rights 131–2
African Union 131–2
aiding and abetting 183
Al Qaeda 14
American Civil War 30–31, 165–6
American Convention on Human
  Rights 131
ancillary liability 183
animal rights 120
apartheid 152
Arab Charter of Human Rights 132
Aristotle 3, 5, 6–7
armed conflict
  agents of 44–50
  deep morality of 9
  ethics of 1–2, 7–9
  international and non-international
    11, 16–23
  legal definition of 10–14
  logic of 2
  morally exceptional character of 1–2
  nexus with 15–16
  and right to life 135–8
  scope of 14–16
  technology in 23, 60, 73, 77
armistice 15
Arrest Warrant case 189
Asian Charter of Human Rights 132
Austin, John 158–9

bacteriological weapons see biological
  weapons
barbarians 6–7
Battle of Solferino 29, 112
Bentham, Jeremy 120
Betancourt, Ingrid 66
biological weapons 38, 60–61
bombardment 59–60
Bond, James 87

Cambodia 27, 171
Cassese, Antonio 149, 160–62
ceasefire 15
chemical weapons 34–5, 52, 60–61
children in armed conflict 91–3
child soldiers 92
China 19, 144, 173
Cicero 4
civil defence organisations 94–5
civilians
  definition of 72–4
  displacement of 84
  internment of 83
  sick and wounded 84–8
Clausewitz, Carl von 2
cluster munitions 42, 52, 61–2
coherence 9, 140–42
collateral damage 76–7
collective punishments 80
Colombia 66
combatant status
  definition of 45
  ethical significance of 54
  legal significance of 46–48
  in non-international conflicts 49–50
command responsibility 184–5
Commonwealth of Independent States
  132
cosmopolitanism 6–7, 23
Council of Europe 130, 157
countermeasures 153

Court of Justice of the European Union 157
crimes against humanity 167, 186
  definition of 177–8
  and universal jurisdiction 170
crimes of aggression 167, 181–2
crossbow 52
cultural protection 69
customary international law
  elements of 25–7
  and international criminal law 174–5
  and international humanitarian law 21–3, 40, 160

deceased combatants 114
deep morality of warfare 9
Democratic Republic of the Congo v Uganda 138
Diogenes the Cynic 6, 23
direct participation in hostilities 46–7, 72
doctrine of double effect 56–7
double jeopardy 190
Draft Articles on State Responsibility 146–53
Draper, GIAD 138
drug trafficking 182
dualism 138–42
dum-dum bullets 33, 52
Dunant, Jean Henri 29–30, 112

East Timor 172
effective control test 19, 147–9
Eichmann, Adolf 169–70
environmental protection 68
  and nuclear weapons 64
erga omnes 152
eudaimonia 4
European Convention on the Protection of Human Rights and Fundamental Freedoms 130–31
European Court of Human Rights 27, 130, 133–4, 157
European Union 157
explosive bullets 31, 52
Extraordinary Chambers in the Courts of Cambodia 27, 171

First World War 34–5, 125, 144, 166
forbidden orders 67

fragmentary weapons 64
fragmentation of international law 139–40
freedom of expression 119, 133–4

Geneva Conventions 28–9
  application of 14–15
  Common Article 1 of 150–52
  Common Article 2 of 10, 21
  Common Article 3 of 14, 17–18, 35, 39, 71, 88, 111, 125, 160–63, 164–5, 180
  development of 30, 35–6
  fundamental guarantees of 49, 81–2, 111
  grave breaches of 170, 179–80
Geneva law 28–9
genocide 27, 126, 133, 152
  crime of 175–7
  incitement to 186
  and universal jurisdiction 170
Genocide Convention 175
German Interests in Polish Upper Silesia case 124
Grotius, Hugo 5
Guantanamo Bay 46

Hagenbach, Peter von 165, 187
Hague law 28–9
Hague Regulations 28, 34, 36, 71, 97
  development of 32–4
Hamdan v Rumsfeld 14
Handyside v United Kingdom 133–4
Hart, HLA 158–9
Hezbollah 22
Hicks, David 46
High Command case 169
Hiroshima 62
Hohfeld, Wesley Newcomb 47, 116
hors de combat 96
Hostage case 169
humanitarianism 2–5, 115
  history of 3–5
  in Ancient Greece 3–4, 6–7
  in Ancient Rome 4
  in the Middle Ages 4–5
human rights
  in armed conflict 134–42
  categories of 122–3
  clashes of 132–4

concept of 119–22
criticisms of 121
generations of 123
negative and positive 122–3
and state sovereignty 22
universality of 121–2
see also animal rights; international human rights law; rights
human shields 78–9

incendiary weapons 64–5
inchoate responsibility 185–6
indiscriminate attacks 57–9, 75–6
and nuclear weapons 63
individual responsibility 182–3
Inter-American Court of Human Rights 27, 131, 157
International Committee of the Red Cross 29–30
see also Red Cross Movement
International Court of Justice 27, 129
and conflicts of norms 137–8
jurisdiction of 155–7
International Covenant on Civil and Political Rights 128, 135–6
International Covenant on Economic, Social and Cultural Rights 128–9
International Criminal Court 27, 129, 143
jurisdiction of 173–5
International Criminal Tribunal for Rwanda 27, 171
International Criminal Tribunal for the Former Yugoslavia 27, 143, 171
international criminal law
and criminal responsibility 182–91
defences in 186–8
development of 165–74
and international humanitarian law 164–5, 191
and procedural guarantees 190–91
standard of proof in 190
and universal jurisdiction 170
see also genocide; crimes against humanity; crimes of aggression; war crimes
international human rights law
in armed conflict 134–42
derogations from 132–3
development of 123–32

focus of 115
and international humanitarian law 124–5
margins of appreciation in 133–4
and the United Nations 126–30
international law
enforcement of 154–9
fragmentation of 139–40
general principles of 27
role of sanctions in 158–9
sources of 24–8
stare decisis in 27
theories of 158–9
International Law Commission 139–40, 146, 168
International Military Tribunal for the Far East 168
International Military Tribunal at Nuremberg 53, 166–8, 175, 185–6, 191
jurisdiction of 167
Israel 22, 144, 169–70
Israeli Wall Advisory Opinion 137–8

journalists 93–4
Juan Carlos Abella v Argentina 12
jus ad bellum 5, 7, 28, 167
jus cogens norms 26–7, 133–4, 152–3
jus contra bellum see *jus ad bellum*
jus in bello 5, 7, 28, 167

Koskenniemi, Martti 139

landmines 41–2, 52, 58, 61–2
laser weapons 65
law of aliens 123–4
League of Arab States 132
League of Nations 34–5, 144
Lebanon 22, 172
Leipzig trials 166
levée en masse 45
lex specialis principle 137–8, 140
Lieber Code 30–31, 78, 165–6
Lieber, Francis 31
Lincoln, Abraham 30–31, 165–6
List, Wilhelm 169
logic of warfare 2

margins of appreciation 133–4
Martens Clause 32–3

Martens, Fyodor Fyodorovich 32–3
McMahan, Jeff 9
McQueen, Steve 106
medical units 85–6, 105, 113–14
mercenaries 98–100
military advantage 76
Military Commissions Act 46–7
military contractors 42
military necessity 52–5, 75–6
  and indiscriminate attacks 57–60
  and proportionality 56
military objectives 73–4
Milosevic, Slobodan 189, 191
Minority Schools in Albania case 125
Monetary Gold case 156
monism 138–42
Montevideo Convention on the Rights and Duties of States 144–6

Nagasaki 62
natural rights 119–20
ne bis in idem 190
Nicaragua v United States 19–20, 147–9, 156–7
non-state groups 11, 42
  liability of 159–63
nuclear weapons 36–7, 41–2, 52, 62–4
Nuclear Weapons Advisory Opinion 63, 137–8, 151
Nuremberg defence 187–8
Nuremberg principles 168
Nuremberg Tribunal see International Military Tribunal at Nuremberg

occupying powers
  definition of 81
  obligations of 10, 15, 80–84, 86
opinio juris 25–6
Organisation of African Unity 131–2
organised crime 14
Organization of American States 131
overall control test 19, 147–9

Palestine 144
Pearl, Daniel 93
peremptory norms 26–7
see also jus cogens norms
perfidy 65–7, 87, 113
Permanent Court of International Justice 124–5

Persian Gulf War 75
persistent objector rule 26
Pinochet, Augusto 188
piracy 182
Plato 3, 6–7
polis 6–7
political community 6–7
precautionary measures 77–9
presumption of innocence 190
principle of complementarity 173–4
principle of distinction 44, 50, 53–5, 70–71, 75
  ethical status of 54–5
  and indiscriminate attacks 57–60
  and nuclear weapons 63
  and proportionality 56
principle of neutrality 7–9
prisoners of war
  capture of 102–3
  communication of 108–9
  conditions of 103–4
  death of 110
  definition of 45, 97–101
  discipline of 105–6
  escape of 106–7
  labour of 107–8
  and medical and religious personnel 105
  in non-international conflicts 110–12
  release of 109–10
  treatment of 101–10
prohibited attacks 74–80
proportionality 55–7, 76–7
  ethical status of 56–7
  and indiscriminate attacks 57–9
  and military necessity 56
  and nuclear weapons 64
  and principle of distinction 56
Prosecutor v Akayesu 186
Prosecutor v Haradinaj 13
Prosecutor v Krstić 176–7
Prosecutor v Kunarac 11, 15–16, 178, 182
Prosecutor v Rajić 74
Prosecutor v Sam Hinga Norman 92
Prosecutor v Tadić 10–15, 18–20, 22, 81, 83, 148–9, 191
protected emblems 41, 65–7, 85–8
  in popular culture 87–8

protected persons regime 48, 80–84
Puntland 19

rape 82, 89–90, 178
Red Cross Movement 29–30, 191
see also protected emblems
refugees 83
Regan, Tom 120
reprisals 79–80, 153
rights
    absolute and non-absolute 117–18
    concept of 47, 116–19
    negative and positive 122–3
    prima facie 118–19
    and reasoning 119
    strength of 117–18
see also animal rights; human rights; natural rights; specificationism
right to life 135–8
rioting 11–12, 18
Rome Statute *see* International Criminal Court
ruses of war 65–7
Rwanda 23, 152
see also International Criminal Tribunal for Rwanda
Ryuichi Shimoda v State 62

Second World War 17, 35–6, 60, 62, 79–80, 83, 88, 94, 125–6, 164–5, 166–70
self-defence
    and ethics of warfare 8–9, 54
sick and wounded combatants 112–14
Sierra Leone 28, 160, 172, 189
Singer, Peter 120, 122–3
slavery 27, 121, 125, 133, 152, 178, 182
Somalia 145
Somaliland 19, 145
sovereign immunity 188–90
Spanish Civil War 17, 36
Special Court for Sierra Leone 28, 160, 172, 189
Special Tribunal for Lebanon 172
specificationism 118
spies 98–100
Srebrenica 176–7
stare decisis 27
statehood
    constitutive theory of 146

declarative theory of 146
definition of 144–6
stateless persons 83
state practice 25–6
state responsibility
    consequences of 153
    principles of 146–52
state sovereignty 22
St Petersburg Declaration 31-3, 37, 51–2, 71
Streicher, Julius 185–6
Stupni Do 74
Sudan 152, 189–90
superfluous injury 51–2, 60–61
    and nuclear weapons 64
superior orders 187–8
systemic integration 139–42

Taiwan 19, 144
Taliban 46
targeting 59–60
Taylor, Charles 172, 189, 191
Tehran Hostages case 149–50
terrorism 13, 49, 182
test of control 147–9
The Great Escape 106
The Living Daylights 87
torture 27, 133, 152, 178
Treaty of Versailles 166
    treaty law 25
    modification of 134

United Nations
    Charter 126, 156
    General Assembly Resolutions 28, 37–8
    and international humanitarian law 36–8
    and international human rights law 126–30
    Security Council 157
United States 46–7, 68, 156–7, 173–4
see also American Civil War
United States Military Tribunal at Nuremberg 169
Universal Declaration of Human Rights 126–8
universal jurisdiction 170
unlawful combatants *see* unprivileged belligerents

unnecessary suffering see superfluous injury
unprivileged belligerents 46–9, 100–101

Vienna Convention on the Law of Treaties 161
Vietnam War 36, 68

war crimes 167
   definition of 179–80
   and universal jurisdiction 170

warfare see armed conflict
wars of national liberation 21, 45
women in armed conflict 88–91
World War I see First World War
World War II see Second World War

Yamashita, Tomoyuki 169, 184
Yugoslavia 13, 22
   see also International Criminal Tribunal for the Former Yugoslavia